SO-EKK-583

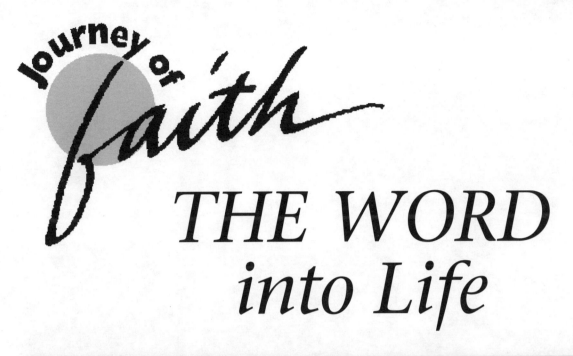

THE WORD
into Life

A GUIDE FOR GROUP REFLECTION ON SUNDAY SCRIPTURE

CYCLE A

JOHN F. CRAGHAN
ELSIE HAINZ MCGRATH
ANN WOLF

Liguori
ONE LIGUORI DRIVE
LIGUORI MO 63057-9999

Imprimi Potest:
Richard Thibodeau, C.Ss.R.
Provincial, Denver Province
The Redemptorists

ISBN 0-7648-0512-6
Library of Congress Catalog Card Number: 2001086326

Copyright © 1994, 1995, 2001 Liguori Publications
One Liguori Drive
Liguori, Missouri 63057-9999

To order, call 1-800-325-9521
www.liguori.org
www.catholicbooksonline.com

All rights reserved. No part of this book may be reproduced, stored in a retrieval system, or transmitted without the written permission of Liguori Publications.

Scripture quotations are taken from the *New Revised Standard Version Bible,* copyright © 1989, Division of Christian Education of the National Council of Churches of Christ in the United States of America. Reprinted with permission. All rights reserved.

Printed in U.S.A.

Design: Wendy Barnes and Evelyn John
Cover photo by: Tony Stone

TABLE OF CONTENTS

Overview 5

✿ ✿ ✿

First Sunday of Advent 10

Second Sunday of Advent 12

Third Sunday of Advent 14

Fourth Sunday of Advent 16

✿ ✿ ✿

Feast of the Holy Family 18

Epiphany of the Lord 20

Baptism of the Lord 22

✿ ✿ ✿

Second Sunday in Ordinary Time 24

Third Sunday in Ordinary Time 26

Fourth Sunday in Ordinary Time 28

Fifth Sunday in Ordinary Time 30

Sixth Sunday in Ordinary Time 32

Seventh Sunday in Ordinary Time 34

Eighth Sunday in Ordinary Time 36

✿ ✿ ✿

First Sunday of Lent 38

Second Sunday of Lent 40

Third Sunday of Lent 42

Fourth Sunday of Lent 44

Fifth Sunday of Lent 46

Passion (Palm) Sunday 48

✿ ✿ ✿

The Resurrection of the Lord (Easter) 52

Second Sunday of Easter 54

Third Sunday of Easter 56

Fourth Sunday of Easter 58

Fifth Sunday of Easter 60

Sixth Sunday of Easter 62

Seventh Sunday of Easter 64

Solemnity of Pentecost 66

✿ ✿ ✿

TABLE OF CONTENTS

The Holy Trinity 68

Body and Blood of Christ 70

❀ ❀ ❀

Ninth Sunday in Ordinary Time 72

Tenth Sunday in Ordinary Time 74

Eleventh Sunday in Ordinary Time 76

Twelfth Sunday in Ordinary Time 78

Thirteenth Sunday in Ordinary Time 80

Fourteenth Sunday in Ordinary Time 82

Fifteenth Sunday in Ordinary Time 84

Sixteenth Sunday in Ordinary Time 86

Seventeenth Sunday in Ordinary Time 88

Eighteenth Sunday in Ordinary Time 90

Nineteenth Sunday in Ordinary Time 92

Twentieth Sunday in Ordinary Time 94

Twenty-first Sunday in Ordinary Time 96

Twenty-second Sunday in Ordinary Time 98

Twenty-third Sunday in Ordinary Time 100

Twenty-fourth Sunday in Ordinary Time 102

Twenty-fifth Sunday in Ordinary Time 104

Twenty-sixth Sunday in Ordinary Time 106

Twenty-seventh Sunday in Ordinary Time 108

Twenty-eighth Sunday in Ordinary Time 110

Twenty-ninth Sunday in Ordinary Time 112

Thirtieth Sunday in Ordinary Time 114

Thirty-first Sunday in Ordinary Time 116

Thirty-second Sunday in Ordinary Time 118

Thirty-third Sunday in Ordinary Time 120

Christ the King 122

❀ ❀ ❀

Thematic Index 124

Supplemental Materials for Easter Triduum and Occasional Sundays 126

Gathering Prayers 174

Dismissal Prayers 176

❀ ❀ ❀

THE HISTORICAL DEVELOPMENT

The decision to become a member of the early Christian community was one laden with serious implications. Becoming Christian meant a break with one's background and often required fracturing relationships with the non-Christian members of one's family. In many cases this decision meant a willingness to suffer persecution even unto death. Stories of the early Christians reveal tales of young Christian women, like Perpetua, who was a noblewoman of Carthage and mother of an infant son, and Felicity, who was a pregnant slavewoman. Both refused to denounce Christianity and were subsequently beheaded during the public games in the amphitheater around A.D. 200.

As the decision to be a Christian was not lightly made, neither was the formation process quick and easy. Catechumens were invited into a step-by-step journey of three or more years with the community before full membership was achieved. During this lengthy process they were expected not only to begin to accept Christian beliefs but also to begin to live the Christian faith. The community shared their faith with the catechumens and celebrated each step along the journey with them.

One period of preparation for the catechumens has remained with the Church throughout the centuries, and that is the season of Lent. Originally this time was one of immediate preparation for the catechumens' baptism, which was celebrated at the Easter Vigil on Holy Saturday. During this forty-day retreat, the entire Christian community, most especially the catechumens, devoted themselves to prayer, fasting, and self-scrutiny. For those already Christian, it was a time to remember and renew their original baptismal commitment.

Following the Lenten preparation, the Church celebrated the solemn Easter Vigil, during which the catechumens received the sacraments of initiation and were welcomed into the community. These sacraments were celebrated only once each year, and only at the Easter Vigil. Formation of the new Christians did not end with the rites of Holy Saturday night, however, but continued with further instruction and the daily living out of Christian values.

This ancient process began to change in the year A.D. 313, when the Emperor Constantine mandated religious tolerance throughout the empire. Not only were Christians no longer persecuted but Christianity actually became fashionable, and people entered the catechumenate for political reasons. The standards for formation were relaxed to the point where baptism was received on demand, and by the fifth century the catechumenate had disappeared altogether. Eventually the sacraments of initiation were separated into the rites we know as baptism, confirmation, and Eucharist. Infant baptism became the norm, and the catechumenate vanished.

The Church published the first *Roman Catechism* in 1566, following the Council of Trent. This book of teachings was presented in question-and-answer form and was used for instruction of the faithful. Such *catechisms* later became the foundation for what came to be called *convert classes*. Using a teacher-student model, the priest met with interested parties in order that they might memorize certain prayers and learn the material contained in the catechism. At the end of a four- to six-month period of time, the priest usually determined that the students had mastered enough doctrinal formulations, and baptism was conferred according to parish custom. The duration of the process, the material to be covered, and the format were left to the priest or parish custom, with few outside directives given.

Successful completion of these convert classes meant either baptism or formal reception into the Catholic Church. This event was usually celebrated in a private ceremony, with only close family in attendance. Those newly received into the Church could be confirmed by the bishop at the cathedral; or they could receive the sacrament in their local parish when the bishop came to confirm the school children. Follow-up for the new Catholics, if there was any, might consist of being sent to a formal course in liturgy, Scripture, dogma, or morality.

The first in modern times to call for a change in the formation of new Catholics was the African Church. Following World War II, the African Church began to apply the ancient form of the catechumenate to modern situations, in order to provide stability in formation and a period of time for faith to mature. Then, between 1962 and 1972, a committee that was formed consequential to Vatican Council II engaged in a formal study and revision of the methods leading to baptism or reception into the Catholic Church. This study resulted in promulgation of the *Latin Rite* in 1972, followed by the provisional English text in 1974.

The catechumenate was reborn: a process of formation, sanctified by liturgical rites that mark progress in the journey of faith and culminate in full membership in the Catholic Christian community. An integral part of the revision is the celebration of the liturgical rites in which the catechumens and the parish community participate. These rites mark *closure* of each stage along the faith journey and *transition* into the next.

THE PROCESS

The catechumenate is rightly called a *process*, rather than a *program*, because catechists and sponsors act as guides in the spiritual journey of adults; also because this journey varies according to time, place, and needs of the catechumens. Rather than centering on a mastery of Church doctrine, the process is one of faith development. Catechumens come to a fuller maturity in their relationship with God, a relationship that now begins to express itself in the form of Roman Catholic beliefs. In addition, the process nourishes the building of relationships, not only among the catechumens and catechists but also among the catechumens and the larger Christian community of the parish.

Inquiry

The first stage in the faith journey is called the *inquiry*. During this period inquirers have the opportunity to form relationships with one another and with their catechists. The sessions are informal and often center upon the life stories of God-with-us that have brought each member to this time and place. Questions such as "What is faith?" "Who is God?" "Why does God care about me?" are considered. There is also the opportunity to ask questions related to *things Catholic*: Why are there statues in many churches? What is the role of Mary in the Catholic Church? How much power does the pope have in the Church?

The set of twelve **JOURNEY OF FAITH** *Inquiry Handouts* assist the questioners through this period. They broadly cover basic questions in such specific areas as: what Catholics believe, the meaning of the Mass, the Bible, the saints, prayer, and practices.

This is a time in which each inquirer can take a long and hard look at the Catholic Church—at the ways in which members worship together, at the ways in which they *live* their Catholic Christian faith. First impressions of the parish community, and of all involved with the catechumenate process, are very important in this stage. Its culmination is the inquirer's commitment to *enter* the catechumenate, the period of formal preparation for entrance into full membership in the Catholic Church.

Catechumenate

Marking the end of the inquiry and the beginning of the catechumenate is the *Rite of Becoming a Catechumen*. At this point the inquirers become *catechumens* (those preparing for baptism) or *candidates* (those already baptized but preparing for full membership in the Catholic Church). They publicly state their wish to continue the process of formation, and the community commits their prayerful support to this second step in the faith journey. Selected members of the parish community join the process to serve as sponsors, who act as companions and models of faith and lend personal support to the catechumens and candidates.

During the catechumenate phase of the process, catechesis usually takes place during the Sunday liturgy. The catechumens and candidates may be prayerfully dismissed after the *Prayers of the Faithful*; the catechists, and sometimes the sponsors, join them in reflecting upon the readings for the day and in connecting the Scripture to the faith life of the Church. A set of sixteen *Catechumenate Handouts* aid the learning process during this period. They address catechetical specifics of our faith: the Church, the sacraments, the moral life, and so forth.

The length of this part of formation is determined by the needs of the catechumen/candidate and of the community; it can last anywhere from several months to three years. During this time the catechumens and candidates not only learn Catholic beliefs, but they are exposed to various forms of prayer; they join the community in worship; they participate in the apostolic life of the Church; and they join in community actions.

When the catechumens and candidates are ready to make a formal request for the sacraments of initiation, and when the catechists and sponsors are ready to recommend them to the bishop and to the parish community for full membership, the *Rite of Election* is celebrated. This celebration is held at the cathedral on the first Sunday of Lent. The *Rite of Election* marks the closure of the catechumenate and the beginning of the *Period of Enlightenment*, the time of immediate preparation for reception of the sacraments of initiation at the Easter Vigil on Holy Saturday.

Lent

The beginning of Lent signals a forty-day retreat in which the parish community joins the *elect* (those whom the Church *elected* for full membership during the *Rite of Election*) in preparation for the Easter Vigil. On the third, fourth, and fifth Sundays the *Rites of the Scrutinies* are celebrated during the liturgy. These rites are prayers of healing in which the elect, as well as the faithful, are reminded that all are in need of continued healing, conversion, and reconciliation. The sessions are marked by increased emphasis on prayer rather than on accumulation of knowledge. Aiding both the catechized and the catechists in this process is a series of eight *Lent Handouts*. Vision is focused upon the events of the Easter Vigil and immediate preparation for reception of the sacraments of initiation. Many parishes allow time during Lent for a day of prayer especially designed for the elect and their sponsors.

Mystagogy

The Easter Vigil does not mark the end of the formation process but the beginning of a commitment to a lifelong discovery and living out of the Christian message. The fifty days from Easter to Pentecost are called the period of *mystagogy*, a Greek word meaning *mystery*. In the early Church, the community used this time to explain the mystery of the sacraments the catechumens had experienced. This post-Easter period serves as a time for today's *neophytes* (newly converted) to form a closer relationship with one another and to come to a deeper experiential understanding of God's Word and the sacraments. The neophytes continue to gather to pray, and the sessions may center more on the apostolic or social justice aspects of Catholic Christianity. Eight *Mystagogy Handouts* assist in redirecting the focus of new Catholics—from learning to living. This might be a time to more fully introduce various service organizations of the parish, the parish council, the school board, the education commissions, and so forth. The newly received Catholics are invited to wholly participate in the life of the parish so that their faith may continue to be nourished by the modeling of other parishioners.

The Catechumenate and the Community

The catechumenate process can provide a means of renewal for the entire parish community. It is a constant reminder of our roots, our heritage, and our traditions. Each beginning offers an opportunity for all to re-journey their own path of faith, an opportunity to share the life story of God-with-us, an opportunity to grow into a more mature relationship with God and with one another as community. The catechumenate can facilitate a continuing conversion process in the life of the parish, so that together the members may reflect more clearly the image of the reign of God in our midst.

THE METHODS

Suggestions for Developing a Catechumenate Process

Flexibility is one of the greatest assets of the new *Order of Christian Initiation of Adults*. The presider is given the freedom to accommodate the rites according to his pastoral judgment in order to fit the needs of the parish community, the catechumens, and the candidates. Catechists are encouraged to use their judgment in developing a process of faith formation suited to the needs of both catechumens and candidates. These materials, presented by *Liguori Publications*, are to act as a guide and an aid to that end.

Though one does not have to be a professor of theology or an experienced teacher to be a successful catechist, there are certain techniques and practical suggestions that can make the experience easier and more enjoyable. While a faith-filled experience is the work of God, it takes planning on the part of the catechumenate team to ensure that the process goes smoothly. It is helpful for the team to meet several weeks prior to the beginning of the process. Create a time line and review the materials. Be open to adapting both in order to meet the needs of those who present themselves as catechumens and candidates.

The team should continue to meet monthly throughout the process. It is helpful if each catechist is aware of the topics discussed, materials covered, and questions raised in each session so that there will be continuity between sessions and among presenters. It is also advisable that catechists contact the following week's presenters in order to brief them on any issues that have surfaced and may need to be addressed the following week.

No one can predict the makeup of any particular group. It is possible to have those who have never had any contact with institutionalized religion, those who have been baptized and active in another Christian denomination, and those who were baptized Catholic but not raised in the Church. Persons never baptized are referred to as *catechumens*, while *candidates* describes previously-baptized people. Generally, both can participate together in the same sessions; the major difference between the two comes in the celebration of the *Rites*, where care is taken to separate the two in prayer and sometimes in physical arrangement of the celebration. Refer to the *Rites* for specific instructions in this regard.

In working with adults it is vital that what is presented and discussed be linked with their life experience, especially in the process of faith formation. Catechists are co-learners, catalysts, and partners rather than directors. When catechists openly share the stories of their own faith journey, the catechumens and candidates experience a sense of trust that makes them comfortable in accepting and sharing who they are and where they are in their own journeys.

Again, flexibility is key to working with the catechumenate. Each session should begin with the opportunity for unfinished business to be addressed from the previous week. Often questions come up between sessions that were not obvious to the participants at the moment the topic was presented.

Communication is vital in establishing a sense of trust among participants, and active listening is one of the catechist's greatest tools in establishing this trust. Catechumens and candidates need to be accepted and affirmed for who they are, and this requires a nonjudgmental attitude on the part of all, especially the catechists. It is important to be aware of one's inner reactions to the speaker and to listen with the eyes and the heart.

Active listening requires **empathy**—an acceptance of the uniqueness of each individual, and a willingness to feel *with* them. It requires **sensitivity**—the ability to pick up the feeling level behind the spoken word. This is a feeling *for* the other in which personal prejudices and emotions are controlled.

It requires **attentiveness**—the ability to look at the person and give undivided attention; and **receptiveness**—the desire to genuinely want to hear and the ability to be open to what is said.

Lectionary-Based

The Sunday Lectionary forms the basis for the journey of faith. This is most appropriate since the Word of God tells the story of the faith experienced by the people of God: the relationship between the chosen people and Yahweh, and the relationship between the early Christian community and Jesus of Nazareth. In the process of reflecting upon these faith stories, our own stories of God-with-us become more clearly perceived and articulated. Because Scripture conveys the stories of a community, it is meant to be encountered in the community as we gather to worship and celebrate together. It is also fitting that the catechumens and candidates gather in community to break open the Word of God and to apply it to their own lives in the here and now.

In their reflection and linking of the Scriptures to their own lives, the early Christians began to develop official summaries and teachings regarding the meaning of their communal religious experiences. Since these doctrines and dogmas were born of theological reflection grounded in Scripture, the Church now links these teachings to Scripture in the catechumenate process. Therefore, the sessions begin with Scripture reflection and move toward an encounter with Catholic belief. Since it is primarily through the Sunday liturgy that the community hands on its traditions and beliefs, this becomes the most opportune time for the catechumens and candidates to be formed by the community. Beginning with the period of the catechumenate, it is strongly suggested that they be dismissed from the liturgy following the *Prayers of the Faithful* in order that they may go apart to reflect together upon the Word of God and the teachings of the Church. Several dismissal prayers can be found in the *Rite of Christian Initiation of Adults* book (see No. 67).

A SUGGESTED GUIDELINE FOR A SUNDAY SESSION FOLLOWS:

30 minutes	Liturgy—all gather in Church. Dismissal after *Prayers of the Faithful*.
10 minutes	Refreshments and settling in.
15 minutes	Prayer and reflection— where are we at this moment?
45 minutes	Reread, reflect upon, and share the Scriptures—either all or the one chosen for this session. Spouses and sponsors can join this session as Eucharist ends.
10 minutes	Evaluation and prayer—how are we going to live the Scripture this week?

Note: During inquiry *or* mystagogy *this format may be adapted for a Sunday morning after Mass or for a weekday evening session.*

Catechist Preparation

In order to prepare for each session, the catechist should make use of both the Scripture commentaries and the handouts covering Catholic beliefs and traditions. For each Sunday a commentary and reflection on the readings is provided. They provide background reading for the catechist in preparing for the session. Throughout the week the catechist should reflect upon the Sunday readings. What are the connections, if any, between the readings? Paying special attention to the gospel reading, who are the characters? What are the sights, sounds, smells, feelings that emerge? Attempt to become a part of the text. What stories of your own faith journey come to the forefront? What is the connection between the readings and the faith-life of today's Church? Are there any questions that are raised in your mind? In between prayer and reflection, the commentary can be consulted. How does the author's reflection resonate with your own prayer and reflection upon the texts? Reread the texts and adapt the discussion questions for your catechumens and candidates.

After you have prayerfully prepared for the session, **relax** and **enjoy** the opportunity to share your faith with those who are eager to be touched by God's Spirit.

THE RITES

Rite of Acceptance Into the Order of Catechumens

This rite marks the first important transition in one's journey of faith—the move from being an interested *inquirer* to becoming a *catechumen*. The importance of this step in one's life is rightly recognized by the Church.

Sponsors have been chosen for all catechumens prior to this initial rite. If the catechumen does not have a particular person in mind to be sponsor, an appropriate person should be selected from among a parish pool of volunteers.

Symbolizing movement into the community, those asking to be received as catechumens, along with their sponsors, usually begin the journey at the doors of the church (see Rite 48). The celebrant introduces them to the worshiping community, who asks, "What do you ask of the Church?" They state their desire for initiation, implying their intent to live, learn, and love with the community. The sign of the cross is then marked on each forehead, symbolizing the love and strength of Christ that accompanies each person (see Rite 54-55).

This sign of faith may also be marked on their ears, that they may hear the voice of the Lord; on their eyes, that they may see God's glory; on their lips, that they may respond to God's Word; on their heart, that Christ may dwell there by faith; on their shoulders, that they may bear the gentle yoke of Christ; on their hands, that their work may witness Christ; and on their feet, that they may walk in Christ's way (see Rite 56).

At the conclusion of the signing, catechumens and sponsors are formally invited to enter the Church and to join in the celebration of the Liturgy of the Word (see Rite 60).

Following the readings and homily, it is recommended that the catechumens be called forward and presented with either a book of the gospels or a cross (see Rite 64). They then are specially included in the community's intercessory prayers before being formally dismissed from the assembly in order to pray and reflect upon the Scriptures (see Rite 65-67).

If some of those seeking full communion in the Church are already baptized, they are to be called candidates and the Rite of Welcoming Baptized but Previously Uncatechized Adults Who are Preparing for Confirmation and/or Eucharist or Reception into the Full Communion of the Catholic Church is to be used. (See Rite 507 and following, Appendix I, for integrating both candidates and catechumens into the introductory celebration rite.)

Rites of the Catechumenate

Other liturgical rites should take place during the period of the catechumenate: celebrations of the Word of God (see Rite 81-89); minor exorcisms (see Rite 90-93); blessings (see Rite 95-96); anointing (see Rite 98-101); sending (see Rite 106-117). These rites, although optional, are very important for the continuing faith development of both the catechumens/candidates and the parish community.

Rite of Election

The importance of this rite is accented by the fact that it is celebrated by the bishop (or bishop's representative), generally on the first Sunday of Lent. The rite marks another transition—one duly noted by a change of "title"—from catechumen to elect. The transition is also noted insofar as godparents have been chosen and approved beforehand.

After all those requesting election have been presented to the bishop (see Rite 130) and approved by the entire people of God there present (see Rite 131), their names are inscribed in the Book of Enrollment (see Rite 132). Intercessory prayers and a special blessing for all the elect follow this sacred moment.

Rites of the Scrutinies

The First Scrutiny takes place on the third Sunday of Lent. Its focus is the gospel of the Samaritan woman at the well. After special intercessory prayers, the celebrant prays that the elect may be exorcised from the powers of sin (see Rite 150-156).

During the week that follows, the Presentation of the Creed should be formally made to the elect, preferably after the homily within Mass (see Rite 157-163).

The Second Scrutiny takes place on the fourth Sunday of Lent. Its focus is the gospel of the man born blind. Again, after special intercessory prayers, the celebrant prays that the elect may be exorcised from the powers of sin (see Rite 164-170).

The fifth Sunday of Lent brings the Third Scrutiny. This Sunday focuses on the raising of Lazarus. Intercessory prayers from all the community and prayers of exorcism from the celebrant again follow (see Rite 171-177). During the week after this rite, the Presentation of the Lord's Prayer should be formally made to the elect, preferably after the reading of the gospel of the Lord's Prayer according to Matthew. Following the homily, which centers on the meaning and importance of the Lord's Prayer, the celebrant calls on the worshiping community to silently pray for all the elect. Before their dismissal, the celebrant bestows a special blessing upon the elect (see Rite 178-184).

Rites of Preparation

When it is possible to bring the elect together on Holy Saturday for reflection and prayer, these are rites that may be considered for use in immediate preparation for the reception of the sacraments (see Rite 185 and following). If either the Presentation of the Creed or the Presentation of the Lord's Prayer has not been celebrated already, they could be celebrated now. An Ephphetha Rite (a rite of opening the ears and mouth, symbolizing the hearing and proclaiming of the Word) is a very fitting preparation rite, as is the rite of Choosing a Baptismal Name. Any or all of these preparatory rites serve to set the stage for the highlight of the catechumenate experience—the reception of the sacraments of initiation.

Rites of Initiation

Months of sharing the journeys of faith of the elect, their sponsors, and their catechists culminate in this very special parish celebration. Holy Saturday is the night to celebrate, and the Church celebrates in style. In the early Church the Easter Vigil lasted until dawn; today's vigil lasts but a few hours (depending on the parish, generally between two and four). It is the most glorious celebration of the entire liturgical year.

This night begins in total darkness. The parish community may assemble outside for the blessing of the fire. Then, as the celebrant processes into the church, proclaiming the Light of Christ, each person lights a taper from the new Easter candle that has been ignited with the new fire. Soon the Church is aglow with tongues of new fire. The Liturgy of the Word begins with only the light of the candles. There are seven readings from the Hebrew Scriptures provided for the occasion, although it is not necessary to proclaim all seven. Psalms are interspersed between each reading.

With the singing of the Gloria, the altar candles and electric lights are lit and the Church bells are joyously rung. Then comes the New Testament epistle, the glorious Alleluia, the gospel, and the homily. The stage is set for the rites of initiation!

The liturgy of baptism begins with the calling forth of those to be baptized. A litany of the saints follows, and then the celebrant blesses the baptismal water by plunging the Easter candle into the pool. Baptism follows, and each of the newly baptized is clothed with a white garment. Then the whole assembly renews their baptismal vows, and the celebrant ritually sprinkles all with the newly blessed waters of baptism.

Once the baptismal rite is concluded, the candidates for

reception are called forward to profess their belief in the holy Catholic Church. They are joined by the newly baptized, and the rite of confirmation is celebrated with laying on of hands and anointing with chrism.

As the initiation rites conclude and the eucharistic prayer for Holy Saturday begins, new Catholics *(neophytes)* take the place of the *catechumens* and *candidates* who worked and prayed so hard in preparation for this night. They, along with their sponsors and godparents and family members, lead their Church, the people of God, to the festive eucharistic banquet. The goal of initiation is this Eucharist—sharing at the table and being sent forth!

Alleluia! Amen!

HOW TO USE *JOURNEY OF FAITH*

The **JOURNEY OF FAITH** process includes catechetical handouts which are separated into the four phases of Christian initiation:

- The *Inquiry* phase, consisting of twelve 4-page handouts
- The *Catechumenate* phase, consisting of sixteen 4-page handouts
- The *Lent* phase, consisting of eight 4-page handouts
- The *Mystagogy* phase, consisting of eight 4-page handouts

Handouts are available for **adult** initiation in both **English** and **Spanish**.

Handouts in English are also available for the Christian initiation of **children**.

Soon to come, handouts will be available for the Christian initiation of **adolescents** in **English**.

There should be a complete set of handouts for every **leader**, for every **sponsor**, and for every **participant**.

In addition to the handouts, there are **Leaders Guides** available for both the **JOURNEY OF FAITH FOR CHILDREN** and the **JOURNEY OF FAITH FOR ADOLESCENTS**. These books will assist all initiation leaders, whether experienced or novices, through the process of guiding catechumens and candidates into the Church.

This book, **THE WORD into Life**, is available for **each liturgical cycle**. It is intended for use by **all leaders** of Christian initiation groups, whether the participants are adults, adolescents, or children. It is also an excellent resource for the **participants** in *adult* initiation classes. Included in each book are:

- The *readings* for all Sundays of the *liturgical year A, B, or C*, Advent through Christ the King
- The *readings* for the *Easter Triduum*
- The *cycle A readings* for the *third, fourth, and fifth Sundays of Lent*
- The *readings* for those occasional *Sundays that supersede ordinary time* readings
- *Scripture commentary* for every set of readings
- *Discussion and/or reflection questions* for every set of readings
- Every set of readings is *cross-referenced to the catechetical handouts*
- An *overview* of Christian initiation that includes a brief *history* of the process, a depiction of the four *phases* of the process, a *methodology*, a description of the *rites*, and the *how-to's* of this program
- A *thematic index*
- A brief collection of short *gathering prayers* and *dismissal prayers* for each phase of the initiation process

THE WORD into Life is a valuable resource unto itself, of course. Whether you are planning homilies, engaged in biblical academics, involved in small group faith-sharing, or simply searching for further enrichment and knowledge through Scripture, **THE WORD into Life** will make it easier.

The readings are taken from the *New Revised Standard Version Bible* (NRSV), approved for lectionary use by the bishops of both the United States and Canada. We have chosen this translation because of its overwhelming worldwide approval. The most universally familiar and accepted translation available today, it is also used in the *Catechism of the Catholic Church*. Because the readings are taken from the NRSV, there are sometimes discrepancies in numbering. For example, the first reading for the third Sunday in Ordinary Time, cycle A, is taken from Is 9:1-4 in the NRSV; the numbering system in your Bible or in your missalette may read Is 8:23—9:3. You are alerted to such discrepancies by the (NRSV) reminder at the end of all citations where different numbering occurs.

This book contains readings for all the Sundays of the year. They are arranged so that there are twenty-eight weeks between the first Sunday of Advent and Pentecost; and there are twenty-eight weeks between Trinity Sunday and Christ the King. Themes that emerge from the readings and the commentaries are listed at the end of each commentary with references back to specific **JOURNEY OF FAITH** handouts. Sundays between the first Sunday of Advent and the eighth Sunday in Ordinary Time refer you to handouts from the *Catechumenate* packet; Sundays between the first Sunday of Lent and Easter refer you to handouts from the *Lent* packet; Sundays between the second Sunday of Easter and Pentecost refer you to handouts from the *Mystagogy* packet. Because the twenty-eight weeks between Trinity and Christ the King may be used either for continuing mystagogy or for beginning a new group of inquirers (or both), all the Sundays between Trinity and Christ the King refer you to both the *Mystagogy* and the *Inquiry* packets.

The commentaries, themes, and prayers contained in this book are helps for preparing you to lead inquirers, catechumens and candidates, and neophytes. You are invited and encouraged to familiarize yourself with these resources, in order to both better anticipate and better stimulate questions and discussion. Leading others to Christ is the most important work you will do in your life; your personal preparation for such significant and rewarding work can never be adequately emphasized.

How the handouts are used is up to you and the format your parish wishes to use for initiation. They could be distributed and discussed at the same session; they could be distributed at the end of the session and discussed at the next session; they could be distributed for home study and only discussed to the extent that they may raise questions. Because the themes listed under your weekly commentary refer you back to specific handouts, the handouts are ongoing tools throughout the process.

We give thanks to our God... praying always with joy...
because of your partnership for the gospel....
And this is our prayer: that your love
may increase ever more and more in knowledge
and every kind of perception...
for the glory and praise of God.
Phil 1:3,4,5,9,11

Enjoy!

Reading 1, Isaiah 2:1-5

The word that Isaiah son of Amoz saw concerning Judah and Jerusalem.

In days to come the mountain of the Lord's house shall be established as the highest of the mountains, and shall be raised above the hills; all the nations shall stream to it.

Many peoples shall come and say, "Come, let us go up to the mountain of the Lord, to the house of the God of Jacob; that he may teach us his ways and that we may walk in his paths."

For out of Zion shall go forth instruction, and the word of the Lord from Jerusalem. He shall judge between the nations, and shall arbitrate for many peoples; they shall beat their swords into plowshares, and their spears into pruning hooks; nation shall not lift up sword against nation, neither shall they learn war any more.

O house of Jacob, come, let us walk in the light of the Lord!

Psalm 122:1-2,3-4,4-5,6-7,8-9

Reading 2, Romans 13:11-14

You know what time it is, how it is now the moment for you to wake from sleep. For salvation is nearer to us now than when we became believers; the night is far gone, the day is near. Let us then lay aside the works of darkness and put on the armor of light; let us live honorably as in the day, not in reveling and drunkenness, not in debauchery and licentiousness, not in quarreling and jealousy. Instead, put on the Lord Jesus Christ, and make no provision for the flesh, to gratify its desires.

Gospel, Matthew 24:37-44

Jesus said to his disciples: "As the days of Noah were, so will be the coming of the Son of Man. For as in those days before the flood they were eating and drinking, marrying and giving in marriage, until the day Noah entered the ark, and they knew nothing until the flood came and swept them all away, so too will be the coming of the Son of Man. Then two will be in the field; one will be taken and one will be left. Two women will be grinding meal together; one will be taken and one will be left.

"Keep awake therefore, for you do not know on what day your Lord is coming. But understand this: if the owner of the house had known in what part of the night the thief was coming, he would have stayed awake and would not have let his house be broken into. Therefore you also must be ready, for the Son of Man is coming at an unexpected hour."

Be Prepared!

ANN WOLF

"The end is coming!" shouts the guy with the sign on the New York City street corner. "Are you ready?" Few people pay any attention; they are all too busy to be bothered with this nonsense. But, as the millennium drew near, more and more people cast a glance in his direction. "Could it be?" they wondered.

Eat, Drink, And...

Unlike the street corner prophet who predicts the exact hour (subject to revision), the gospel tells us no one knows the day nor the time when the end will come. It is in everyone's best interest to be in a constant state of preparedness. Otherwise you might end up like Noah's neighbors, who weren't ready to sail when the waters came. "The Son of Man is coming at an unexpected hour," warns Jesus. Only those who are awake and ready will enjoy the fullness of the reign of God.

The early Christians believed they were already living in the "end time." They were convinced that the Second Coming would follow shortly after the death/resurrection event. Paul warned that Christians could not afford to be scantily-clothed sleepers caught up in sensual vices and weak mental attitudes. They must live as though they had truly "put on the Lord Jesus Christ."

Climbing God's Mountain

Isaiah too describes the end time which, for the Israelites, was called *Yom Yahweh* ("the Day of the Lord"). It was then that Jerusalem would become the center of God's reign on earth. All would "go up to the mountain of the Lord, to the house of the God of Jacob" to learn God's ways that they may walk in God's path. The Law that had been given to Moses and the "chosen people" on Mount Sinai was enshrined and studied in the Jerusalem Temple. But it was not enough to study and honor the Law: it must be lived. The Law was to manifest itself most clearly in the relationships of God's people with one another, and in their relationship with Yahweh. Isaiah tries to convince the people that true peace—that sense of personal security and the possibility of achieving wholeness for which the people yearned—could only become a reality when God's Law took priority in the lives of the people. This firm grounding in God's way would enable all peoples to live together in harmony: "Nation shall not lift up sword against nation, neither shall they learn war any more." The reign of God would become a reality.

Although filled with a sense of hope, Isaiah also saw the facts. The monarchy was corrupt, and the people continued to oppress one another. True peace—a sense of security and wholeness—was not a reality in Isaiah's time; perhaps it could become a reality only with the coming of the Messiah.

Today's Good News

The Israelites could look around and say, "When the Messiah comes, God's reign will begin." Christians, however, believe that the Messiah *has* come—in the person of Jesus of Nazareth. And yet, is the reign of God a reality? We still long for a day of peace, a day when all nations and all peoples can live together as one human family. Continued unrest in many parts of the world speaks to us of a lack of peace, a lack of respect for one another. Just as both Isaiah and Paul's communities were, we too are unwilling to make God and God's ways the center of our lives.

What are those things that keep us from making God the focus of our lives, the center of our being? In the Western world, we are often caught up in the desire to make more money and own more "stuff." We are often overcome by our busyness; we forget the importance of family and friends in our lives. We forget that in forming relationships with one another, we form a relationship with God.

The words *Advent* and *adventure* come from the same root word. *Advent* means to come, to approach. An *adventure* is a bold undertaking during which one may encounter hazards. One takes chances—risks. During this Advent season, are we willing to risk making God the center of our lives?

Points for Reflection and Discussion

1. Name some obstacles that must be overcome if all peoples are to become one human family. What do we have to do to bring it about?

_____

_____

_____

_____

2. Make a list of: three persons/places/things that interfere with your making God the center of your life; and three persons/places/things that draw you into a closer relationship with God.

_____

_____

_____

_____

Themes

Preparedness
    C1, The Sacraments: An Introduction
    C5, The Sacrament of Penance
Reign of God
    C9, The People of God
    C10, Who is Jesus Christ?
Relationship
    C11, The Early Church
    C16, The Dignity of Life

Reading 1, Isaiah 11:1-10

On that day: A shoot shall come out from the stump of Jesse, and a branch shall grow out of his roots. The spirit of the Lord shall rest on him, the spirit of wisdom and understanding, the spirit of counsel and might, the spirit of knowledge and the fear of the Lord. His delight shall be in the fear of the Lord.

He shall not judge by what his eyes see, or decide by what his ears hear; but with righteousness he shall judge the poor, and decide with equity for the meek of the earth; he shall strike the earth with the rod of his mouth, and with the breath of his lips he shall kill the wicked. Righteousness shall be the belt around his waist, and faithfulness the belt around his loins.

The wolf shall live with the lamb, the leopard shall lie down with the kid, the calf and the lion and the fatling together, and a little child shall lead them. The cow and the bear shall graze, their young shall lie down together; and the lion shall eat straw like the ox. The nursing child shall play over the hole of the asp, and the weaned child shall put its hand on the adder's den. They will not hurt or destroy on all my holy mountain; for the earth will be full of the knowledge of the Lord as the waters cover the sea.

On that day the root of Jesse shall stand as a signal to the peoples; the nations shall inquire of him, and his dwelling shall be glorious.

Psalm 72:1-2,7-8,12-13,17

Reading 2, Romans 15:4-9

Whatever was written in former days was written for our instruction, so that by steadfastness and by the encouragement of the scriptures we might have hope.

May the God of steadfastness and encouragement grant you to live in harmony with one another, in accordance with Christ Jesus, so that together you may with one voice glorify the God and Father of our Lord Jesus Christ.

Welcome one another, therefore, just as Christ has welcomed you, for the glory of God. For I tell you that Christ has become a servant of the circumcised on behalf of the truth of God in order that he might confirm the promises given to the patriarchs, and in order that the Gentiles might glorify God for his mercy. As it is written, "Therefore I will confess you among the Gentiles, and sing praises to your name."

Gospel, Matthew 3:1-12

In those days John the Baptist appeared in the wilderness of Judea, proclaiming, "Repent, for the kingdom of heaven has come near." This is the one of whom the prophet Isaiah spoke when he said, "The voice of one crying out in the wilderness: 'Prepare the way of the Lord, make his paths straight.' "

Now John wore clothing of camel's hair with a leather belt around his waist, and his food was locusts and wild honey. Then the people of Jerusalem and all Judea were going out to him, and all the region along the Jordan, and they were baptized by him in the river Jordan, confessing their sins.

But when he saw many Pharisees and Sadducees coming for baptism, he said to them, "You brood of vipers! Who warned you to flee from the wrath to come? Bear fruit worthy of repentance. Do not presume to say to yourselves, 'We have Abraham as our ancestor'; for I tell you, God is able from these stones to raise up children to Abraham. Even now the ax is lying at the root of the trees; every tree therefore that does not bear good fruit is cut down and thrown into the fire.

"I baptize you with water for repentance, but one who is more powerful than I is coming after me; I am not worthy to carry his sandals. He will baptize you with the Holy Spirit and fire. His winnowing fork is in his hand, and he will clear his threshing floor and will gather his wheat into the granary; but the chaff he will burn with unquenchable fire."

The Law of Love

ANN WOLF

Today's gospel reading confronts us with the message and person of John the Baptist. Dining on locusts and decked out in a camel's hair tunic with a leather belt, John's extreme appearance was matched only by his radical message: "Repent!" John didn't mean just a simple adjustment—he meant a profound transformation, a 180-degree turnaround.

Despite his fanatical behavior, the gospel tells us that the whole region flocked to the Jordan to hear John, including many Pharisees and Sadducees. It was for members of those two groups that John reserved his harshest tongue-lashing.

The Pharisees enforced observance of the oral tradition as well as the written law. The Sadducees were concerned with strict compliance to ritual law and Temple practices. John reminded both that blind observance of law and ritual did not guarantee salvation; neither did direct lineage with Abraham alone provide favor with Yahweh. The religious leadership of the Jewish people had become dangerously rigid and exclusive. Rather than leading people to God, they were creating barriers between Yahweh and the people.

John preached a baptism of repentance. He did not practice Jewish baptism, which was a rite of purification, or cleansing, rooted in the Hebrew Scriptures. While he kept the idea of purification, he added the element of a complete turning away from sin—a radical change of heart. Ritual purity and adherence to the law were not enough. Good works alone were no longer sufficient. Above all there must be pure intent.

Neither Jew nor Gentile...

Paul's Letter to the Romans also speaks of law ("whatever was written in former days was written for our instruction"). Many Jewish Christians continued to observe the Mosaic Law, especially those concerning circumcision and those governing dietary customs. Some of the Gentile Christians, however, did not conform to the Mosaic Law, and this became a source of division among the community. While Paul did not discount the Mosaic Law, he also did not exclude Gentiles from the reign of God solely because they did not conform to the Mosaic Law. Jesus first preached to the Jews in order to fulfill the covenant with their ancestors, but Paul understood the promise was to be extended to the Gentiles as well. Contrary to our human prejudices, God shows no ethnic preference in the plan of salvation. The reign of God is open to all.

Although Paul did not insist that the "letter" of the Mosaic Law be followed by Gentiles, he did demand they follow the "spirit" of the Law. Acceptance of one another's human dignity, and reconciliation among the community, far outweighed adherence to ritual and dietary laws. Paul called upon the community to "live in harmony with one another, in accordance with Christ Jesus."

Peace on Earth

Isaiah too looked forward to a time of harmony among God's people—a harmony symbolized by a spirit of justice and righteousness. There would be no more chaos, no harm or ruin in the land, but the land and its people would be filled with knowledge of the Lord. Like the symbol of water permeating every crack and crevice, knowledge of the Lord's ways—justice and righteousness—seeped into the core of all creation, to be absorbed into the very being of all God's creatures. All creation would be reconciled to itself and the harmony present at the beginning of time be returned: wild animals dwelling together without fear, children guiding them without danger. Chaos gives way to a sense of perfect peace.

Today's Good News

The early Church needed guidelines to promote harmony. Today's Catholic Church is no exception. These "laws" are not meant to coerce members into conformity; they are meant to be guidelines for moral living. Adherence to laws alone does not guarantee salvation. Participation in the reign of God demands a freely given Christian response to the spirit of these guidelines.

Responding to the spirit of the law requires relational living. We are called to experience the life, the essence of another human person. In doing this, we allow that person to touch our private space. We share the pain and sorrow, the joy and excitement, the hopes and dreams of the other. Barriers crumble, common threads are woven. This can be a frightening venture. It is much easier to quote laws than to allow ourselves to become vulnerable, to place our very selves in the hands of another. Isaiah's vision, Paul's challenge, John the Baptist's warning...all are as startlingly relevant today as they were when first issued. Can we envision perfect peace? If we heed the warning and *"Repent!"*...if we accept the challenge and *"live in harmony"*...perhaps *"on that day...the earth will be full of the knowledge of the Lord...and his dwelling shall be glorious."*

Points for Reflection and Discussion

1. Name one potential source of chaos in your personal life. What steps can you take to bring interior peace?

_____

_____

_____

_____

_____

2. Name one "law" of the Catholic Church that causes you difficulty. How can this difficulty be resolved?

_____

_____

_____

_____

_____

Themes
Authority
   C8, The Sacrament of Holy Orders
   C13, Christian Moral Living
Ecumenism
   C11, The Early Church
Repentance
   C2, The Sacrament of Baptism
   C5, The Sacrament of Penance

Reading 1, Isaiah 35:1-6,10

The wilderness and the dry land shall be glad, the desert shall rejoice and blossom; like the crocus it shall blossom abundantly, and rejoice with joy and singing. The glory of Lebanon shall be given to it, the majesty of Carmel and Sharon. They shall see the glory of the Lord, the majesty of our God.

Strengthen the weak hands, and make firm the feeble knees. Say to those who are of a fearful heart, "Be strong, do not fear! Here is your God. He will come with vengeance, with terrible recompense. He will come and save you." Then the eyes of the blind shall be opened, and the ears of the deaf unstopped; then the lame shall leap like a deer, and the tongue of the speechless sing for joy.

And the ransomed of the Lord shall return, and come to Zion with singing; everlasting joy shall be upon their heads; they shall obtain joy and gladness, and sorrow and sighing shall flee away.

Psalm 146:6-7,8-9,9-10

Reading 2, James 5:7-10

Be patient, beloved, until the coming of the Lord. The farmer waits for the precious crop from the earth, being patient with it until it receives the early and the late rains. You also must be patient. Strengthen your hearts, for the coming of the Lord is near. Beloved, do not grumble against one another, so that you may not be judged. See, the Judge is standing at the doors! As an example of suffering and patience, beloved, take the prophets who spoke in the name of the Lord.

Gospel, Matthew 11:2-11

When John heard in prison what the Messiah was doing, he sent word by his disciples and said to him, "Are you the one who is to come, or are we to wait for another?" Jesus answered them, "Go and tell John what you hear and see: the blind receive their sight, the lame walk, the lepers are cleansed, the deaf hear, the dead are raised, and the poor have good news brought to them. And blessed is anyone who takes no offense at me."

As they went away, Jesus began to speak to the crowds about John: "What did you go out into the wilderness to look at? A reed shaken by the wind? What then did you go out to see? Someone dressed in soft robes? Look, those who wear soft robes are in royal palaces. What then did you go out to see? A prophet? Yes, I tell you, and more than a prophet. This is the one about whom it is written, 'See, I am sending my messenger ahead of you, who will prepare your way before you.' Truly I tell you, among those born of women no one has arisen greater than John the Baptist; yet the least in the kingdom of heaven is greater than he."

Patience, People...

ANN WOLF

"Be patient!" How many times have we heard those words or spoken them to another? Sometimes we lose our patience at minor irritations. Traffic slows to a standstill on the freeway when we are already ten minutes late for an appointment. A coworker fails to finish a project, causing us to work overtime to complete it. We drop a container of milk in the midst of preparing dinner. Patience is even more difficult when the issue at stake is greater, as it was for the people who awaited liberation from their Babylonian captivity.

Isaiah preaches patience as he reminds the people that they were once before liberated from captivity. Just as the wilderness and the crocus rejoiced at their release from slavery in Egypt, present desolation shall give way to an abundance of joy likened to the beauty and luxuriant vegetation of Carmel and Sharon. "Be strong, do not fear!" Isaiah says to frightened hearts, for God will "come with vengeance." Then shall the blind see, the lame leap, the deaf hear, and the mute rejoice in giving praise to God. The faithful ones will be ransomed and will enter Zion singing for joy. Sorrow and mourning will be no more.

Are You the One?

It is no wonder that John the Baptist and his followers were seized with a sense of excitement and expectation when they began to see and hear of Jesus' healing miracles. "Are you the one who is to come, or are we to wait for another?" And Jesus replied, "Go and tell John what you see and hear...".

Could it be that the long-awaited Messiah had come? Would all the predictions of the prophets be realized? Would Israel once again become a glorious and powerful nation?

Should We Look for Another?

All the questions were soon answered, but the answers came in surprising form. Not only was there no military coup to overthrow the Roman oppressors and restore Israel's claim to power, but there were still the poor, the hungry, and the disabled for whom to care. The glory of the messianic promise had not been fulfilled, and hopes had been dashed with Jesus' execution. But the promise still remained, and now the expectation was for the Second Coming. Be patient until Jesus comes again, the disciples began to say.

"Patience" dictates the author of the Letter of James. Just as the farmer waits for rain upon the crops, so the Christian community must wait for the coming of the Lord. Living some thirty-five years after the death/ resurrection of Jesus, this community of Christians was filled with a sense of expectation for the Second Coming. As time passed and Jesus did not return, they began to realize that their "temporary" religious community was evolving into an institution—a church—preparing to wait, to be patient. The steadfast faith of the persecuted Christians living in the shadow of death slowly gave way to the quiet faith that sustained the everyday life of the next-century Christians.

Today's Good News

Perhaps it is easiest to have faith in the face of difficult circumstances. In times of both personal and natural disaster, there is often a sense of God-with-us. We hear the phrase: "It can't get any worse," meaning we anticipate a movement toward better times and situations. It is only when no movement can be discerned that patience is easily lost.

We lose patience during those times when we are unable to exert control over our lives and our future; we are engulfed with a sense of helplessness. Waiting for the decision of another—a decision that might result in a radical change in our lives—can cause us much anxiety and many sleepless nights. Acceptance or rejection of a job application, notification of admission to a college or university, results of a medical examination—all these are circumstances beyond our control. We do what we can do, and we wait. Learning to wait in patience helps to create the sense of steadfastness that we find in the Letter of James.

We can recount many examples of persecuted people being supported by a steadfast faith. James calls attention to the prophets of the Hebrew Scriptures who continued to speak out against injustice at the risk of losing their lives. Throughout the centuries, history records the names of women and men who have given their lives defending their faith, defending the rights of others. Lost to us are the names of many who have remained steadfast in ordinary times. And yet, if we stop to think about it, those people surround us. They are listed in the family tree contained in our Bible. They are pictured in the photograph album of our grandparents. They came as immigrants seeking a new life; they continue to come as undocumented people seeking to survive. These are the people who nourish our weakness with their steadfast patience and faith. Yes, the Lord is coming, but for those who wait in steadfastness, the coming is already in process.

Points for Reflection and Discussion

1. Describe one person who has influenced your life with his or her steadfast faithfulness.

_____

_____

_____

_____

_____

2. Have you ever experienced a disaster in your life that turned out to be a blessing? Tell about it.

_____

_____

_____

_____

_____

Themes
Early Church
    C11, The Early Church
Messiah
    C10, Who is Jesus Christ?
Waiting
    C12, History of the Church

Reading 1, Isaiah 7:10-14

The Lord spoke to Ahaz, saying, "Ask a sign of the Lord your God; let it be deep as Sheol or high as heaven." But Ahaz said, "I will not ask, and I will not put the Lord to the test."

Then Isaiah said: "Hear then, O house of David! Is it too little for you to weary mortals, that you weary my God also? Therefore the Lord himself will give you a sign. Look, the young woman is with child and shall bear a son, and shall name him Immanuel."

Psalm 24:1-2,3-4,5-6

Reading 2, Romans 1:1-7

[From] Paul, a servant of Jesus Christ, called to be an apostle, set apart for the gospel of God, which he promised beforehand through his prophets in the holy scriptures, the gospel concerning his Son, who was descended from David according to the flesh and was declared to be Son of God with power according to the spirit of holiness by resurrection from the dead, Jesus Christ our Lord, through whom we have received grace and apostleship to bring about the obedience of faith among all the Gentiles for the sake of his name, including yourselves who are called to belong to Jesus Christ.

To all God's beloved in Rome, who are called to be saints: Grace to you and peace from God our Father and the Lord Jesus Christ.

Gospel, Matthew 1:18-24

The birth of Jesus the Messiah took place in this way. When his mother Mary had been engaged to Joseph, but before they lived together, she was found to be with child from the Holy Spirit. Her husband Joseph, being a righteous man and unwilling to expose her to public disgrace, planned to dismiss her quietly. But just when he had resolved to do this, an angel of the Lord appeared to him in a dream and said, "Joseph, son of David, do not be afraid to take Mary as your wife, for the child conceived in her is from the Holy Spirit. She will bear a son, and you are to name him Jesus, for he will save his people from their sins."

All this took place to fulfill what had been spoken by the Lord through the prophet: "Look, the virgin shall conceive and bear a son, and they shall name him Emmanuel," which means, "God is with us."

When Joseph awoke from sleep, he did as the angel of the Lord commanded him; he took her as his wife.

Come, Emmanuel!

ANN WOLF

Today's readings recount the birth of two children: the first, the son of a king and queen; the second, the son of peasants who at his death would be *called* King. A descendent of the Davidic line, the son of Ahaz and his wife was a sign of the covenant God made with the "chosen people." I will be your God, and you will be my people, Yahweh promised (see, for example, Lv 26:12; Jer 7:23;11:4;30:22; Ez 36:28; Hos 2:25); and so this child bears God's promise in the name *Emmanuel* (God with us). Joseph's dream, recounted today in Matthew's Gospel, echoes Isaiah's words to Ahaz in order to demonstrate that Jesus is the ultimate fulfillment of God's promise. Paul too, reminds us in his Letter to the Romans, that the prophets had long ago promised a Messiah who would be born of the Davidic line. But Paul goes farther than the prophets did. He calls this Messiah "Son of God."

Miracles of Birth

Anticipating the feast we will celebrate in a few days, today's gospel tells the story of the birth of Jesus of Nazareth. This is the story of a maiden becoming a mother and God becoming a baby, a story in which Matthew preserves the foundation of the Christian faith. Through his eyes we enter into the most sacred space in the lives of Mary and Joseph, the conception of the child Jesus, the Christ.

Miracle birth was not an uncommon theme in the Jewish tradition. Among others, we have the stories of Sarah and Elizabeth, two women who were generations apart and much too old to be (humanly) capable of childbearing. Mary's miracle birth, however, differed profoundly from the experience of either Sarah or Elizabeth. Their sons were but signs of the covenant: Mary's son was to be the fulfillment of that covenant.

Overhearing the prediction that she would become pregnant, Sarah laughed at the incredibility of Yahweh's power over her old body's barrenness (Gn 18:12). Thus the child born to Sarah and Abraham was called Isaac, which means *laughter*. He was firstborn of the covenant Yahweh made with Abraham and Sarah: "Look toward heaven and count the stars, if you are able to count them....So shall your descendants be" (Gn 15:5).

Matthew's conception account does not mention Elizabeth, but Luke precedes the Annunciation story with the birth of John the Baptist, son of Elizabeth and Zechariah. Barren and advanced in age, Elizabeth bore a son. This child too was consecrated to the service of God, to be "called the prophet of the Most High; for you will go before the Lord to prepare his ways" (Lk 1:76). The covenant is once more renewed.

Mary was neither of advanced age nor known to be barren when her child was conceived. Quite the contrary, tradition has it that she could have been as young as twelve years of age, and she was a virgin betrothed to a man named Joseph of the house of David. Today's gospel account is told from the perspective of Joseph, "a righteous man," knowledgeable of the Law. Though Judean betrothal custom granted the right of sexual intimacy, it is not clear if sexual relations were permitted between betrothed couples in Galilee. At any rate, Joseph clearly knows that he is not the biological father of the child Mary carries. But Joseph's compassion outweighs requirements of the Law because rather than permit her to be stoned as an adulteress according to the Law of Deuteronomy (22:20-21), Joseph decides to spare her life and divorce her quietly.

In a dream, Joseph is assured not only of Mary's fidelity, but of the fact that the child to be born is a part of God's marvelous plan—"The young woman is with child and shall bear a son, and shall name him Immanuel" (Is 7:14). Joseph's acceptance of Mary as his wife joined his "yes" to hers—and a final link in the messianic chain was forged. Through the power of the Spirit, Jesus thus became *Emmanuel*—God with us.

When we think of the Annunciation, we usually focus upon Mary and her response to God's call. In Matthew's story, however, Joseph is brought to the forefront, and it is through his family that Jesus is usually identified with the Davidic line. The success of God's plan depends upon the positive response of both Joseph and Mary.

Today's Good News

The same is true today. God's presence is dependent upon our response, and God's presence is most often made known in our lives through persons closest to us. It is through our family traditions and our ancestors that God's salvation history becomes our sacred story. Many of us can recount the story of our ancestors' journey to their "promised land"—some seeking a better life, some fleeing persecution. Our family heritage, reflected in our stories of birth and death, sorrow and expectation, reveal the truth of "God with us" on the journey. The promise of *Emmanuel* becomes a reality for us all.

Points for Reflection and Discussion

1. When have you said "yes," allowing God to become present in a very real way in your life or in that of another?

_____

_____

_____

_____

2. Recall the birth of a special child in your life. How did you feel the first time you held that child in your arms? How has God touched you through that child?

_____

_____

_____

_____

_____

Themes

Children
    C7, The Sacrament of Marriage
Christmas
    C10, Who is Jesus Christ?
Promise
    C1, The Sacraments: An Introduction
    C12, History of the Church

Reading 1, Sirach 3:2-6,12-14

The Lord honors a father above his children, and he confirms a mother's right over her children. Those who honor their father atone for sins, and those who respect their mother are like those who lay up treasure. Those who honor their father will have joy in their own children, and when they pray they will be heard. Those who respect their father will have long life, and those who honor their mother obey the Lord.

My child, help your father in his old age, and do not grieve him as long as he lives; even if his mind fails, be patient with him; because you have all your faculties do not despise him. For kindness to a father will not be forgotten, and will be credited to you against your sins.

Psalm 128:1-2,3,4-5

Reading 2, Colossians 3:12-21

As God's chosen ones, holy and beloved, clothe yourselves with compassion, kindness, humility, meekness, and patience. Bear with one another and, if anyone has a complaint against another, forgive each other; just as the Lord has forgiven you, so you also must forgive. Above all, clothe yourselves with love, which binds everything together in perfect harmony. And let the peace of Christ rule in your hearts, to which indeed you were called in the one body. And be thankful. Let the word of Christ dwell in you richly; teach and admonish one another in all wisdom; and with gratitude in your hearts sing psalms, hymns, and spiritual songs to God. And whatever you do, in word or deed, do everything in the name of the Lord Jesus, giving thanks to God the Father through him.

Wives, be subject to your husbands, as is fitting in the Lord. Husbands, love your wives and never treat them harshly. Children, obey your parents in everything, for this is your acceptable duty in the Lord. Fathers, do not provoke your children, or they may lose heart.

Gospel, Matthew 2:13-15,19-23

After [the wise men] had left, an angel of the Lord appeared to Joseph in a dream and said, "Get up, take the child and his mother, and flee to Egypt, and remain there until I tell you; for Herod is about to search for the child, to destroy him." Then Joseph got up, took the child and his mother by night, and went to Egypt, and remained there until the death of Herod. This was to fulfill what had been spoken by the Lord through the prophet, "Out of Egypt I have called my son."

When Herod died, an angel of the Lord suddenly appeared in a dream to Joseph in Egypt and said, "Get up, take the child and his mother, and go to the land of Israel, for those who were seeking the child's life are dead." Then Joseph got up, took the child and his mother, and went to the land of Israel. But when he heard that Archelaus was ruling over Judea in place of his father Herod, he was afraid to go there. And after being warned in a dream, he went away to the district of Galilee. There he made his home in a town called Nazareth, so that what had been spoken through the prophets might be fulfilled, "He will be called a Nazorean."

Families

Ann Wolf

Although the Church today celebrates the Feast of the Holy Family, our gospel reading tells us very little about life within the Holy Family, and it does not give us much guidance as to what family life today should entail. We are told only that Mary, Joseph, and Jesus settled in the town of Nazareth. Given the fact that Jesus was considered to be the Messiah by his disciples, we might question why we have no detailed information about him prior to his ministry. Perhaps this is so because the daily life of the Holy Family was not extraordinary. Rather, they were a typical Jewish family who quietly modeled faithfulness to the Word of God and to Jewish law and tradition. They observed the Law, they celebrated the feasts, and they kept Yahweh as the center of their lives.

Roots

Our first reading, from the Book of Sirach, paints a portrait of what the author believed family life to be for those who observed the Law and kept Yahweh as the center of their being. Sirach's aim was to demonstrate that true religion involves moral duties to others, first of all to one's parents. Hebrew society at that time in history believed that God rewarded the just and punished the evil in this lifetime. Those who lived moral lives were blessed with many children, long life, healthy animals, and good crops. The immoral person was cursed with infertility, a short life, sickly animals, and crop failure. It was therefore in one's best interest to follow Sirach's advice.

Relationships with other persons, especially with members of our family, shape and express the quality of our lives. There is a sense of interdependence in which we are responsible not only for our own lives, but also for the well-being of others.

The Tie that Binds

While many would point to today's selection from the Letter to the Colossians to support the accusation that Paul was a male chauvinist, let us examine the passage in view of what has just been said about interdependence and responsibility for one another's well-being. True, the letter does use the words "subject to" when describing the ideal behavior of wives. Let us look beyond that phrase, however, to the roles of the husband and the children in nurturing family life. Husbands are to love their wives and to avoid any bitterness toward them. Children are to obey parents, while fathers are to refrain from nagging their children.

The core of successful family life, however, is found at the beginning of the second reading (verses 12-17). Compassion, kindness, humility, meekness, and patience are all virtues necessary to harmonious family life. All these virtues signify an interior change of heart; and they are redemptive virtues, or signs of the need for reconciliation. They do not focus on private spirituality, but rather include a care for others, and they are lived out within the family. Added to these virtues is love, that which not only reconciles, but brings relationships closer to perfection.

Today's Good News

All families are called to live as one body rooted in peace. We all know that the lives of individuals within families are not always peaceful in the sense of absence of conflict. The sense of peace called for here is that state of wholeness in which security, both physical and spiritual, can be realized.

Paul invokes that "the word of Christ dwell in you richly...in all wisdom" (Col 3:16). *Word* suggests the power of creation: by the Creator's *word* we came into being. Thus "in all wisdom" through "the word of Christ" calls each family member to nurture one another into the fullness of what God has created each to be.

At first glance, the Letter to the Colossians might not seem to be very revolutionary in content. If, however, these words were taken seriously, they could transform family life. Imagine what it would mean for family members to nurture one another into a true sense of peace, a state of both physical and spiritual security. We wouldn't need laws protecting us from spousal and/or child abuse. The term *dysfunctional family* would disappear from our rhetoric. Our homes would become havens of refreshment, enabling us to bravely face worldly stresses. If all individual families were to take to heart the message of this letter, the entire human family would be revolutionized. In calling one another to wholeness, entire societies could be nurtured into a familial bond that would surpass divisions caused by racism, poverty, and oppression. If we were to strive for world peace in the sense of physical and spiritual security for all human beings, we would approach the promise of end time redemption. We would have contributed to the coming of the reign of God in our day.

Points for Reflection and Discussion

1. Why does the presentation of the Holy Family as an "ordinary" family give us a sense of encouragement?

_____

_____

_____

_____

2. What are some things that form the focus for family life in the United States? What is the main focus of your family life?

_____

_____

_____

_____

_____

Themes

Family
    C9, The People of God
    C16, The Dignity of Life
Love
    C13, Christian Moral Living
    C14, Social Justice
Marriage
    C7, The Sacrament of Marriage
    C15, The Consistent Life Ethic

Reading 1, Isaiah 60:1-6

Arise, [Jerusalem], shine; for your light has come, and the glory of the Lord has risen upon you. For darkness shall cover the earth, and thick darkness the peoples; but the Lord will arise upon you, and his glory will appear over you.

Nations shall come to your light, and kings to the brightness of your dawn. Lift up your eyes and look around; they all gather together, they come to you; your sons shall come from far away, and your daughters shall be carried on their nurses' arms.

Then you shall see and be radiant; your heart shall thrill and rejoice, because the abundance of the sea shall be brought to you, the wealth of the nations shall come to you. A multitude of camels shall cover you, the young camels of Midian and Ephah; all those from Sheba shall come. They shall bring gold and frankincense, and shall proclaim the praise of the Lord.

Psalm 72:1-2,7-8,10-11,12-13

Reading 2, Ephesians 3:2-3,5-6

Surely you have already heard of the commission of God's grace that was given me for you, and how the mystery was made known to me by revelation. In former generations this mystery was not made known to humankind, as it has now been revealed to his holy apostles and prophets by the Spirit: that is, the Gentiles have become fellow heirs, members of the same body, and sharers in the promise in Christ Jesus through the gospel.

Gospel, Matthew 2:1-12

In the time of King Herod, after Jesus was born in Bethlehem of Judea, wise men from the East came to Jerusalem, asking, "Where is the child who has been born king of the Jews? For we observed his star at its rising, and have come to pay him homage." When King Herod heard this, he was frightened, and all Jerusalem with him; and calling together all the chief priests and scribes of the people, he inquired of them where the Messiah was to be born. They told him, "In Bethlehem of Judea; for so it has been written by the prophet: 'And you, Bethlehem, in the land of Judah, are by no means least among the rulers of Judah; for from you shall come a ruler who is to shepherd my people Israel.'"

Then Herod secretly called for the wise men and learned from them the exact time when the star had appeared. Then he sent them to Bethlehem, saying, "Go and search diligently for the child; and when you have found him, bring me word so that I may also go and pay him homage."

When they had heard the king, they set out; and there, ahead of them, went the star that they had seen at its rising, until it stopped over the place where the child was. When they saw that the star had stopped, they were overwhelmed with joy. On entering the house, they saw the child with Mary his mother; and they knelt down and paid him homage. Then, opening their treasure chests, they offered him gifts of gold, frankincense, and myrrh.

And having been warned in a dream not to return to Herod, they left for their own country by another road.

Unity in Diversity

ANN WOLF

Currently many religious denominations are experiencing tensions among their members for a variety of reasons. Some tensions involve issues of gender (male/female ordinations), others of marital status (celibate/married clergy), and still others of sexual preference (heterosexual/homosexual orientation). Tensions were also a fact of life in the early Church. Nor were they absent from the Jewish communities of the Hebrew Scriptures.

Rise Up, Jerusalem

Our first reading recounts the tension present among Abraham's family members. The last two verses of today's selection point to a reconciliation of the children of Abraham. The descendants of his third wife, Keturah, who settled in the lands of Midian, Ephah, and Sheba, will return to Jerusalem bearing gifts (verse 6). The following verse, which we do not hear today, names the children of Abraham's second wife, Hagar, who will come from Kedar and Nebaioth to join in sacrifice before Yahweh. Isaiah's intent is to show reconciliation between the offspring of Isaac, child of promise, and Ishmael, child of the desert. While Isaiah's new Jerusalem may not regain the political power of Solomon's era, the prophet looks forward to a day when Jerusalem's religious and moral influence will be felt worldwide. Isaiah no longer measures Jerusalem's greatness in terms of military and political power. Its future greatness will be found in its sense of moral values, which will reconcile diverse ethnic and cultural traditions so that all peoples may proclaim the praises of the Lord.

Reconciliation of ethnic and cultural traditions was one of the challenges of the early Christian community as well, as it struggled to unite the Gentile Christians with the Jewish Christians. Even though today's second reading bears the name of the community of Ephesus, it is more likely that this Letter to the Ephesians was a "circular" letter, sent from one community to the next.

Such a letter would address issues common to all communities in the area. We may assume, therefore, that the tension between Jews and Gentiles, which is a focal point in this correspondence, was an issue for most of the communities of Asia Minor.

The writer of the Letter to the Ephesians explains that God gave Paul the responsibility to make known the salvation mystery—a salvation which included both Jew and Gentile. Paul is very adamant about the fact that Gentiles have full and equal participation with the Jews. They are co-heirs with one another and members of one and the same body.

From East and From West

It is believed that Matthew included the story of the Magi in today's gospel specifically to address this struggle between the Jews and Gentiles in the community of believers. Later traditions called the Magi "kings," and the Western Church gave them the names of Caspar, Balthasar, and Malchior. To emphasize their diversity, they were described as an African and two Arabs. Matthew echoes Paul's sentiments by showing that Christianity has neither ethnic nor cultural boundary. All should be welcomed into the Christian family as the Magi were welcomed by Mary and Joseph.

Stories of the early Church confirm that not all agreed with Paul that the Jews and Gentiles were equal members within the community. In fact, the subject of equality was the focus of more than one heated discussion between Peter and Paul. Likewise, the communities were often divided regarding the Gentiles' adherence to Jewish custom and law before they could be admitted to Christianity.

Today's Good News

Ethnic diversity was not a mark of only the early Christian Church. Today the Roman Catholic Church ministers to people of a wider range of cultures than perhaps any other religion or denomination. Unlike some Christian denominations, which have established national branches, the Roman Catholic Church retains an international structure and mission.

Until Vatican Council II, liturgical rites and celebrations, and a worldwide Latin Mass, made for more "uniform" and static practices. Since the Council, the liturgy has adapted to more local ethnic customs and traditions. The common language of the people is now used in liturgy. In addition, efforts are being made to incorporate more ethnically traditional music and dress in community liturgies.

Incorporating ethnic traditions into prayer has worked well within Catholic communities that are basically ethnically homogeneous. However, a challenge still remains insofar as ascertaining the best methods of integrating a variety of ethnic cultures and traditions within a culturally mixed worshiping community.

Beyond celebrations of liturgy, the challenge is even greater. How do we celebrate parish life itself as one family, a family blessed with a diverse heritage? Paul refused to have the Gentiles assimilated into Jewish culture to such an extent that their own identity as a people was lost. Do we approach our parish community with the sense of celebrating our diversity and with the hope of complementing one another's giftedness of culture?

Points for Reflection and Discussion

1. What types of cultural and ethnic traditions are represented within your parish?

_____

_____

_____

_____

2. What responsibility does the Catholic Church have in the process of racial/ethnic integration in our neighborhoods and schools, both public and private?

_____

_____

_____

_____

Themes

Conciliation
   C5, The Sacrament of Penance
   C9, The People of God
Mission
   C13, Christian Moral Living
   C14, Social Justice
Unity
   C11, The Early Church
   C12, History of the Church

Reading 1, Isaiah 42:1-4,6-7

Here is my servant, whom I uphold, my chosen, in whom my soul delights; I have put my spirit upon him; he will bring forth justice to the nations. He will not cry or lift up his voice, or make it heard in the street; a bruised reed he will not break, and a dimly burning wick he will not quench; he will faithfully bring forth justice. He will not grow faint or be crushed until he has established justice in the earth; and the coastlands wait for his teaching.

I am the Lord, I have called you in righteousness, I have taken you by the hand and kept you; I have given you as a covenant to the people, a light to the nations, to open the eyes that are blind, to bring out the prisoners from the dungeon, from the prison those who sit in darkness.

Psalm 29:1-2,3-4,3,9-10

Reading 2, Acts 10:34-38

Peter began to speak to [those assembled in the house of Cornelius]: "I truly understand that God shows no partiality, but in every nation anyone who fears him and does what is right is acceptable to him. You know the message he sent to the people of Israel, preaching peace by Jesus Christ—he is Lord of all. That message spread throughout Judea, beginning in Galilee after the baptism that John announced: how God anointed Jesus of Nazareth with the Holy Spirit and with power; how he went about doing good and healing all who were oppressed by the devil, for God was with him."

Gospel, Matthew 3:13-17

Jesus came from Galilee to John at the Jordan, to be baptized by him. John would have prevented him, saying, "I need to be baptized by you, and do you come to me?" But Jesus answered him, "Let it be so now; for it is proper for us in this way to fulfill all righteousness." Then he consented.

And when Jesus had been baptized, just as he came up from the water, suddenly the heavens were opened to him and he saw the Spirit of God descending like a dove and alighting on him. And a voice from heaven said, "This is my Son, the Beloved, with whom I am well pleased."

"Ordinary" Time

ANN WOLF

Today the Church celebrates the Feast of the Baptism of the Lord. It marks the official ending of the Christmas Season and the beginning of what the Church terms "Ordinary Time." During Ordinary Time the gospel readings tell us of the public life and ministry of Jesus which began with his baptism. Theologically, Jesus' baptism is so important that the story is told by all four evangelists. This event introduces Jesus as the New Covenant, and baptism eventually becomes part of the initiation rite of all Christians into that covenant.

My Chosen One

In the first reading, Isaiah too speaks of covenant and names the Servant as a sign of Yahweh's covenant with the people. While it is difficult to determine whether Isaiah is referring to a single person, a king, or the state of Israel as the Servant, it is easy to determine the impact that the Servant figure will have upon the life of Israel: "He [will establish] justice in the earth; and the coastlands [will] wait for his teaching." The eyes of the blind will be opened, prisoners will be freed, light will burst forth from the darkness. Yahweh chose this Servant from among many, and being so chosen carried with it the challenge to respond.

While the author of this portion of the Book of Isaiah was not predicting the ministry of Jesus when this passage was written, it is easy to see how the early Christians could see similarities between the ministry of the Servant, and that of Jesus of Nazareth. In the second reading, from Acts of the Apostles, Peter reminds us of Isaiah's Servant when he refers to Jesus' going "about doing good and healing all who were oppressed by the devil." During his baptism "God anointed (him) with the Holy Spirit and with power." Thus Jesus became the proclamation of the Good News of peace.

Matthew's Gospel reading gives us his version of the story of Jesus' baptism, at the hands of John, in the Jordan River. Just as the crossing of the Jordan marked the transition from wilderness to Promised Land for the "chosen people" (see Jos 1:1-3;3:14-17), Jesus' baptism marked the transition from his ordinary life as a carpenter's son in Nazareth to his extraordinary ministry as the beloved Son of God.

Being Baptized

The baptismal rite speaks of death and rising to new life. It marks the beginning of new life as a member of the Christian community. But baptism is not a sacrament that is received once and then forgotten. There is a

continuation of this first commitment to the Christian life, and this commitment manifests itself through action.

For both Isaiah's Servant and Jesus of Nazareth, the response to the call centered upon acts of justice. We are not told exactly how the Servant was to establish justice on the earth, but we are told that it would not be through crying out and shouting in the street, nor through the breaking of a reed. It seems that witness through example and teaching, rather than through radical acts, were what the Servant was called to do. We know that Jesus responded by means of teaching and quiet witness, as well as through healing, casting out of demons, and confrontation of both religious and government leaders.

Today's Good News

In today's society response to the baptismal commitment comes in many forms. Through faithful support of one's spouse and responsible parenting one can live out baptismal promises within the family. Baptismal promises can become a reality in the workplace through ethically responsible business practices. Employers who offer fair wages and good working conditions and employees who take their jobs seriously can become witnesses to their baptismal covenant.

In the community at large supporting projects that address societal needs (homelessness, health care, illiteracy) with financial aid or the gift of one's time or talent is one way to live out the call to Christianity. Even responsible voting could be considered a response to the baptismal call.

Within the Christian community those who choose religious life (priests, brothers, sisters) are responding in a special way to their baptismal commitment. But so are those who offer their talents in teaching religion to children, in visiting the elderly of the parish, in visiting the sick. Those who serve on finance commissions, parish councils, education commissions—all are responding to the call of baptism.

Response to the baptismal call is any public statement of word or action through which we make known our belief in and commitment to Christianity. Through baptism we are called to be a chosen people. Through baptism we receive the gift of the Spirit, which empowers us to respond to this call, to being "chosen" ones. The response can be as unique as the individual from whom it comes; but a response is demanded of each and every baptized person.

Points for Reflection and Discussion

1. What kind of support do you need from family, friends, Church in order to live out your baptismal commitment or to respond to your call to receive the sacrament of baptism?

_____

_____

_____

_____

2. What has been the most difficult response to your baptismal commitment (or call to receive baptism) that you have had to make in your life? What gave you the strength to respond in the way you did?

_____

_____

_____

_____

Themes
Baptism
   C2, The Sacrament of Baptism
Holy Orders
   C8, The Sacrament of Holy Orders
Matrimony
   C7, The Sacrament of Marriage

Reading 1, Isaiah 49:3,5-6

[The Lord] said to me, "You are my servant, Israel, in whom I will be glorified." And now the Lord says, who formed me in the womb to be his servant, to bring Jacob back to him, and that Israel might be gathered to him, for I am honored in the sight of the Lord, and my God has become my strength—he says, "It is too light a thing that you should be my servant to raise up the tribes of Jacob and to restore the survivors of Israel; I will give you as a light to the nations, that my salvation may reach to the end of the earth."

Psalm 40:1,3,6,7-8,9 (NRSV)

Reading 2, 1 Corinthians 1:1-3

Paul, called to be an apostle of Christ Jesus by the will of God, and our brother Sosthenes. To the church of God that is in Corinth, to those who are sanctified in Christ Jesus, called to be saints, together with all those who in every place call on the name of our Lord Jesus Christ, both their Lord and ours: Grace to you and peace from God our Father and the Lord Jesus Christ.

Gospel, John 1:29-34

[John the Baptist] saw Jesus coming toward him and declared, "Here is the Lamb of God who takes away the sin of the world! This is he of whom I said, 'After me comes a man who ranks ahead of me because he was before me.' I myself did not know him; but I came baptizing with water for this reason, that he might be revealed to Israel."

And John testified, "I saw the Spirit descending from heaven like a dove, and it remained on him. I myself did not know him, but the one who sent me to baptize with water said to me, 'He on whom you see the Spirit descend and remain is the one who baptizes with the Holy Spirit.' And I myself have seen and have testified that this is the Son of God."

Called to Be Holy

ANN WOLF

Today's readings continue the theme of call/response that we saw last week in the Baptism of the Lord narrative. Today we focus on the element of empowerment through the Spirit and confirmation of the call to ministry.

The reading from Isaiah is the second of four Servant Songs. Although the Servant relates being called by the Lord in the intimacy of the womb, that call was not meant to remain a private spiritual experience. The strength of God empowered the servant to announce himself as a "light to the nations" and a bearer of God's salvation to the "end of the earth." The Lord has spoken, and thus confirms the servant as a specially chosen representative, granting legitimacy to the mission of evangelization.

In the second reading, Paul extends the call to the people of the Church of God in Corinth, those who have been "sanctified in Christ Jesus (and) called to be saints." This sanctification conveys a public dimension as holiness manifests itself through action within the Christian community of Corinth. The gift of the "grace...and peace from God our Father and the Lord Jesus Christ" confirms the call to discipleship.

The Spirit Descending

Confirmation by the Spirit of the call/response is also related in the account of Jesus' baptism found today in John's Gospel. Last week's baptism narrative, from Matthew's Gospel, gave us the account from the vantage point of Jesus. This week, John the Evangelist describes the event through the eyes of John the Baptist. While Jesus' baptism in the Jordan was a very intense personal experience for him, the Baptizer observes a public confirmation of the Spirit to Jesus' response to the call to ministry. "I saw the Spirit descending from heaven like a dove, and it remained on him." The power of the Spirit gave Jesus the sense of internal confirmation for his movement from private life to public ministry. This same Spirit gave John external confirmation of Jesus as God's Son, the one who had authority to baptize with the Holy Spirit.

Today's Good News

Few of us experience the descent of the Holy Spirit in the form of a dove as confirmation of God's call or our response. How, then, can we know that God truly has confirmed a response to a perceived call? Though "call" can be an intensely personal experience, it is often accompanied by a sense of empowerment that prompts a public manifestation or response to that call. There is inner assurance that we no longer represent only our own interests, but now must speak and act as the children of God.

Some calls in life are major events that demand significant responses. These could include calls to ordained ministry, religious life, or married life. Confirmation of such responses does not necessarily come instantly. It can come during the process of formation for seminarians and religious, or during the engagement period for those contemplating marriage. Is one well-suited for a lifestyle of celibacy and lifelong commitment to serve the Church and the people of God at the expense of one's personal goals and desires? Are the personalities and family backgrounds of the engaged couple well-suited to a lifelong commitment to nourishing each other in faith and love? An absence of serious doubts and questions, a sense of inner peace, seem to confirm one's call and support one's response as genuine.

Often people are faced with a less permanent call/response, such as whether to take a certain job. Sometimes it is only after we begin a new job that confirmation comes. There is a sense of comfortableness in surroundings. We are confident that we have the skills to accomplish the tasks; coworkers seem supportive. This is to us a sign that we have made a good decision.

Confirmation through the Spirit doesn't mean that our course of action will be permanently free from all tension and doubt. But we are assured that the Spirit will give us the strength and endurance necessary to face the challenges that come our way in trying to make a faithful response to the call to be Christian disciples.

Points for Reflection and Discussion

1. Paul calls the Corinthians to be "saints." Name one person in your life whom you consider to be a saint. What about them causes you to think of them in that way?

_____

_____

_____

_____

2. Have you ever had an experience in your life in which you knew without a doubt that a certain course of action was one you should follow? How could you be so certain? Describe that experience.

_____

_____

_____

_____

_____

Themes

Confirmation
   C3, The Sacrament of Confirmation
Holy Spirit
   C9, The People of God

Reading 1, Isaiah 9:1-4 (NRSV)

There will be no gloom for those who were in anguish. In the former time [the Lord] brought into contempt the land of Zebulun and the land of Naphtali, but in the latter time he will make glorious the way of the sea, the land beyond the Jordan, Galilee of the nations.

The people who walked in darkness have seen a great light; those who lived in a land of deep darkness—on them light has shined. You have multiplied the nation, you have increased its joy; they rejoice before you as with joy at the harvest, as people exult when dividing plunder. For the yoke of their burden, and the bar across their shoulders, the rod of their oppressor, you have broken as on the day of Midian.

Psalm 27:1,4,13-14

Reading 2, 1 Corinthians 1:10-13,17

I appeal to you, brothers and sisters, by the name of our Lord Jesus Christ, that all of you be in agreement and that there be no divisions among you, but that you be united in the same mind and the same purpose. For it has been reported to me by Chloe's people that there are quarrels among you, my brothers and sisters. What I mean is that each of you says, "I belong to Paul," or "I belong to Apollos," or "I belong to Cephas," or "I belong to Christ." Has Christ been divided? Was Paul crucified for you? Or were you baptized in the name of Paul? For Christ did not send me to baptize but to proclaim the gospel, and not with eloquent wisdom, so that the cross of Christ might not be emptied of its power.

Gospel, Matthew 4:12-23

When Jesus heard that John had been arrested, he withdrew to Galilee. He left Nazareth and made his home in Capernaum by the sea, in the territory of Zebulun and Naphtali, so that what had been spoken through the prophet Isaiah might be fulfilled: "Land of Zebulun, land of Naphtali, on the road by the sea, across the Jordan, Galilee of the Gentiles—the people who sat in darkness have seen a great light, and for those who sat in the region and shadow of death light has dawned." From that time Jesus began to proclaim, "Repent, for the kingdom of heaven has come near."

As he walked by the Sea of Galilee, he saw two brothers, Simon, who is called Peter, and Andrew his brother, casting a net into the sea—for they were fishermen. And he said to them, "Follow me, and I will make you fish for people." Immediately they left their nets and followed him.

As he went from there, he saw two other brothers, James son of Zebedee and his brother John, in the boat with their father Zebedee, mending their nets, and he called them. Immediately they left the boat and their father, and followed him.

Jesus went throughout Galilee, teaching in their synagogues and proclaiming the good news of the kingdom and curing every disease and every sickness among the people.

Learning to Fish

ANN WOLF

Matthew's Gospel on this day recounts the beginning of Jesus' public ministry and the call of the first disciples. Seeing John the Baptist's arrest as a sign to begin his public ministry, Jesus withdrew to Capernaum, a city in his homeland of Galilee. Since Galilee was part of the land previously called Zebulun and Naphtali, Matthew considers Jesus' ministry as a fulfillment of the first reading from Isaiah: The people of Zebulun and Naphtali will see a great light which will rise above the land overshadowed by death.

The land of Zebulun and Naphtali mentioned by both Isaiah and Matthew lay at the northernmost edge of the kingdom of the Twelve Tribes of Israel. These lands were the first to fall to the Assyrians and to be overrun by the forces of Tiglath-Pilesar III. During the 730's B.C., this despised ruler deported the Israelites and resettled the area with a diverse mixture of Gentiles. From that time forward the region of Galilee began to be looked upon as a "heathen" area. Thus, the prophet refers to the contemptible lands. This passage from Isaiah holds out hope for a future time when a ruler of the Davidic line will once again raise the people to their former glory. The yoke that burdened them, the rod of slavery, will be replaced by abundant joy and great rejoicing.

Come After Me

Matthew sees Isaiah's promise of restoration realized in the person of Jesus of Nazareth and in his proclamation, "Repent, for the kingdom of heaven has come near." But Jesus was not to be the only proclaimer of the Good News. He calls Simon (Peter), Andrew, James, and John to follow him. In his Letter to the Corinthians, Paul adds another preacher of the gospel, Apollos, who joins Cephas (Peter) and Paul himself in proclaiming the Good News.

Though the gospel seems to imply that the disciples of Jesus immediately abandoned their nets and took on new lives as followers of Jesus, it could not have been that simple. They were not called to merely spend an afternoon with the Lord, but to radically change—to reform—their entire lives. No longer were they fishermen, but now "fishers of people." This commitment to discipleship required leaving family, home, and friends to take up life on the road with an itinerant preacher.

Today's Good News

It is not always easy to be a faithful witness to the gospel message, as Paul hints at in his Letter to the Corinthians. Sometimes factions develop within families or within the Church that make the living out of gospel values difficult. Paul tells us that when tensions arise, our rootedness in Christ raises us above petty arguments. We are called to continually reform our lives so that we may reflect the light of Christ.

While we may consider the disciples' responses to be a bit radical—an immediate abandonment of their former lives—all of us have known someone who has reformed a past life in order to follow the call to Christian marriage or to the life of an ordained or vowed religious. It is through the faithful living out of those vocations that we become the bearers of the Good News, the proclaimers of the reign of God in our midst.

In spreading the gospel, all vocations are of equal importance. As Saint Paul says, there are different gifts, but the same Spirit, there are varied functions, but one body (see 1 Cor 12). While the Church needs ordained clergy to mediate sacramental blessings, the Church also needs trained catechists, visitors of the sick and elderly, and advocates for the marginalized. None of these ministers can meet all the needs of the people of God on their own.

While we often look to the Church to take the lead in spreading the gospel message, let us not forget that parents are the first and best teachers of their children when it comes to the passing on of gospel values. The love and concern that a married couple shows for one another is a concrete reflection to children of God's love for them.

Likewise, those committed to religious life or to the single state can be reminders to us that Jesus of Nazareth was neither married nor a consecrated rabbi. The gifts of all people are valued and needed as we work together to bring about the coming of God's reign in our world.

Points for Reflection and Discussion

1. Jesus commanded all his followers to preach the gospel "to the end of the earth." Are you comfortable or uncomfortable with this command? Why?

_____

_____

_____

_____

2. What is the greatest gift you bring to the effort of spreading the Good News?

_____

_____

_____

_____

Themes

Reconciliation
    C5, The Sacrament of Penance
Vocations
    C7, The Sacrament of Marriage
    C8, The Sacrament of Holy Orders

Reading 1, Zephaniah 2:3;3:12-13

Seek the Lord, all you humble of the land, who do his commands; seek righteousness, seek humility; perhaps you may be hidden on the day of the Lord's wrath. For I will leave in the midst of you a people humble and lowly. They shall seek refuge in the name of the Lord—the remnant of Israel; they shall do no wrong and utter no lies, nor shall a deceitful tongue be found in their mouths. Then they will pasture and lie down, and no one shall make them afraid.

Psalm 146:6-7,8-9,9-10

Reading 2, 1 Corinthians 1:26-31

Consider your own call, brothers and sisters: not many of you were wise by human standards, not many were powerful, not many were of noble birth. But God chose what is foolish in the world to shame the wise; God chose what is weak in the world to shame the strong; God chose what is low and despised in the world, things that are not, to reduce to nothing things that are, so that no one might boast in the presence of God. He is the source of your life in Christ Jesus, who became for us wisdom from God, and righteousness and sanctification and redemption, in order that, as it is written, "Let the one who boasts, boast in the Lord."

Gospel, Matthew 5:1-12

When Jesus saw the crowds, he went up the mountain; and after he sat down, his disciples came to him. Then he began to speak, and taught them, saying:

"Blessed are the poor in spirit, for theirs is the kingdom of heaven.

"Blessed are those who mourn, for they will be comforted.

"Blessed are the meek, for they will inherit the earth.

"Blessed are those who hunger and thirst for righteousness, for they will be filled.

"Blessed are the merciful, for they will receive mercy.

"Blessed are the pure in heart, for they will see God.

"Blessed are the peacemakers, for they will be called children of God.

"Blessed are those who are persecuted for righteousness' sake, for theirs is the kingdom of heaven.

"Blessed are you when people revile you and persecute you and utter all kinds of evil against you falsely on my account. Rejoice and be glad, for your reward is great in heaven."

The Option for the Poor

ANN WOLF

All three of today's readings speak to us of God's preferential option for the lowly. Zephaniah speaks of the faithful "remnant of Israel," while Matthew and Paul point to the lowly and despised Christians living in Roman-occupied lands.

The selection from Zephaniah was written within the 630's B.C., a time during which the Jewish people had become particularly lax in their observation of ritual law. The prophet warns that on the *Yom Yahweh* (the "Day of the Lord") God's anger will rain down upon those who have been unfaithful to the covenant. They will be consumed in darkness and distress and surrounded by ruin and devastation. Only the remnant of faithful ones shall be saved. Those who speak truthfully and without deceit are the ones who shall be considered faithful to Yahweh. These lowly and humble shall live in Yahweh's care and safety. "They will pasture and lie down, and no one shall make them afraid."

The Lowly and the Humble

Although Jesus ushers in a new era in salvation history, his message is a replay of the justice and righteousness proclamation of the Hebrew prophets. According to the Hebrew concept of kingship, the ruler's first duty was to protect and care for the weak. Jesus extends this obligation to all those who seek to participate in the reign of God. Matthew's Beatitudes talk not necessarily of the materially poor, but of those who choose voluntary poverty. He moves from socio-economic poverty to a sense of personal and moral humility. Poverty of spirit gives rise to pureness of heart, which includes not only acts of justice and righteousness but also sincere worship. Acts of justice spring from prayer and are celebrated in offering praise to God.

Though Jesus promised rewards to the faithful, these blessings would be realized only with the coming of the reign of God. In the life and ministry of Jesus, we witness the dawn of a new era, the beginning of the reign of God. But the reign has yet to reach completion. Even Jesus' death/resurrection did not bring about the raising of the lowly and the blessing of the despised, for Paul echoes this promise of better times to come for the first century Christians of Corinth. Just as God had chosen the lowly of Israel to be a people of promise, God renews that covenant with the weak and despised Christians in Roman society. Paul renews God's promise of redemption and sanctification through life in Christ Jesus.

Today's Good News

The Church today continues to remind us of God's preferential option for the poor and the marginalized. More than one hundred years ago, in 1891, Pope Leo XIII issued the first encyclical to address social issues, entitled *The Condition of Labor*, or *Rerum Novarum*. This document supported worker's rights to organize and called for fair labor practices on the part of employers.

In our own time, the U.S. bishops have issued a number of documents that have dealt with social issues, among them *The Challenge of Peace: The U.S. Catholic Bishops' Pastoral Letter on War and Peace*; *Economic Justice for All: U.S. Catholic Bishops' Pastoral Letter on Catholic Social Teaching and the U.S. Economy*; and *Brothers and Sisters to Us: U.S. Catholic Bishops' Pastoral Letter on Racism in Our Day*. And Pope John Paul II, on the occasion of the one-hundreth anniversary of *Rerum Novarum*, issued a new encyclical on human rights, *Centesimus Annus*.

It is the responsibility of the pope and the bishops to challenge us, especially, to examine structures of society with an eye toward the manner in which we treat the poor and marginalized of our world. It is our responsibility to respond to such challenges with actions that can lead to structural change. In an urban setting one may become aware that a lending institution refuses loans to certain ethnic groups. In a rural area similar discrimination may be found against a certain class of farmers or migrant workers. One action could be to withdraw personal funds if the institution continued such practices. Boycotting companies and retail stores that engage in unfair labor practices has also been shown to be effective in accomplishing structural change.

In addition, the pope and bishops call each of us to examine our own attitude toward the poor and marginalized. Do we cross the street in order to avoid an encounter with a shabbily dressed person? If we do speak, is it in a condescending manner?

God does not necessarily call us to choose material poverty for ourselves and our families, but God does call us to be one with each other in poverty of spirit—a poverty where *each* human being is valued and treated as an image of the Creator.

Points for Reflection and Discussion

1. Is the word "marginalized" used only to describe the materially poor? To whom could it also refer?

_____

_____

_____

_____

2. The dictionary defines the word "solidarity" in the following manner: complete unity, as of opinion, purpose, interest, feeling. What does being in solidarity with the marginalized mean for your life?

_____

_____

_____

_____

Themes

Beatitudes
    C16, The Dignity of Life
Social Justice
    C14, Social Justice
    C15, The Consistent Life Ethic

Reading 1, Isaiah 58:7-10

[Thus says the Lord:] Share your bread with the hungry, and bring the homeless poor into your house; when you see the naked, cover them, and [do] not hide yourself from your own kin. Then your light shall break forth like the dawn, and your healing shall spring up quickly; your vindicator shall go before you, the glory of the Lord shall be your rear guard. Then you shall call, and the Lord will answer; you shall cry for help, and he will say, "Here I am."

If you remove the yoke from among you, the pointing of the finger, the speaking of evil, if you offer your food to the hungry and satisfy the needs of the afflicted, then your light shall rise in the darkness and your gloom be like the noonday.

Psalm 112:4-5,6-7,8-9

Reading 2, 1 Corinthians 2:1-5

When I came to you, brothers and sisters, I did not come proclaiming the mystery of God to you in lofty words or wisdom. For I decided to know nothing among you except Jesus Christ, and him crucified. And I came to you in weakness and in fear and in much trembling. My speech and my proclamation were not with plausible words of wisdom, but with a demonstration of the Spirit and of power, so that your faith might rest not on human wisdom but on the power of God.

Gospel, Matthew 5:13-16

[Jesus said to his disciples:] "You are the salt of the earth; but if salt has lost its taste, how can its saltiness be restored? It is no longer good for anything, but is thrown out and trampled under foot.

"You are the light of the world. A city built on a hill cannot be hid. No one after lighting a lamp puts it under the bushel basket, but on the lampstand, and it gives light to all in the house. In the same way, let your light shine before others, so that they may see your good works and give glory to your Father in heaven."

Life's Necessities

ANN WOLF

One of the darkest times in the history of the Jewish people was the age of the Babylonian captivity. The prophets of that era preached a message of hope. One day, they said, Yahweh will restore God's chosen people to their former glory. The exile will end; we will return to Jerusalem in triumph. But the actual deliverance from the snares of Babylon was not as joyous as had been the expectation of freedom. The land lay in ruin; Jerusalem was devastated. The greatest heartache of all was the pain of no longer being able to offer sacrifice to Yahweh in Solomon's Temple; the Temple was no more. For a people whose worship had centered around sacrifice, there was little hope of reestablishing the same type of ritual experience that had been theirs prior to the exile. Isaiah attempts to convey a sense of hope to these people who had expected joy, but were now consumed by despair.

Light...

In today's reading the prophet assures the people that what Yahweh seeks most from them is not sacrifice, but acts of justice and righteousness. While sacrifice was seen as a renewal of the covenant, acts of justice and righteousness were proper responses to that covenant. They were the signs that the people were in right relationship with one another and with Yahweh. Sheltering the homeless, clothing the naked, feeding the hungry, and alleviating oppression were all acts that would allow Yahweh's people to bring light to those who lived in the midst of darkness.

And Salt...

Today's passage from Matthew's Gospel speaks of God's people acting as "the salt of the earth" and "the light of the world." These words follow that portion of the gospel that contains the Beatitudes, in which Jesus blesses those whose actions flow from a sense of justice and righteousness. Ritual is not enough; it must be complemented by concrete actions. The oppressed must be set free, the marginalized must be cared for. Jesus echoes Isaiah in stressing that acts of righteousness are signs of the covenant in action.

When Matthew uses the image of salt, he is stating that moral living is as necessary an ingredient in bringing about the reign of God as salt was to surviving the desert climate of Palestine. While we commonly use salt to flavor our food, all those who lived before the era of refrigeration depended upon salt to preserve their food from spoilage. Without salt one would quickly die of starvation.

Salt also played a role in the ritual sacrifices of the Jewish people. They not only preserved their food with salt, but they salted their sacrificial offerings in order to symbolize the preservation of their covenant with Yahweh.

Today's Good News

Christians today also place great emphasis on moral living as a sign of the continuation and renewal of our covenant with Yahweh in the person of Jesus of Nazareth. Jesus is referred to as the new covenant, and a major ritual sign of that new covenant in the Catholic Church is the sacrament of the Eucharist. This celebration, often called the Mass, not only nourishes and strengthens the relationship between the worshipers and God, but it facilitates the building of relationships among the Catholic Christian community. The prayers, and often the readings, emphasize the fact that we Christians too are called to acts of justice and righteousness in society. We cannot be in right relationship with God unless we are in right relationship with one another.

Saint Paul reminds us in the second reading that being in right relationship with God and with one another does not necessarily manifest itself through "wisdom." It is not through acts of power or a sense of triumph that we are united as Christians. Rather, it is through our own weakness and acceptance of the poverty of the cross of Jesus that we become one with another. It is then that we become like the salt that preserved life in the desert. It is then that our covenant relationship with God is preserved and nourished.

Rather than desiring to be in relationship with one another, many today seek the affluence of solitude. Those who once gathered on front porches during a summer's eve to chat with neighbors now lounge in air conditioned dens mesmerized by the television set. Children no longer play softball in the alleys and streets but "exercise" their minds by means of video and computer games.

This same sense of isolation spills over into our worship centers, where we must stretch over empty space to greet one another at the sign of peace. For some, the distance is so great that a wave of the hand or nod of the head is the only possible greeting. Are we really a "community" of believers?

Points for Reflection and Discussion

1. What do you think is the main cause for the lack of "community spirit" in our society today? How can this be addressed?

_____

_____

_____

_____

2. What actions could be taken in your parish to increase the sense of community, especially at celebrations of the Eucharist?

_____

_____

_____

_____

Themes

Community
  C9, The People of God
  C11, The Early Church
Eucharist
  C4, The Eucharist
  C10, Who is Jesus Christ?
Harmony
  C1, The Sacraments: An Introduction
  C15, The Consistent Life Ethic

Reading 1, Sirach 15:15-20

If you choose, you can keep the commandments, and to act faithfully is a matter of your own choice. [The Lord] has placed before you fire and water; stretch out your hand for whichever you choose. Before each person are life and death, and whichever one chooses will be given.

For great is the wisdom of the Lord; he is mighty in power and sees everything; his eyes are on those who fear him, and he knows every human action. He has not commanded anyone to be wicked, and he has not given anyone permission to sin.

Psalm 119:1-2,4-5,17-18,33-34

Reading 2, 1 Corinthians 2:6-10

Among the mature we do speak wisdom, though it is not a wisdom of this age or of the rulers of this age, who are doomed to perish. But we speak God's wisdom, secret and hidden, which God decreed before the ages for our glory. None of the rulers of this age understood this; for if they had, they would not have crucified the Lord of glory.

But, as it is written, "What no eye has seen, nor ear heard, nor the human heart conceived, what God has prepared for those who love him"—these things God has revealed to us through the Spirit; for the Spirit searches everything, even the depths of God.

Gospel, Matthew 5:17-37

[Jesus said to his disciples:] "Do not think that I have come to abolish the law or the prophets; I have come not to abolish but to fulfill. For truly I tell you, until heaven and earth pass away, not one letter, not one stroke of a letter, will pass from the law until all is accomplished. Therefore, whoever breaks one of the least of these commandments, and teaches others to do the same, will be called least in the kingdom of heaven; but whoever does them and teaches them will be called great in the kingdom of heaven. For I tell you, unless your righteousness exceeds that of the scribes and Pharisees, you will never enter the kingdom of heaven.

"You have heard that it was said to those of ancient times, 'You shall not murder'; and 'whoever murders shall be liable to judgment.' But I say to you that if you are angry with a brother or sister, you will be liable to judgment; and if you insult a brother or sister, you will be liable to the council; and if you say, 'You fool,' you will be liable to the hell of fire. So when you are offering your gift at the altar, if you remember that your brother or sister has something against you, leave your gift there before the altar and go; first be reconciled to your brother or sister,

and then come and offer your gift. Come to terms quickly with your accuser while you are on the way to court with him, or your accuser may hand you over to the judge, and the judge to the guard, and you will be thrown into prison. Truly I tell you, you will never get out until you have paid the last penny.

"You have heard that it was said, 'You shall not commit adultery.' But I say to you that everyone who looks at a woman with lust has already committed adultery with her in his heart. If your right eye causes you to sin, tear it out and throw it away; it is better for you to lose one of your members than for your whole body to be thrown into hell. And if your right hand causes you to sin, cut it off and throw it away; it is better for you to lose one of your members than for your whole body to go into hell.

"It was also said, 'Whoever divorces his wife, let him give her a certificate of divorce.' But I say to you that anyone who divorces his wife, except on the ground of unchastity, causes her to commit adultery; and whoever marries a divorced woman commits adultery.

"Again, you have heard that it was said to those of ancient times, 'You shall not swear falsely, but carry out the vows you have made to the Lord.' But I say to you, Do not swear at all, either by heaven, for it is the throne of God, or by the earth, for it is his footstool, or by Jerusalem, for it is the city of the great King. And do not swear by your head, for you cannot make one hair white or black. Let your word be 'Yes, Yes' or 'No, No'; anything more than this comes from the evil one."

Law

ANN WOLF

When we think about a wise person, we are generally reminded of someone who is closer to the end of life than to the beginning; one who has lived long and experienced many joys and sorrows along the way. The wise person is not a walking encyclopedia, who can repeat page after page of mathematical formulas or who can recite dates of great events in history. Rather, the wise person is one who can take knowledge and apply it to the everyday events of life. This ability comes not from being a student of life's processes, but from being in relationship with other people in the midst of God's created world. Saint Paul describes a wise person as one who is spiritually mature; one who has learned to get in touch with God's wisdom, which has been present in creation from all eternity, and to bring that wisdom to the reality of daily life.

The Jewish people believed the totality of God's will was contained in the 613 precepts of the Torah, which were to be strictly observed. To follow the Law exactly was to please God. Sometimes following the Law conflicted with interpersonal relationships, however. An example was the priest who passed by the unconscious Samaritan in Jesus' parable. He was following the Law, which forbade the touching of a dead person. If he had tried to help the Samaritan, and had found that he was dead, the Law would have prevented him from conducting worship services. In this case, following the letter of the Law directly contributed to the physical suffering of another person.

Today's Good News

Jesus addresses the Law in today's gospel reading, but it is not to do away with laws that might be considered unjust or unwarranted. Rather, Jesus expands the Law—to encompass seemingly lesser, and even more common, everyday experiences.

Jesus realizes that while few of us may be personally confronted with the violent act of murder, many of us find ourselves in the situation of being able to destroy another person's spirit through bursts of angry words. He reminds us that abusive language and contempt for the dignity of another human person will quickly kill a relationship between people. Bemoaning the fact that conditions of society require courts of law, Jesus asks: Wouldn't it be better if we could settle our differences between one another without resorting to legal battles? Wouldn't it be better if we didn't have to resort to the taking of oaths, but that we could trust that one another's word would be honored?

Jesus addresses family relationships when he extends the laws of divorce to cover lustful thoughts. While divorce legally terminates the life of a marriage, lustful thoughts, treating another human being as a sex object, using another person for one's own pleasure—all these "lesser" acts slowly eat away at a relationship. The death of such a marriage actually comes long before the divorce decree, and it often is the result of nothing more than too many seemingly small singular actions. Marriage in Christ is a sacrament, indissoluble because the couple forges a covenant with God that dissallows sins such as lust to pervade and erode the relationship.

While Jesus often criticized those who enforced strict observance of the Law, we find him to be more demanding than many would expect when it comes to enforcing laws that touch the substance of human life and relationships with one another. He does not abolish or even reduce these laws, but he brings them to greater fullness.

The reading from Sirach reminds us that we alone have the freedom to choose to do God's will by respecting and honoring others as creations in God's image. We have the option of bringing life and nourishing each other, or of destroying one another through words and acts that violate human dignity. The new morality that Jesus proclaims is not in terms of what is explicitly commanded or forbidden; rather, it requires radical respect for all members of the human family without exception.

In most of our cities, violent acts are increasing at an alarming rate. Our prisons are crowded to overflowing with offenders who have yet to see their twenty-fifth birthday. Yet we know that people are not born wishing harm for one another. Violent behavior, in most cases, is learned. It is a reaction to the devaluing of one's own sense of dignity. It is a reaction to being treated as an object, to being treated with contempt. Do we wonder that Jesus could see the connection between feelings of frustration and anger and acts of murder?

Points for Reflection and Discussion

1. Have you or a member of your family ever been the victim of a violent act? What was your response?

_____

_____

_____

_____

2. Does the Church have any obligation to address the rising incidence of violent acts that plagues our cities? What should its involvement be? Should your local parish take any action to address the issue of violent acts in your neighborhood?

_____

_____

_____

_____

Themes
Commandments
  C13, Christian Moral Living
  C14, Social Justice
Magisterium
  C12, History of the Church
  C8, The Sacrament of Holy Orders

Reading 1, Leviticus 19:1-2,17-18

The Lord spoke to Moses, saying: "Speak to all the congregation of the people of Israel and say to them: You shall be holy, for I the Lord your God am holy.

"You shall not hate in your heart anyone of your kin; you shall reprove your neighbor, or you will incur guilt yourself. You shall not take vengeance or bear a grudge against any of your people, but you shall love your neighbor as yourself: I am the Lord."

Psalm 103:1-2,3-4,8,10,12-13

Reading 2, 1 Corinthians 3:16-23

Do you not know that you are God's temple and that God's Spirit dwells in you? If anyone destroys God's temple, God will destroy that person. For God's temple is holy, and you are that temple.

Do not deceive yourselves. If you think that you are wise in this age, you should become fools so that you may become wise. For the wisdom of this world is foolishness with God. For it is written, "He catches the wise in their craftiness," and again, "The Lord knows the thoughts of the wise, that they are futile."

So let no one boast about human leaders. For all things are yours, whether Paul or Apollos or Cephas or the world or life or death or the present or the future—all belong to you, and you belong to Christ, and Christ belongs to God.

Gospel, Matthew 5:38-48

[Jesus said to his disciples:] "You have heard that it was said, 'An eye for an eye and a tooth for a tooth.' But I say to you, Do not resist an evildoer. But if anyone strikes you on the right cheek, turn the other also; and if anyone wants to sue you and take your coat, give your cloak as well; and if anyone forces you to go one mile, go also the second mile. Give to everyone who begs from you, and do not refuse anyone who wants to borrow from you.

"You have heard that it was said, 'You shall love your neighbor and hate your enemy.' But I say to you, Love your enemies and pray for those who persecute you, so that you may be children of your Father in heaven; for he makes his sun rise on the evil and on the good, and sends rain on the righteous and on the unrighteous. For if you love those who love you, what reward do you have? Do not even the tax collectors do the same? And if you greet only your brothers and sisters, what more are you doing than others? Do not even the Gentiles do the same? Be perfect, therefore, as your heavenly Father is perfect."

A Holy People

ANN WOLF

Today's readings speak to us of what it means to be holy as God is holy. For the writer of Leviticus, to be holy is to love one's neighbor as oneself; for Paul, it is to become a fool in the world's eyes; for Jesus, it is to love one's enemies and pray for one's persecutors.

The progression that we see between today's Hebrew Scriptures and gospel reading gives us an example of the evolution of biblical thought on retaliation and love. Violence has been a curse upon humankind since the fall of Adam and Eve. We recall the story of the first murder told to us in the Book of Genesis (chapter 4). Cain killed his brother, Abel, because he was angered that Abel's offering was more pleasing to God than the sacrifice that Cain offered. The author of Genesis tells us that God put a special mark upon Cain, and that if anyone should avenge Abel's death by killing Cain, Cain would be avenged sevenfold (4:15).

The Book of Deuteronomy presents a development of the idea of revenge when the author describes the *law of talion*, or "limited" revenge. According to this practice, one could inflict no greater punishment than the injury or damage that had been suffered by the victim. "Life for life, eye for eye, tooth for tooth, hand for hand, foot for foot" (19:21). While this may seem barbaric to us, it represents a humanitarian effort when compared with the sevenfold revenge of Genesis.

In Tobit 4:15 we see a further development: "What you hate, do not do to anyone." By the time of Jesus the rabbis tended to believe that even retribution according to the *talion* was too harsh, and they began to commute penalties to fines. But Jesus takes justice and revenge to new heights when he proclaims: "Love your enemies and pray for those who persecute you."

Fools for God

The motivation for moral behavior described in Leviticus is to be holy as God is holy, and the reflection of Yahweh's holiness set the Chosen People apart from all others. The implication was that if one acted as God wished, blessings would follow. For the Israelites, these blessings included good health, long life, many children, good crops, healthy animals, and protection from one's enemies. Tobit reflects yet another motivation, that of helping someone so that they will be obligated to someday help you.

Jesus extends an expectation to the ultimate of heroic behavior, namely, love your enemies and pray for those who persecute you. This would be one of those "foolish" acts Saint Paul speaks of in his Letter to the Corinthians.

Here God's wisdom seems an absurdity to the world while the world's wisdom is absurd in God's eyes.

Matthew's Gospel, in which Jesus asks his followers to turn the other cheek, appears to also present a ridiculous request, especially when asked of those who had been victims of violent acts. Yet, violence tends to spiral indefinitely. What Jesus suggests here is that the compassion of a generous heart can bring a sense of healing and redemption to broken, hostile relationships.

Avoiding physical violence, however, does not necessarily mean not responding to the presence of evil in the world. Jesus' strategy is not passive resignation or indifference, but rather an attitude of kindness, forbearance, generosity, and an open acceptance of other people. Such an attitude can bring the power of conversion into play in a hostile situation.

Today's Good News

Does an attitude of extraordinary forgiveness make a difference in our contemporary world, which is often marked by open hostility? We need only to recall the heroes of the civil rights movement, who were not only jeered but attacked with rocks and clubs, as they marched peacefully down city streets in an attempt to gain the freedom to use public restrooms and drinking fountains. Even when members of the civil rights movement were slain, the leaders did not resort to violent acts of retaliation. Rather, they continued peaceful marches and held candlelight vigils to pray for those who continued to oppress and attack them.

Today, Jesus continues to call his followers to move beyond natural inclinations of reciprocal love. Jesus asks for the extraordinary love and forgiveness shown by parents who, at the burial of their murdered son, pray for mercy for the teenaged gang members who shot him to death. Absurdity? Yes, in the eyes of the world. But the reign of God demands that the absurdity of God's wisdom become the rule for us all.

Points for Reflection and Discussion

1 There are those who say that "modern" warfare is an act of violence that can never be tolerated. How would you respond to that statement?

_____

_____

_____

_____

2. The official teaching of the Catholic Church does not categorically condemn the death penalty legally imposed by civil law (see CCC 2269). Should the Church change its position? Why or why not?

_____

_____

_____

_____

_____

Themes
Conscience
    C5, The Sacrament of Penance
    C13, Christian Moral Living
Catholic Social Teachings
    C14, Social Justice

Reading 1, Isaiah 49:14-15

Zion said, "The Lord has forsaken me, my Lord has forgotten me."

Can a woman forget her nursing child, or show no compassion for the child of her womb? Even these may forget, yet I will not forget you.

Psalm 62:1-2,5-6,7-8 (NRSV)

Reading 2, 1 Corinthians 4:1-5

Think of us in this way, as servants of Christ and stewards of God's mysteries. Moreover, it is required of stewards that they be found trustworthy. But with me it is a very small thing that I should be judged by you or by any human court. I do not even judge myself. I am not aware of anything against myself, but I am not thereby acquitted. It is the Lord who judges me.

Therefore do not pronounce judgment before the time, before the Lord comes, who will bring to light the things now hidden in darkness and will disclose the purposes of the heart. Then each one will receive commendation from God.

Gospel, Matthew 6:24-34

[Jesus said to his disciples:] "No one can serve two masters; for a slave will either hate the one and love the other, or be devoted to the one and despise the other. You cannot serve God and wealth.

"Therefore I tell you, do not worry about your life, what you will eat or what you will drink, or about your body, what you will wear. Is not life more than food, and the body more than clothing? Look at the birds of the air; they neither sow nor reap nor gather into barns, and yet your heavenly Father feeds them. Are you not of more value than they? And can any of you by worrying add a single hour to your span of life? And why do you worry about clothing? Consider the lilies of the field, how they grow; they neither toil nor spin, yet I tell you, even Solomon in all his glory was not clothed like one of these. But if God so clothes the grass of the field, which is alive today and tomorrow is thrown into the oven, will he not much more clothe you—you of little faith? Therefore do not worry, saying, 'What will we eat?' or 'What will we drink?' or 'What will we wear?' For it is the Gentiles who strive for all these things; and indeed your heavenly Father knows that you need all these things. But strive first for the kingdom of God and his righteousness, and all these things will be given to you as well.

"So do not worry about tomorrow, for tomorrow will bring worries of its own. Today's trouble is enough for today."

Promises, Promises!

ANN WOLF

Today's first reading is from the *Book of Consolation*, a selection from the prophet Isaiah addressed to the Jewish people who had been demoralized by the Babylonian exile. Their land had been confiscated, and their Temple had been desecrated. Furthermore, their families had been wrenched apart and exiled to various localities in the Babylonian empire. The nation of Israel, once powerful and glorious, had been physically and emotionally abused. Through the words of the prophet, Yahweh now reminds the people that they continue to be the chosen ones and remain precious in God's eyes. The verses prior to today's selection describe a conversation between Yahweh and the unnamed Servant, who is called to be a sign of glory to the world. Yahweh promises deliverance, at which time families will be reunited, kings and princes shall bow before those who were once slaves, the land will be restored, and God's people will no longer hunger or thirst (verses 6-10).

"Promises, promises!" seems to be a reasonable response on the part of the Servant. In reality, Israel is a broken people who cannot bear to hope. "The Lord has forsaken me," replies the Servant. And with the tenderness of a God whose love knows no limits, Yahweh speaks: "Can a woman forget her nursing child, or show no compassion for the child of her womb? Even these may forget, yet I will not forget you."

Birds and Flowers

The gospel also speaks of trust, but the time and place is changed. Had Jesus spoken to those living in the midst of the Babylonian captivity, he would have been called insensitive. Jesus speaks, however, to the people of Galilee during a time of prosperity, and he addresses basic human needs: eating, drinking, and clothing. Shelter is not mentioned because it was not critical to life in the Near Eastern climate. To those whose basic survival is not threatened, Jesus says, do not be anxious, and do not be preoccupied with or absorbed by your desire to have more than you need. Your basic needs are already met. Do not toil and spin beyond what is necessary to support your family. Surely work in the field and house is necessary in order to survive, but examine your priorities. Beware of the temptation to be consumed by worldly possessions, which can cloud the view of what is important in life. The highest priority belongs to preserving your relationship as daughters and sons of God.

Saint Paul speaks to us of the practical side of life when he calls us to be faithful stewards of the mysteries of God. Part of the mystery of God is creation itself. As God cares for the birds of the air and the flowers of the field, so too are we to care for all of creation. A part of being good stewards of creation is to care for one another's needs.

Today's Good News

Life is not perfect this side of the fullness of the reign of God. We will always have to work. One tragedy is that there are those among us who must be consumed by work in order merely to survive. If we think hard enough we can all probably bring to mind a family in which a wage earner must work two or three jobs in order to provide food and shelter for a family. Often these are single parents, who must not only shoulder the burden of the workplace, but must also provide a nurturing environment for children. Such families dream of a life which, for many of us, represents no more than a common middle-class existence.

An even greater tragedy is the plight of the senior citizen who has worked hard, raised a family, and now looks forward to the peaceful days of retirement. Rather than enjoying a sense of security, many are faced with the unfathomable choice between buying food or needed medication. Every year the winter death toll includes at least a few elderly who freeze to death because they cannot pay for a basic need such as heat.

Being aware that the basic needs of all take priority over the luxury of some is a call to stewardship. Beyond awareness, we are called to action. The ultimate goal of all activity must be to seek the reign of God. And there can be no authentic search for the reign of God apart from the quest for justice in which the basic needs of all members of the human family are met. We cannot look for justice in God alone. We are the ones to produce that justice.

Points for Reflection and Discussion

1. If you were to compile a list of those things basic to survival in today's society, what would you include? Be specific.

_____

_____

_____

_____

2. Who has the major responsibility for caring for the needs of the poor: the persons themselves, the Church, or the state? Explain your answer.

_____

_____

_____

_____

Themes

Stewardship
    C15, The Consistent Life Ethic
Trust
    C10, Who is Jesus Christ?

Reading 1, Genesis 2:7-9;3:1-7

The Lord God formed man from the dust of the ground, and breathed into his nostrils the breath of life; and the man became a living being.

And the Lord God planted a garden in Eden, in the east; and there he put the man whom he had formed. Out of the ground the Lord God made to grow every tree that is pleasant to the sight and good for food, the tree of life also in the midst of the garden, and the tree of the knowledge of good and evil.

Now the serpent was more crafty than any other wild animal that the Lord God had made. He said to the woman, "Did God say, 'You shall not eat from any tree in the garden'?" The woman said to the serpent, "We may eat of the fruit of the trees in the garden; but God said, 'You shall not eat of the fruit of the tree that is in the middle of the garden, nor shall you touch it, or you shall die.' " But the serpent said to the woman, "You will not die; for God knows that when you eat of it your eyes will be opened, and you will be like God, knowing good and evil." So when the woman saw that the tree was good for food, and that it was a delight to the eyes, and that the tree was to be desired to make one wise, she took of its fruit and ate; and she also gave some to her husband, who was with her, and he ate.

Then the eyes of both were opened, and they knew that they were naked; and they sewed fig leaves together and made loincloths for themselves.

Psalm 51:1-2,3-4,10-11,12,15 (NRSV)

Reading 2, Romans 5:12-19

Just as sin came into the world through one man, and death came through sin, and so death spread to all because all have sinned—sin was indeed in the world before the law, but sin is not reckoned when there is no law. Yet death exercised dominion from Adam to Moses, even over those whose sins were not like the transgression of Adam, who is a type of the one who was to come.

But the free gift is not like the trespass. For if the many died through the one man's trespass, much more surely have the grace of God and the free gift in the grace of the one man, Jesus Christ, abounded for the many. And the free gift is not like the effect of the one man's sin. For the judgment following one trespass brought condemnation, but the free gift following many trespasses brings justification. If, because of the one man's trespass, death exercised dominion through that one, much more surely will those who receive the abundance of grace and the free gift of righteousness exercise dominion in life through the one man, Jesus Christ. Therefore just as one man's trespass

led to condemnation for all, so one man's act of righteousness leads to justification and life for all. For just as by the one man's disobedience the many were made sinners, so by the one man's obedience the many will be made righteous.

Gospel, Matthew 4:1-11

Jesus was led up by the Spirit into the wilderness to be tempted by the devil. He fasted forty days and forty nights, and afterwards he was famished. The tempter came and said to him, "If you are the Son of God, command these stones to become loaves of bread." But he answered, "It is written, 'One does not live by bread alone, but by every word that comes from the mouth of God.' "

Then the devil took him to the holy city and placed him on the pinnacle of the temple, saying to him, "If you are the Son of God, throw yourself down; for it is written, 'He will command his angels concerning you,' and 'On their hands they will bear you up, so that you will not dash your foot against a stone.' " Jesus said to him, "Again it is written, 'Do not put the Lord your God to the test.' "

Again, the devil took him to a very high mountain and showed him all the kingdoms of the world and their splendor; and he said to him, "All these I will give you, if you will fall down and worship me." Jesus said to him, "Away with you, Satan! for it is written, 'Worship the Lord your God, and serve only him.' "

Then the devil left him, and suddenly angels came and waited on him.

Promote Life

JOHN F. CRAGHAN

In our modern world, a full life often means the rejection of limitations or restraints. We are overwhelmed with the media's message that we only go around once and hence should grab all the gusto we can. Unfortunately, this may mean that we will jeopardize the person and property of fellow humans.

Today's readings deal with the pivotal issue(s) of life and death. They offer both positive and negative experiences of the reality of coping with limitations. They powerfully intimate that a life without limits is not a genuine life.

The author of the Garden of Eden account possibly drew his inspiration from the life/death style of King David. David was an exceptionally gifted man, possessing beauty (1 Sm 16:12) and wisdom (2 Sm 14:17,20). Nonetheless, David chose to commit adultery and murder (2 Sm 11). It was this kind of a graced and disgraced individual who became the model of all humans.

Limitation is a fact of life; indeed it is the condition for living. To live to the fullest means to exercise freedom by accepting restraints. To be fully alive means to opt for good in the face of evil.

To *know* good and evil means to realize the difference between the two. To *live* means to enjoy physical existence. The dilemma of the couple in the garden (and hence the dilemma of us all) is to accept full life by acknowledging the limits necessary in our authentic existence. Reflecting on the experience of David, the Yahwist author of today's Genesis story demands we promote life by accepting its necessary limits.

Life Through Death

In his Letter to the Romans, Paul chooses to comment on the garden story against the background of the life and death of Jesus. By *sin,* Paul understands that tremendous power unleashed upon the world from the time of the first sin which has grown at avalanche proportions because of individual sins. By *death,* Paul means the deprivation of community with God. This death is a demonic power, acting like a king and making authentic living impossible. By contrast, *life* means intimacy with God and the capacity to lead a truly authentic existence.

Because Jesus accepted the limitations of death on a cross, there has arisen for all persons the opportunity to be truly alive. Whereas Adam brought about condemnation, Jesus has brought acquittal. Because Jesus chose to be limited by his obedience unto death, he has made it possible for all to be in right relationship with God.

Death Through Life

In Matthew's desert presentation, the newly baptized Jesus must choose what his ministry will be like. In the temptations, Jesus rejects several possibilities. He will not accept the popular notion of a temporal, political messiah. He realizes full well that the Father's plan for the kingdom involves limitations.

The temptation account contrasts the infidelity of Israel in the desert with the fidelity of Jesus to his Father's will. The first temptation recalls Israel's grumbling against the Lord in the matter of food (Ex 16:1-15; Dt 8:3). Jesus is tempted to repeat the wilderness miracles and win popular acclaim. Since this would mean manipulating the people, Jesus rejects it. The second temptation brings to mind Israel's complaint to Moses about the lack of water (Ex 17:1-7; Dt 6:16). The devil's use of Psalm 91 implies a popular messianic figure who would leap from the Temple and land unscathed. Jesus once again rejects the offer, because it would involve forcing his Father's hand to perform a miracle. The third temptation looks to Israel's idolatry in the promised land (Dt 6:13). Jesus is tempted to adore Satan in person since Satan is in control of the world. Once again Jesus refuses. The kingdom will be realized through a different kind of power.

Today's Good News

In life, temptations abound. We experience those times when we are tempted to reject limitations in the matter of our neighbor's spouse or our neighbor's money. We are tempted to exceed the limits of justice in accepting racism and prejudice. We are even duped into thinking that we are truly living a full life when we overstep these limits. Nonetheless, the Scriptures consistently teach us to make our temptations the raw material for our genuine existence. They endorse the idea that to promote life is to accept limits.

Points for Reflection and Discussion

1. Reflect on some of the choices you have recently made in your life. How do your choices represent your Christian faith?

_____

_____

_____

_____

2. Many people have found God in desert experiences. Have you had a desert experience that marked a conversion for you? Talk about it.

_____

_____

_____

_____

_____

Themes

Prayer
   L6, The Lord's Prayer
Temptation
   L1, What is Lent?

Reading 1, Genesis 12:1-4

The Lord said to Abram, "Go from your country and your kindred and your father's house to the land that I will show you. I will make of you a great nation, and I will bless you, and make your name great, so that you will be a blessing. I will bless those who bless you, and the one who curses you I will curse; and in you all the families of the earth shall be blessed."

So Abram went, as the Lord had told him; and Lot went with him. Abram was seventy-five years old when he departed from Haran.

Psalm 33:4-5,18-19,20,22

Reading 2, 2 Timothy 1:8-10

Join with me in suffering for the gospel, relying on the power of God, who saved us and called us with a holy calling, not according to our works but according to his own purpose and grace. This grace was given to us in Christ Jesus before the ages began, but it has now been revealed through the appearing of our Savior Christ Jesus, who abolished death and brought life and immortality to light through the gospel.

Gospel, Matthew 17:1-9

Jesus took with him Peter and James and his brother John and led them up a high mountain, by themselves. And he was transfigured before them, and his face shone like the sun, and his clothes became dazzling white. Suddenly there appeared to them Moses and Elijah, talking with him.

Then Peter said to Jesus, "Lord, it is good for us to be here; if you wish, I will make three dwellings here, one for you, one for Moses, and one for Elijah." While he was still speaking, suddenly a bright cloud overshadowed them, and from the cloud a voice said, "This is my Son, the Beloved; with him I am well pleased; listen to him!" When the disciples heard this, they fell to the ground and were overcome by fear. But Jesus came and touched them, saying, "Get up and do not be afraid." And when they looked up, they saw no one except Jesus himself alone.

As they were coming down the mountain, Jesus ordered them, "Tell no one about the vision until after the Son of Man has been raised from the dead."

Suffering Servants

JOHN F. CRAGHAN

How often we find relief in being removed from the problems of the world. We tend to isolate and insulate ourselves from the needs of others. We tend to see ourselves—even when we suffer—as quarantined from the concerns of others. In such circumstances, blessing consists in being left alone. How difficult it can be to see that the union of our pain and our call to service leads the way to real blessing.

Today's readings understand that serving others and enduring pain go hand in hand. They also see such experiences as the source of blessing.

Pain and Gain

Abram (later Abraham, see Gn 17:5) first moved from southern to northwestern Mesopotamia (11:31). In today's passage, he is asked to endure the pain of leaving his kinsfolk and his father's house and travel to the land of Canaan. Yet the author is careful to link Abram's movements with a message of blessing for others.

Between chapters three and eleven of Genesis, a constant emphasis was the increase of human sin. In the Tower of Babel account (11:1-9), for example, haughty humanity attempted to make a name for itself, but the result was the further scattering of humankind. By contrast, God promised Abram: "I will make your name great, so that you will be a blessing." In turn, by helping and benefitting its neighbors, Israel will indeed be a source of blessing (see 19:17-18;26:4,28): "In you all the families of the earth shall be blessed."

Give and Live

The author of Second Timothy presents Paul as the model of apostolic devotion in the preaching of the gospel. He exhorts the recipients of the letter to "join...in suffering for the gospel." He adds that God's call is a gratuitous gift which, like Christ's deeds, should benefit others.

The author elsewhere links personal pain with the preaching of the Good News. Thus Paul suffered as a criminal in chains, "but the word of God is not chained" (2:9). Furthermore, he endured suffering in order that God's chosen may "obtain the salvation that is in Christ Jesus, with eternal glory" (2:10). The true follower of Christ is a soldier (2:4) and a worker (2:15) whose painful efforts advance the gospel.

It is likely that the transfiguration of Jesus captured a moment of very intense prayer. Matthew, by describing Jesus' face and clothes, makes him a part of the heavenly realm (see 13:43;28:3). Matthew enhances this heavenly atmosphere with the mention of tents and the cloud (see Ex 40:34-38). As at the baptism, Jesus is fittingly acknowledged as the Son of God (see 3:17;17:5). It is only appropriate that Matthew should have Peter address Jesus as Lord, not rabbi (see Mk 9:5).

In descending the mountain, Matthew links the glorified Son of God with the suffering Son of Man: "So also the Son of Man is about to suffer at their hands" (17:12). To acknowledge Jesus as Son of God is to accept him as suffering Son of Man. The transfigured one of the heavenly realm is also the humiliated one of the earthly sphere.

Today's Good News

In our daily living we are asked to find our identity by interacting with others and by becoming partners with them, especially with their pain and frustration. By accepting baptism, we accept the cross of others. We are not isolated. Rather, we are necessarily involved, and because we are willing to accept pain and service the words spoken to Abram are also applicable to us: "In you all the families of the earth shall be blessed."

Points for Reflection and Discussion

1. As we learn to trust, we begin to see more and more transfigurations all around us. How have you met God in a transfiguring experience?

_____

_____

_____

_____

2. "In you all the families of the earth shall be blessed." How does that make you feel?

_____

_____

_____

_____

Themes

Blessing
    L7, The Meaning of Holy Week
Service
    L2, Saying Yes to Jesus (Rite of Election)
Suffering
    L5, The Way of the Cross

Reading 1, Exodus 17:3-7

The people thirsted [in the wilderness] for water; and the people complained against Moses and said, "Why did you bring us out of Egypt, to kill us and our children and livestock with thirst?" So Moses cried out to the Lord, "What shall I do with this people? They are almost ready to stone me."

The Lord said to Moses, "Go on ahead of the people, and take some of the elders of Israel with you; take in your hand the staff with which you struck the Nile, and go. I will be standing there in front of you on the rock at Horeb. Strike the rock, and water will come out of it, so that the people may drink." Moses did so, in the sight of the elders of Israel.

He called the place Massah and Meribah, because the Israelites quarreled and tested the Lord, saying, "Is the Lord among us or not?"

Psalm 95:1-2,6-7,7-9 (NRSV)

Reading 2, Romans 5:1-2,5-8

Since we are justified by faith, we have peace with God through our Lord Jesus Christ, through whom we have obtained access to this grace in which we stand; and we boast in our hope of sharing the glory of God.

And hope does not disappoint us, because God's love has been poured into our hearts through the Holy Spirit that has been given to us. For while we were still weak, at the right time Christ died for the ungodly. Indeed, rarely will anyone die for a righteous person—though perhaps for a good person someone might actually dare to die. But God proves his love for us in that while we still were sinners Christ died for us.

Gospel, John 4:5-42

[Jesus] came to a Samaritan city called Sychar, near the plot of ground that Jacob had given to his son Joseph. Jacob's well was there, and Jesus, tired out by his journey, was sitting by the well. It was about noon.

A Samaritan woman came to draw water, and Jesus said to her, "Give me a drink." (His disciples had gone to the city to buy food.) The Samaritan woman said to him, "How is it that you, a Jew, ask a drink of me, a woman of Samaria?" (Jews do not share things in common with Samaritans.) Jesus answered her, "If you knew the gift of God, and who it is that is saying to you, 'Give me a drink,' you would have asked him, and he would have given you living water." The woman said to him, "Sir, you have no bucket, and the well is deep. Where do you get that living water? Are you greater than our ancestor Jacob, who gave us the well, and with his sons and his flocks drank from it?" Jesus said to her, "Everyone who drinks of this water will be thirsty again, but those who drink of the water that I will give them will never be thirsty. The water that I will give will become in them a spring of water gushing up to eternal life." The woman said to him, "Sir, give me this water, so that I may never be thirsty or have to keep coming here to draw water."

Jesus said to her, "Go, call your husband, and come back." The woman answered him, "I have no husband." Jesus said to her, "You are right in saying, 'I have no husband'; for you have had five husbands, and the one you have now is not your husband. What you have said is true!"

The woman said to him, "Sir, I see that you are a prophet. Our ancestors worshiped on this mountain, but you say that the place where people must worship is in Jerusalem." Jesus said to her, "Woman, believe me, the hour is coming when you will worship the Father neither on this mountain nor in Jerusalem. You worship what you do not know; we worship what we know, for salvation is from the Jews. But the hour is coming, and is now here, when the true worshipers will worship the Father in spirit and truth, for the Father seeks such as these to worship him. God is spirit, and those who worship him must worship in spirit and truth."

The woman said to him, "I know that Messiah is coming" (who is called Christ). "When he comes, he will proclaim all things to us." Jesus said to her, "I am he, the one who is speaking to you."

Just then his disciples came. They were astonished that he was speaking with a woman, but no one said, "What do you want?" or, "Why are you speaking with her?" Then the woman left her water jar and went back to the city. She said to the people, "Come and see a man who told me everything I have ever done! He cannot be the Messiah, can he?" They left the city and were on their way to him.

Meanwhile the disciples were urging him, "Rabbi, eat something." But he said to them, "I have food to eat that you do not know about." So the disciples said to one another, "Surely no one has brought him something to eat?" Jesus said to them, "My food is to do the will of him who sent me and to complete his work. Do you not say, 'Four months more, then comes the harvest'? But I tell you, look around you, and see how the fields are ripe for harvesting. The reaper is already receiving wages and is gathering fruit for eternal life, so that sower and reaper may rejoice together. For here the saying holds true, 'One sows and another reaps.' I sent you to reap that for which you did not labor. Others have labored, and you have entered into their labor."

Many Samaritans from that city believed in him because of the woman's testimony, "He told me everything I have ever done." So when the Samaritans came to him, they asked him to stay with them; and he stayed there two days. And many more believed because of his word. They said to the woman, "It is no longer because of what you said that we believe, for we have heard for ourselves, and we know that this is truly the Savior of the world."

Wellsprings

JOHN F. CRAGHAN

Love is its own reward. We live in a world of progress reports, work evaluations, and periodic reassessments. We hope to get a higher wage and/or a better position because of our improved output or more efficient management. We thereby assume that better performance means a better reward. In our *quid pro quo* atmosphere, it is hard to believe love can be its own reward.

Today's readings treat the graciousness of our God, a graciousness not prompted by our work ethic or motivated by our compelling desire to succeed. It is a graciousness that is only explicable on the basis of our God's capacity to love for the sake of loving.

A second level in the narrative of Massah and Meribah is Israel's dispute with Yahweh over the question of the exodus from Egypt. On this level, the people's thirst serves as the occasion for attacking the very purpose of the exodus: "Why did you bring us out of Egypt?" On this level, Israel rejects God's whole plan of salvation.

The primary tradition concentrates on Yahweh's graciousness for the people. In the primary tradition, the people merely quarrel with Moses and constrain him to meet their demands. Moses' cry to the Lord results in a positive and prompt reply. There is no threat of punishment for the people. God meets their needs because it is the nature of God to do so.

Love Is Its Own Reward

In his Letter to the Romans, Paul observes that the state of being right with God brings about unshakable peace. Through Christ Jesus, the Christian has access to God's presence. Despite the ups and downs of life, the Christian has a hope rooted in God's Spirit. The gift of the Spirit is the assurance of God's love.

Paul insists that Christ freely chose to die for godless humans. The self-giving of Christ seems so incomprehensible, his death is the great proof of God's love.

John demonstrates in today's gospel the truth that the sending of the Son is grounded in God's love for the world (see 3:16). It is only this love that can adequately explain the happenings in this episode.

Jesus brings living water, that is, God's revelation, to the Samaritans—renegade or at least second-class Jews. It is significant that Jesus chooses to talk not only with a Samaritan but with a Samaritan woman—this is indeed a reversal of acceptable practice in first-century Judaism in Palestine. The outcome is that the woman brings the message of Jesus to her people, who end up by accepting Jesus as the Savior of the world. John sees this as the fulfillment of Jesus' mission: "God did not send the Son into the world to condemn the world, but in order that the world might be saved through him" (3:17).

Today's Good News

We are directed to reach out to our family, to assist our friends, to love and work with all peoples, not simply because we will be amply compensated but because it is the nature of our God to love with no strings attached. Hence, to accept God is to accept God's worldview. Our family, our friends, and our business associates are worthy of gratuitous love because the essence of our God is to look to the welfare of others. In our pragmatic world, the upsetting message is that love is its own reward.

Points for Reflection and Discussion

1. Try to imagine loving some one as unconditionally as God loves every one. How would your life change?

_____

_____

_____

_____

2. The water of life is imaged throughout today's readings. Who has been a source of life-giving water for you?

_____

_____

_____

_____

Themes
Hope
    L1, What is Lent?
Love
    L2, Saying Yes to Jesus (Rite of Election)
Water
    L3, Take a Look (The Scrutinies)

Reading 1, 1 Samuel 16:1,6-7,10-13

The Lord said to Samuel, "Fill your horn with oil and set out; I will send you to Jesse the Bethlehemite, for I have provided for myself a king among his sons."

When [the sons of Jesse] came, [Samuel] looked on Eliab and thought, "Surely the Lord's anointed is now before the Lord." But the Lord said to Samuel, "Do not look on his appearance or on the height of his stature, because I have rejected him; for the Lord does not see as mortals see; they look on the outward appearance, but the Lord looks on the heart."

Jesse made seven of his sons pass before Samuel, and Samuel said to Jesse, "The Lord has not chosen any of these." Samuel said to Jesse, "Are all your sons here?" And he said, "There remains yet the youngest, but he is keeping the sheep." And Samuel said to Jesse, "Send and bring him; for we will not sit down until he comes here." He sent and brought him in. Now he was ruddy, and had beautiful eyes, and was handsome. The Lord said, "Rise and anoint him; for this is the one."

Then Samuel took the horn of oil, and anointed him in the presence of his brothers; and the spirit of the Lord came mightily upon David from that day forward.

Psalm 23:1-3,3-4,5,6

Reading 2, Ephesians 5:8-14

Once you were darkness, but now in the Lord you are light. Live as children of light—for the fruit of the light is found in all that is good and right and true.

Try to find out what is pleasing to the Lord. Take no part in the unfruitful works of darkness, but instead expose them. For it is shameful even to mention what such people do secretly; but everything exposed by the light becomes visible, for everything that becomes visible is light. Therefore it says, "Sleeper, awake! Rise from the dead, and Christ will shine on you."

Gospel, John 9:1-41

As [Jesus] walked along, he saw a man blind from birth. His disciples asked him, "Rabbi, who sinned, this man or his parents, that he was born blind?" Jesus answered, "Neither this man nor his parents sinned; he was born blind so that God's works might be revealed in him. We must work the works of him who sent me while it is day; night is coming when no one can work. As long as I am in the world, I am the light of the world." When he had said this, he spat on the ground and made mud with the saliva and spread the mud on the man's eyes, saying to him,

"Go, wash in the pool of Siloam" (which means Sent). Then he went and washed and came back able to see.

The neighbors and those who had seen him before as a beggar began to ask, "Is this not the man who used to sit and beg?" Some were saying, "It is he." Others were saying, "No, but it is someone like him." He kept saying, "I am the man." But they kept asking him, "Then how were your eyes opened?" He answered, "The man called Jesus made mud, spread it on my eyes, and said to me, 'Go to Siloam and wash.' Then I went and washed and received my sight." They said to him, "Where is he?" He said, "I do not know."

They brought to the Pharisees the man who had formerly been blind. Now it was a sabbath day when Jesus made the mud and opened his eyes. Then the Pharisees also began to ask him how he had received his sight. He said to them, "He put mud on my eyes. Then I washed, and now I see." Some of the Pharisees said, "This man is not from God, for he does not observe the sabbath." But others said, "How can a man who is a sinner perform such signs?" And they were divided. So they said again to the blind man, "What do you say about him? It was your eyes he opened." He said, "He is a prophet."

The Jews did not believe that he had been blind and had received his sight until they called the parents of the man who had received his sight and asked them, "Is this your son, who you say was born blind? How then does he now see?" His parents answered, "We know that this is our son, and that he was born blind; but we do not know how it is that now he sees, nor do we know who opened his eyes. Ask him; he is of age. He will speak for himself." His parents said this because they were afraid of the Jews; for the Jews had already agreed that anyone who confessed Jesus to be the Messiah would be put out of the synagogue. Therefore his parents said, "He is of age; ask him."

So for the second time they called the man who had been blind, and they said to him, "Give glory to God! We know that this man is a sinner." He answered, "I do not know whether he is a sinner. One thing I do know, that though I was blind, now I see." They said to him, "What did he do to you? How did he open your eyes?" He answered them, "I have told you already, and you would not listen. Why do you want to hear it again? Do you also want to become his disciples?" Then they reviled him, saying, "You are his disciple, but we are disciples of Moses. We know that God has spoken to Moses, but as for this man, we do not know where he comes from."

The man answered, "Here is an astonishing thing! You do not know where he comes from, and yet he opened my eyes. We know that God does not listen to sinners, but he does listen to one who worships him and obeys his will. Never since the world began has it been heard that anyone *opened the eyes of a person born blind. If this man were not from God, he could do nothing." They answered him, "You were born entirely in sins, and are you trying to teach us?" And they drove him out. Jesus heard that they had driven him out, and when he found him, he said, "Do you believe in the Son of Man?" He answered, "And who is he, sir? Tell me, so that I may believe in him." Jesus said to him, "You have seen him, and the one speaking with you is he." He said, "Lord, I believe." And he worshiped him. Jesus said, "I came into this world for judgment so that those who do not see may see, and those who do see may become blind."*

Some of the Pharisees near him heard this and said to him, "Surely we are not blind, are we?" Jesus said to them, "If you were blind, you would not have sin. But now that you say, 'We see,' your sin remains."

Points of View

JOHN F. CRAGHAN

Day after day we are offered a great number of facts, situations, events—especially in the media. We learn of murders, revolutions, natural disasters, and are required to assess all this material. Our conclusions to this process form our point of view about the world.

Today's readings dwell on light and darkness, sight and blindness, seeing and not seeing. They are timely reminders to reexamine our priorities and retest our standards for making judgments. They urge us to look within and ask whether our decisions are really Christian.

The author of 1 Sm 16:1—2 Sm 5:5 begins his narrative by painting an enthusiastic portrait of David's rise from a nobody to a royal somebody. He captures the upward movement of Israel's youthful hero. At the same time, he endorses key values of the decision-making process.

The story warns against judging by mere appearances since the well-to-do tend to be the elite. Hence, there is the process whereby Samuel reviews the available sons of Jesse. The story highlights the motif of the selection of the most unlikely candidate. The shepherd boy, a marginal person, enters into the process and is ultimately chosen. Although the author notes David's handsome appearance, this is not the decisive factor because "the Lord looks on the heart."

Let There Be Light

The author of Ephesians contrasts the previously pagan lives of his audience with their new Christian lives by using the images of light and darkness, and the account from the Gospel of John contrasts the perceptions of the blind man and the Pharisees/Jews. The blind man progresses from darkness to light. Initially he regards Jesus as a man, but then calls him a prophet. He further acknowledges that Jesus comes from God, and finally confesses that he is the Son of Man. The blind man sees (faith) that Jesus is "the light of the world."

The Pharisees/Jews first appear to accept the healing, but then begin to doubt that the man was blind from birth. They next deny Jesus' heavenly origins, and go on to mock the blind man. They adamantly refuse to see and thus end up blind.

Today's Good News

Taking this message to heart, modern Christians are called to look beyond appearances. We must decide whether the helpless, the indigent, the derelict are worthy of respect; or whether they are merely objects of disdain. These people are also the sisters and brothers of Jesus. It all depends on our point of view.

Modern Christians must judge wayward members of the family. Are they merely a disgrace to the family name? Or do they exhibit genuine human qualities that we choose to ignore in order to concentrate on their clear excesses? It all depends on our point of view.

Modern Christians must evaluate the policies and programs of both Church and state. Are they right merely because authority has endorsed them? Do they really benefit the community? Or do too many people get hurt in the process of protecting the administration's policy? It all depends on our point of view.

Points for Reflection and Discussion

1. Do you generally derive your criteria for judgment from the gospel, or from the standard business procedures of our environment?

_____

_____

_____

2. Imagine yourself blind. Whom do you trust to lead you?

_____

_____

_____

Themes
Blindness
　　L2, Saying Yes to Jesus (Rite of Election)
Conversion
　　L3, Take a Look (The Scrutinies)
Light
　　L1, What is Lent?

Reading 1, Ezekiel 37:12-14

Thus says the Lord God: "I am going to open your graves, and bring you up from your graves, O my people; and I will bring you back to the land of Israel. And you shall know that I am the Lord, when I open your graves, and bring you up from your graves, O my people. I will put my spirit within you, and you shall live, and I will place you on your own soil; then you shall know that I, the Lord, have spoken and will act," says the Lord.

Psalm 130:1-2,3-4,5-6,7-8

Reading 2, Romans 8:8-11

Those who are in the flesh cannot please God. But you are not in the flesh; you are in the Spirit, since the Spirit of God dwells in you. Anyone who does not have the Spirit of Christ does not belong to him. But if Christ is in you, though the body is dead because of sin, the Spirit is life because of righteousness. If the Spirit of him who raised Jesus from the dead dwells in you, he who raised Christ from the dead will give life to your mortal bodies also through his Spirit that dwells in you.

Gospel, John 11:1-45

Now a certain man was ill, Lazarus of Bethany, the village of Mary and her sister Martha. Mary was the one who anointed the Lord with perfume and wiped his feet with her hair; her brother Lazarus was ill.

So the sisters sent a message to Jesus, "Lord, he whom you love is ill." But when Jesus heard it, he said, "This illness does not lead to death; rather it is for God's glory, so that the Son of God may be glorified through it." Accordingly, though Jesus loved Martha and her sister and Lazarus, after having heard that Lazarus was ill, he stayed two days longer in the place where he was.

Then after this he said to the disciples, "Let us go to Judea again." The disciples said to him, "Rabbi, the Jews were just now trying to stone you, and are you going there again?" Jesus answered, "Are there not twelve hours of daylight? Those who walk during the day do not stumble, because they see the light of this world. But those who walk at night stumble, because the light is not in them."

After saying this, he told them, "Our friend Lazarus has fallen asleep, but I am going there to awaken him." The disciples said to him, "Lord, if he has fallen asleep, he will be all right." Jesus, however, had been speaking about his death, but they thought that he was referring merely to sleep. Then Jesus told them plainly, "Lazarus is dead. For your sake I am glad I was not there, so that you may believe. But let us go to him." Thomas, who was called the Twin, said to his fellow disciples, "Let us also go, that we may die with him."

When Jesus arrived, he found that Lazarus had already been in the tomb four days. Now Bethany was near Jerusalem, some two miles away, and many of the Jews had come to Martha and Mary to console them about their brother. When Martha heard that Jesus was coming, she went and met him, while Mary stayed at home. Martha said to Jesus, "Lord, if you had been here, my brother would not have died. But even now I know that God will give you whatever you ask of him." Jesus said to her, "Your brother will rise again." Martha said to him, "I know that he will rise again in the resurrection on the last day." Jesus said to her, "I am the resurrection and the life. Those who believe in me, even though they die, will live, and everyone who lives and believes in me will never die. Do you believe this?" She said to him, "Yes, Lord, I believe that you are the Messiah, the Son of God, the one coming into the world." When she had said this, she went back and called her sister Mary, and told her privately, "The Teacher is here and is calling for you." And when she heard it, she got up quickly and went to him. Now Jesus had not yet come to the village, but was still at the place where Martha had met him. The Jews who were with her in the house, consoling her, saw Mary get up quickly and go out. They followed her because they thought that she was going to the tomb to weep there.

When Mary came where Jesus was and saw him, she knelt at his feet and said to him, "Lord, if you had been here, my brother would not have died." When Jesus saw her weeping, and the Jews who came with her also weeping, he was greatly disturbed in spirit and deeply moved. He said, "Where have you laid him?" They said to him, "Lord, come and see." Jesus began to weep. So the Jews said, "See how he loved him!" But some of them said, "Could not he who opened the eyes of the blind man have kept this man from dying?"

Then Jesus, again greatly disturbed, came to the tomb. It was a cave, and a stone was lying against it. Jesus said, "Take away the stone." Martha, the sister of the dead man, said to him, "Lord, already there is a stench because he has been dead four days." Jesus said to her, "Did I not tell you that if you believed, you would see the glory of God?" So they took away the stone. And Jesus looked upward and said, "Father, I thank you for having heard me. I knew that you always hear me, but I have said this for the sake of the crowd standing here, so that they may believe that you sent me."

When he had said this, he cried with a loud voice, "Lazarus, come out!" The dead man came out, his hands and feet bound with strips of cloth, and his face wrapped in a cloth. Jesus said to them, "Unbind him, and let him *go." Many of the Jews therefore, who had come with Mary and had seen what Jesus did, believed in him.*

Dry Bones

JOHN F. CRAGHAN

We sometimes reach a point where despair takes over and depression reigns supreme. We feel overwhelmed by life's shocks and incapacitated by our own failure. Self-pity often becomes the expression of our profound misery. We feel we are old bones incapable of new life.

Today's readings deal with the very real problems of anxiety and hopelessness. Yet they clearly announce a God who becomes involved in human tragedy. This is the God of the living who chooses to become concerned because concern is a manifestation of life. This God unequivocally enables old bones to have new life.

Preaching to a depressed exilic audience in the aftermath of the destruction of Jerusalem, Ezekiel personally experiences their sense of frustration. He even quotes their expression of despair: "Our bones are dried up, and our hope is lost; we are cut off completely" (37:11). The prophet is transported by God's Spirit to a place littered with dry human bones. At the prophet's word, the bones are reconstituted into human bodies and the breath/spirit/wind brings the bodies to life. In Ezekiel's interpretation, the vision is applied to God's despondent people. The bones are the graves of that people who now come back to life and are promised resettlement in their own land. The message is that old bones can have new life.

In Romans 7:14-25, Paul paints a vivid picture of human agony. "I do not do the good I want, but the evil I do not want is what I do" (7:19). In chapter eight of Romans, however, Paul develops the theme of new hope because of the life-giving Spirit. Christians experience God's power, whereby a genuine moral life is possible and the threat of condemnation is lifted.

In today's reading, Paul teaches that Christians who allow the Spirit to determine their moral values actually live out their profound association with Christ. Even though the Spirit does not remove physical death, the Spirit does bring to human life that transforming experience of being right with God (justice—a gratuitous gift) that leads to resurrection. For Paul, the message of God in Christ is that old bones can have new life.

The Glory of God

John recounts the raising of Lazarus as a sign that transforms tragedy into hope. Lazarus' illness and subsequent death are an occasion for the manifestation of God's glory. God's presence is made visible through deeds of power. The primary focus of this incident is the glory of the Father, not the assistance of a friend.

Faith goes hand in hand with glory. The miracle also glorifies Jesus, and the disciples' faith in Jesus will lead to the further display of God's glory (see also Jn 2:11). To accept Jesus is to make oneself open to that whole process of transformation. The disciple glorifies the Father just as the Son did by sharing in the passion/death/resurrection.

Today's Good News

Human despair takes many forms. Whatever form it takes, the process of overcoming despair is fundamentally the same. It is to be in the presence of God and to breathe the Spirit upon our world. Hope then becomes possible and life becomes livable.

To provide jobs for the unemployed is clearly in the tradition of Ezekiel: Graves open and the Spirit breathes new life. To care for the elderly and the shut-ins is certainly in the tradition of Paul: The Spirit influences our moral choices and outreach to others implies we belong to Christ. To alleviate the hunger of the world's stricken is obviously in the tradition of John. So too are the many acts of charity we all are called upon to perform. We thus manifest the glory of God and strengthen the faith of our sisters and brothers. We participate in God's great work of giving old bones new life.

Points for Reflection and Discussion

1. God is a God of the living. What area in your existence needs to be untied, as Lazarus was, in order to come back to life?

_____

_____

_____

_____

2. Do you fear death? Talk about your experiences of death.

_____

_____

_____

_____

Themes
Death
   L1, What is Lent?
Spirit
   L7, The Meaning of Holy Week

Procession With Palms, Matthew 21:1-11

When they had come near Jerusalem and had reached Bethphage, at the Mount of Olives, Jesus sent two disciples, saying to them, "Go into the village ahead of you, and immediately you will find a donkey tied, and a colt with her; untie them and bring them to me. If anyone says anything to you, just say this, 'The Lord needs them.' And he will send them immediately." This took place to fulfill what had been spoken through the prophet, saying, "Tell the daughter of Zion, Look, your king is coming to you, humble, and mounted on a donkey, and on a colt, the foal of a donkey."

The disciples went and did as Jesus had directed them; they brought the donkey and the colt, and put their cloaks on them, and he sat on them. A very large crowd spread their cloaks on the road, and others cut branches from the trees and spread them on the road. The crowds that went ahead of him and that followed were shouting, "Hosanna to the Son of David! Blessed is the one who comes in the name of the Lord! Hosanna in the highest heaven!"

When he entered Jerusalem, the whole city was in turmoil, asking, "Who is this?" The crowds were saying, "This is the prophet Jesus from Nazareth in Galilee."

Reading 1, Isaiah 50:4-7

The Lord God has given me the tongue of a teacher, that I may know how to sustain the weary with a word. Morning by morning he wakens—wakens my ear to listen as those who are taught. The Lord God has opened my ear, and I was not rebellious, I did not turn backward. I gave my back to those who struck me, and my cheeks to those who pulled out the beard; I did not hide my face from insult and spitting. The Lord God helps me; therefore I have not been disgraced; therefore I have set my face like flint, and I know that I shall not be put to shame.

Psalm 22:7-8,16-17,18-19,22-23 (NRSV)

Reading 2, Philippians 2:5-11 (NRSV)

Let the same mind be in you that was in Christ Jesus, who, though he was in the form of God, did not regard equality with God as something to be exploited, but emptied himself, taking the form of a slave, being born in human likeness. And being found in human form, he humbled himself and became obedient to the point of death—even death on a cross. Therefore God also highly exalted him and gave him the name that is above every name, so that at the name of Jesus every knee should bend, in heaven and on earth and under the earth, and every tongue should confess that Jesus Christ is Lord, to the glory of God the Father.

Gospel, Matthew 26:14—27:66

One of the twelve, who was called Judas Iscariot, went to the chief priests and said, "What will you give me if I betray him to you?" They paid him thirty pieces of silver. And from that moment he began to look for an opportunity to betray him.

On the first day of Unleavened Bread the disciples came to Jesus, saying, "Where do you want us to make the preparations for you to eat the Passover?" He said, "Go into the city to a certain man, and say to him, 'The Teacher says, My time is near; I will keep the Passover at your house with my disciples.' " So the disciples did as Jesus had directed them, and they prepared the Passover meal.

When it was evening, he took his place with the twelve; and while they were eating, he said, "Truly I tell you, one of you will betray me." And they became greatly distressed and began to say to him one after another, "Surely not I, Lord?" He answered, "The one who has dipped his hand into the bowl with me will betray me. The Son of Man goes as it is written of him, but woe to that one by whom the Son of Man is betrayed! It would have been better for that one not to have been born." Judas, who betrayed him, said, "Surely not I, Rabbi?" He replied, "You have said so."

While they were eating, Jesus took a loaf of bread, and after blessing it he broke it, gave it to the disciples, and said, "Take, eat; this is my body." Then he took a cup, and after giving thanks he gave it to them, saying, "Drink from it, all of you; for this is my blood of the covenant, which is poured out for many for the forgiveness of sins. I tell you, I will never again drink of this fruit of the vine until that day when I drink it new with you in my Father's kingdom." When they had sung the hymn, they went out to the Mount of Olives.

Then Jesus said to them, "You will all become deserters because of me this night; for it is written, 'I will strike the shepherd, and the sheep of the flock will be scattered.' But after I am raised up, I will go ahead of you to Galilee." Peter said to him, "Though all become deserters because of you, I will never desert you." Jesus said to him, "Truly I tell you, this very night, before the cock crows, you will deny me three times." Peter said to him, "Even though I must die with you, I will not deny you." And so said all the disciples.

Then Jesus went with them to a place called Gethsemane; and he said to his disciples, "Sit here while I go over there and pray." He took with him Peter and the two sons of Zebedee, and began to be grieved and agitated.

Then he said to them, "I am deeply grieved, even to death; remain here, and stay awake with me." And going a little farther, he threw himself on the ground and prayed, "My Father, if it is possible, let this cup pass from me; yet not what I want but what you want." Then he came to the disciples and found them sleeping; and he said to Peter, "So, could you not stay awake with me one hour? Stay awake and pray that you may not come into the time of trial; the spirit indeed is willing, but the flesh is weak." Again he went away for the second time and prayed, "My Father, if this cannot pass unless I drink it, your will be done." Again he came and found them sleeping, for their eyes were heavy. So leaving them again, he went away and prayed for the third time, saying the same words. Then he came to the disciples and said to them, "Are you still sleeping and taking your rest? See, the hour is at hand, and the Son of Man is betrayed into the hands of sinners. Get up, let us be going. See, my betrayer is at hand."

While he was still speaking, Judas, one of the twelve, arrived; with him was a large crowd with swords and clubs, from the chief priests and the elders of the people. Now the betrayer had given them a sign, saying, "The one I will kiss is the man; arrest him." At once he came up to Jesus and said, "Greetings, Rabbi!" and kissed him. Jesus said to him, "Friend, do what you are here to do." Then they came and laid hands on Jesus and arrested him.

Suddenly, one of those with Jesus put his hand on his sword, drew it, and struck the slave of the high priest, cutting off his ear. Then Jesus said to him, "Put your sword back into its place; for all who take the sword will perish by the sword. Do you think that I cannot appeal to my Father, and he will at once send me more than twelve legions of angels? But how then would the scriptures be fulfilled, which say it must happen in this way?"

At that hour Jesus said to the crowds, "Have you come out with swords and clubs to arrest me as though I were a bandit? Day after day I sat in the temple teaching, and you did not arrest me. But all this has taken place, so that the scriptures of the prophets may be fulfilled." Then all the disciples deserted him and fled.

Those who had arrested Jesus took him to Caiaphas the high priest, in whose house the scribes and the elders had gathered.

But Peter was following him at a distance, as far as the courtyard of the high priest; and going inside, he sat with the guards in order to see how this would end. Now the chief priests and the whole council were looking for false testimony against Jesus so that they might put him to death, but they found none, though many false witnesses came forward. At last two came forward and said, "This fellow said, 'I am able to destroy the temple of God and to build it in three days.'" The high priest stood up and said, "Have you no answer? What is it that they testify against you?" But Jesus was silent. Then the high priest said to him, "I put you under oath before the living God, tell us if you are the Messiah, the Son of God."

Jesus said to him, "You have said so. But I tell you, From now on you will see the Son of Man seated at the right hand of Power and coming on the clouds of heaven." Then the high priest tore his clothes and said, "He has blasphemed! Why do we still need witnesses? You have now heard his blasphemy. What is your verdict?" They answered, "He deserves death." Then they spat in his face and struck him; and some slapped him, saying, "Prophesy to us, you Messiah! Who is it that struck you?" Now Peter was sitting outside in the courtyard. A servant-girl came to him and said, "You also were with Jesus the Galilean." But he denied it before all of them, saying, "I do not know what you are talking about." When he went out to the porch, another servant-girl saw him, and she said to the bystanders, "This man was with Jesus of Nazareth." Again he denied it with an oath, "I do not know the man." After a little while the bystanders came up and said to Peter, "Certainly you are also one of them, for your accent betrays you." Then he began to curse, and he swore an oath, "I do not know the man!" At that moment the cock crowed. Then Peter remembered what Jesus had said: "Before the cock crows, you will deny me three times." And he went out and wept bitterly.

When morning came, all the chief priests and the elders of the people conferred together against Jesus in order to bring about his death. They bound him, led him away, and handed him over to Pilate the governor.

When Judas, his betrayer, saw that Jesus was condemned, he repented and brought back the thirty pieces of silver to the chief priests and the elders. He said, "I have sinned by betraying innocent blood." But they said, "What is that to us? See to it yourself." Throwing down the pieces of silver in the temple, he departed; and he went and hanged himself. But the chief priests, taking the pieces of silver, said, "It is not lawful to put them into the treasury, since they are blood money." After conferring together, they used them to buy the potter's field as a place to bury foreigners. For this reason that field has been called the Field of Blood to this day. Then was fulfilled what had been spoken through the prophet Jeremiah, "And they took the thirty pieces of silver, the price of the one on whom a price had been set, on whom some of the people of Israel had set a price, and they gave them for the potter's field, as the Lord commanded me."

Now Jesus stood before the governor; and the governor asked him, "Are you the King of the Jews?" Jesus said, "You say so." But when he was accused by the chief priests and elders, he did not answer. Then Pilate said to him, "Do you not hear how many accusations they make against you?" But he gave him no answer, not even to a single charge, so that the governor was greatly amazed.

Now at the festival the governor was accustomed to release a prisoner for the crowd, anyone whom they wanted. At that time they had a notorious prisoner, called Jesus Barabbas. So after they had gathered, Pilate said to them, "Whom do you want me to release for you, Jesus Barabbas or Jesus who is called the Messiah?" For he realized that it was out of jealousy that they had handed him over.

While he was sitting on the judgment seat, his wife sent word to him, "Have nothing to do with that innocent man, for today I have suffered a great deal because of a dream about him."

Now the chief priests and the elders persuaded the crowds to ask for Barabbas and to have Jesus killed. The governor again said to them, "Which of the two do you want me to release for you?" And they said, "Barabbas." Pilate said to them, "Then what should I do with Jesus who is called the Messiah?" All of them said, "Let him be crucified!" Then he asked, "Why, what evil has he done?" But they shouted all the more, "Let him be crucified!"

So when Pilate saw that he could do nothing, but rather that a riot was beginning, he took some water and washed his hands before the crowd, saying, "I am innocent of this man's blood; see to it yourselves." Then the people as a whole answered, "His blood be on us and on our children!" So he released Barabbas for them; and after flogging Jesus, he handed him over to be crucified.

Then the soldiers of the governor took Jesus into the governor's headquarters, and they gathered the whole cohort around him. They stripped him and put a scarlet robe on him, and after twisting some thorns into a crown, they put it on his head. They put a reed in his right hand and knelt before him and mocked him, saying, "Hail, King of the Jews!" They spat on him, and took the reed and struck him on the head. After mocking him, they stripped him of the robe and put his own clothes on him. Then they led him away to crucify him.

As they went out, they came upon a man from Cyrene named Simon; they compelled this man to carry his cross.

And when they came to a place called Golgotha (which means Place of a Skull), they offered him wine to drink, mixed with gall; but when he tasted it, he would not drink it. And when they had crucified him, they divided his clothes among themselves by casting lots; then they sat down there and kept watch over him.

Over his head they put the charge against him, which read, "This is Jesus, the King of the Jews." Then two bandits were crucified with him, one on his right and one on his left. Those who passed by derided him, shaking their heads and saying, "You who would destroy the temple and build it in three days, save yourself! If you are the Son of God, come down from the cross."

In the same way the chief priests also, along with the scribes and elders, were mocking him, saying, "He saved others; he cannot save himself. He is the King of Israel; let him come down from the cross now, and we will believe in him. He trusts in God; let God deliver him now, if he wants to; for he said, 'I am God's Son.'" The bandits who were crucified with him also taunted him in the same way.

From noon on, darkness came over the whole land until three in the afternoon. And about three o'clock Jesus cried with a loud voice, "Eli, Eli, lema sabachthani?" that is, "My God, my God, why have you forsaken me?" When some of the bystanders heard it, they said, "This man is calling for Elijah." At once one of them ran and got a sponge, filled it with sour wine, put it on a stick, and gave it to him to drink. But the others said, "Wait, let us see whether Elijah will come to save him." Then Jesus cried again with a loud voice and breathed his last.

At that moment the curtain of the temple was torn in two, from top to bottom. The earth shook, and the rocks were split. The tombs also were opened, and many bodies of the saints who had fallen asleep were raised. After his resurrection they came out of the tombs and entered the holy city and appeared to many.

Now when the centurion and those with him, who were keeping watch over Jesus, saw the earthquake and what took place, they were terrified and said, "Truly this man was God's Son!"

Many women were also there, looking on from a distance; they had followed Jesus from Galilee and had provided for him. Among them were Mary Magdalene, and Mary the mother of James and Joseph, and the mother of the sons of Zebedee. When it was evening, there came a rich man from Arimathea, named Joseph, who was also a disciple of Jesus. He went to Pilate and asked for the body of Jesus; then Pilate ordered it to be given to him. So Joseph took the body and wrapped it in a clean linen cloth and laid it in his own new tomb, which he had hewn in the rock. He then rolled a great stone to the door of the tomb and went away. Mary Magdalene and the other Mary were there, sitting opposite the tomb.

The next day, that is, after the day of Preparation, the chief priests and the Pharisees gathered before Pilate and said, "Sir, we remember what that impostor said while he was still alive, 'After three days I will rise again.' Therefore command the tomb to be made secure until the third day; otherwise his disciples may go and steal him away, and tell the people, 'He has been raised from the dead,' and the last deception would be worse than the first." Pilate said to them, "You have a guard of soldiers; go, make it as secure as you can." So they went with the guard and made the tomb secure by sealing the stone.

Non-Violence

JOHN F. CRAGHAN

We have the innate tendency to react to violence with violence. We suffer personal hurt and so we strike back. We are the innocent victims of prejudice and so we lash out. We are put down by stronger opponents and so we retaliate. "Arm yourself with compassion, not violence" seems a foolhardy slogan at best.

Today's readings take up the problem of violence. They challenge us about our "get even" policy. Even in the face of pain and frustration, today's readings advocate that we arm ourselves with compassion, not violence.

A Suffering Servant

The first reading is part of the third Suffering Servant Song (Is 50:4-9). It was spoken toward the end of the exile of God's people in Babylon. The poem depicts Israel as a servant who is obedient to God's Word, but not all obeyed the call of the prophet. This refusal led to frequent humiliations (beating, plucking of the beard, buffets, spitting). Yet the Servant did not react to violence with violence. Rather, he continued to hope that God would support him in his trial and utterly vindicate him. He is an example of non-violence.

At the time of his arrest, Jesus practiced what he had preached in the Sermon on the Mount. There he had called blest those who are insulted and persecuted because of him (Mt 5:11). Instead of "an eye for an eye and a tooth for a tooth" Jesus advocated offering no resistance and turning the other cheek (5:38-40). Further, Jesus taught his disciples to love their enemies and pray for their persecutors (5:44). Now Jesus rejects the use of violence even to save himself. He could have called down twelve legions of angels to defend his cause. But he did not. Instead of striking back with violence as human kings do (see 2:16-18), Jesus teaches that the purpose of power is to serve others. "The Son of Man came not to be served but to serve, and to give his life a ransom for many" (20:28).

Today's Good News

The modern Christian does not have to look far in order to discover the use of violence. Not infrequently, we employ subtle forms of violence. When we are hurt by friends and family members, we resort to violence when we refuse to speak. Our silence thus becomes our principle way of crippling the enemy.

In our working world, we can be the innocent victims of harassment and exploitation. Instinctively, we look for the opportunity to retaliate against the perpetrators.

Slander and deceit may become our lethal weapons as we take the offensive.

On the world scene, we witness an alarming escalation of violence. We seem to take it for granted that only violence can overcome violence. Bigger and better arms and better planned strategy appear to be the only reasonable response.

Jesus urges us to review our violent ways. Today's gospel implies an attitude of patient endurance, even death if necessary. Jesus' message is to arm yourself with compassion, not violence. And he practiced his message to the ultimate.

Points for Reflection and Discussion

1. Have you, or anyone close to you, ever been personally exposed to violence? How did you react? How did it change your life, or your lifestyle?

_____

_____

_____

_____

2. Have you, like Jesus, experienced the fickleness of people who vacillate between admiration and condemnation? Have you ever been among the fickle?

_____

_____

_____

_____

Themes

Revenge
   L6, The Lord's Prayer
Violence
   L5, The Way of the Cross

Reading 1, Acts 10:34,37-43

Peter began to speak to them: "The message spread throughout Judea, beginning in Galilee after the baptism that John announced: how God anointed Jesus of Nazareth with the Holy Spirit and with power; how he went about doing good and healing all who were oppressed by the devil, for God was with him. We are witnesses to all that he did both in Judea and in Jerusalem. They put him to death by hanging him on a tree; but God raised him on the third day and allowed him to appear, not to all the people but to us who were chosen by God as witnesses, and who ate and drank with him after he rose from the dead. He commanded us to preach to the people and to testify that he is the one ordained by God as judge of the living and the dead. All the prophets testify about him that everyone who believes in him receives forgiveness of sins through his name."

Psalm 118:1-2,16-17,22-23

Reading 2, Colossians 3:1-4 *

If you have been raised with Christ, seek the things that are above, where Christ is, seated at the right hand of God. Set your minds on things that are above, not on things that are on earth, for you have died, and your life is hidden with Christ in God. When Christ who is your life is revealed, then you also will be revealed with him in glory.

**alternate reading - 1 Corinthians 5:6-8*

Gospel, Matthew 28:1-10 **

After the sabbath, as the first day of the week was dawning, Mary Magdalene and the other Mary went to see the tomb. And suddenly there was a great earthquake; for an angel of the Lord, descending from heaven, came and rolled back the stone and sat on it. His appearance was like lightning, and his clothing white as snow. For fear of him the guards shook and became like dead men. But the angel said to the women, "Do not be afraid; I know that you are looking for Jesus who was crucified. He is not here; for he has been raised, as he said. Come, see the place where he lay. Then go quickly and tell his disciples, 'He has been raised from the dead, and indeed he is going ahead of you to Galilee; there you will see him.' This is my message for you." So they left the tomb quickly with fear and great joy, and ran to tell his disciples. Suddenly Jesus met them and said, "Greetings!" And they came to him, took hold of his feet, and worshiped him. Then Jesus said to them, "Do not be afraid; go and tell my brothers to go to Galilee; there they will see me."

***alternate reading - John 20:1-9**

His Love Endures Forever

JOHN F. CRAGHAN

Some see Easter merely as the harbinger of spring. We reach that part of our yearly cycle where longer days and warmer weather are upon us. Hence, we rejoice in this phase of nature, equating Easter Sunday with the vernal equinox. It is difficult to admit that Easter has other connotations.

Today's readings demand that we view Easter more in terms of personal conversion and less in terms of seasonal changes. They help us to understand Easter as the transformation experience of Jesus, which in turn is to become the transformation experience of Christians. The empty tomb is the invitation to a fuller life.

Psalm 118 is a psalm of declarative praise, one that announces the abrupt newness in one's life that calls for immediate celebration. The "I" of the psalm is quite likely a king who, having experienced some social or political upheaval, now sings of Yahweh's miraculous deliverance. To be sure, Yahweh has been faithful to the covenant commitment ("his steadfast love endures forever"). The psalmist speaks of Yahweh's intervention: his right hand has struck with power. Death, that is, the disruption in the life of the king and the citizenry, has been conquered.

Amazement and bewilderment are described in masonry terms: The stone rejected by the builders is nothing less than the cornerstone. Fittingly, the New Testament interprets the masonry imagery in terms of Jesus' exaltation (see Mt 21:42; Acts 4:11; 1 Pt 2:7). Easter is thus the reversal of Jesus' passion and death—it is the celebration of new life.

Bread of Life

In this section of First Corinthians, Paul has just scolded that community for tolerating an incestuous marriage (5:1-6). Paul compares such sinfulness to a little yeast that leavens all the dough. Now he appeals to the combined feasts of Passover and Unleavened Bread. In the latter the Jews had to remove all the leaven of the previous year. Likewise the Corinthians are to get rid of the wicked.

Paul then uses the imagery of Passover to motivate the moral behavior of his community. Just as the Passover celebrates the journey from the land of bondage to the land of freedom, so too Easter, the Christian Passover, celebrates a journey: Jesus' trek from death to new life. But the trek also demands a radical change in the life of Christians: "Not with the old yeast, the yeast of malice and evil, but with the unleavened bread of sincerity and truth" (1 Cor 5:8).

In Matthew's account of Easter morning, there is a mighty earthquake that calls to mind the earthquake at the death of Jesus (27:51-54). The earthquake and the clothing of the angel (see Dt 7:9; Rv 1:14-16) proclaim the shaking of the earth's foundation at Jesus' triumph over death. This position is clearly the proclamation of victory. God has conquered death in the Resurrection of Jesus—the rejected stone has become the cornerstone.

Matthew quickly links the stone imagery with a call to a new life. Jesus' command to the women to bring the news to "my brothers" is his communication of forgiveness to the sinful disciples. The focus on Galilee as the place of Jesus' appearance conjures up the mission to the Gentiles (see Mt 28:16-20). The Resurrection of Jesus is thus the catalyst that welcomes all into God's kingdom.

Today's Good News

Easter Sunday is not intended to be a quiet reflection on the emptiness of the tomb. It is, rather, the remembering of Jesus' transformation that calls for a similar transformation in the lives of modern Christians. The stones of Psalm 118 and Matthew 28, as well as the dough of 1 Corinthians 5, are powerful images designed to bring about change in daily living.

Husbands and wives who deepen their mutual love and commitment are indeed fresh dough. They transform their own lives as well as the lives of others. Those who overcome drug or alcohol dependency, or similar dependencies, were once the stones rejected by the builders. Their new lifestyle, however, indicates that they have become cornerstones. All those who labor for the transformation of the poor, the indigent, the disenfranchised, are the new stone of the empty tomb, announcing the defeat of death and the victory of a truly human life. These and similar people are caught up in the experience of Easter.

Points for Reflection and Discussion

1. You are a disciple. How will you share the joy of being an Easter person?

_____

_____

_____

_____

2. Imagine you are one of those who saw the empty tomb and then met Jesus on the road. Describe your experience.

_____

_____

_____

_____

_____

Themes

Life
   L7, The Meaning of Holy Week
Resurrection
   L8, Catechumenate Retreat Day

Reading 1, Acts 2:42-47

[The baptized] devoted themselves to the apostles' teaching and fellowship, to the breaking of bread and the prayers. Awe came upon everyone, because many wonders and signs were being done by the apostles. All who believed were together and had all things in common; they would sell their possessions and goods and distribute the proceeds to all, as any had need. Day by day, as they spent much time together in the temple, they broke bread at home and ate their food with glad and generous hearts, praising God and having the goodwill of all the people. And day by day the Lord added to their number those who were being saved.

Psalm 118:2-4,13-15,22-24

Reading 2, 1 Peter 1:3-9

Blessed be the God and Father of our Lord Jesus Christ! By his great mercy he has given us a new birth into a living hope through the resurrection of Jesus Christ from the dead, and into an inheritance that is imperishable, undefiled, and unfading, kept in heaven for you, who are being protected by the power of God through faith for a salvation ready to be revealed in the last time.

In this you rejoice, even if now for a little while you have had to suffer various trials, so that the genuineness of your faith—being more precious than gold that, though perishable, is tested by fire—may be found to result in praise and glory and honor when Jesus Christ is revealed.

Although you have not seen him, you love him; and even though you do not see him now, you believe in him and rejoice with an indescribable and glorious joy, for you are receiving the outcome of your faith, the salvation of your souls.

Gospel, John 20:19-31

When it was evening on the first day of the week, and the doors of the house where the disciples had met were locked for fear of the Jews, Jesus came and stood among them and said, "Peace be with you." After he said this, he showed them his hands and his side. Then the disciples rejoiced when they saw the Lord.

Jesus said to them again, "Peace be with you. As the Father has sent me, so I send you."

When he had said this, he breathed on them and said to them, "Receive the Holy Spirit. If you forgive the sins of any, they are forgiven them; if you retain the sins of any, they are retained."

But Thomas (who was called the Twin), one of the twelve, was not with them when Jesus came. So the other disciples told him, "We have seen the Lord." But he said to them, "Unless I see the mark of the nails in his hands, and put my finger in the mark of the nails and my hand in his side, I will not believe."

A week later his disciples were again in the house, and Thomas was with them. Although the doors were shut, Jesus came and stood among them and said, "Peace be with you." Then he said to Thomas, "Put your finger here and see my hands. Reach out your hand and put it in my side. Do not doubt but believe." Thomas answered him, "My Lord and my God!"

Jesus said to him, "Have you believed because you have seen me? Blessed are those who have not seen and yet have come to believe."

Now Jesus did many other signs in the presence of his disciples, which are not written in this book. But these are written so that you may come to believe that Jesus is the Messiah, the Son of God, and that through believing you may have life in his name.

An Easter People

JOHN F. CRAGHAN

We often like to sit back and review the gospel stories about the third day. We recall the visit of the women, the discovery of the empty tomb, and the subsequent appearance of the risen Lord. The danger is that, while we can recite the stories, we may not be able to act upon them. Our temptation is to be Easter spectators but not Easter participants.

Today's readings are powerful reminders that faith is much more than a sterile, passive recollection of a key event. They show, in their own upsetting way, that the celebration of Easter is a call to action. They demand that believers express the transformation of Jesus in the transformation of their own lives. They assert that faith in the Resurrection means faith in action.

In this major summary of the Acts of the Apostles (see also 4:32-35;5:11-16), Luke paints a picture of the Christian community in the aftermath of Easter and Pentecost (see 2:1-13). He reveals some of those basic elements that make the community specifically Christian. He shows that such a community finds its source of unity in the apostolic teaching. He also speaks of the breaking of bread, which has clear eucharistic overtones. In addition, he mentions prayer and (in this Jerusalem setting) attendance at the Temple.

Luke elaborates, however, on the *communal life.* This is that camaraderie by which one places one's own goods, without reservation, at the service of the needy. It is significant that the basis for such sharing is Easter faith: those who *believed* held all things in common. For Luke's audience, the clear message is that faith in the Resurrection means faith in action.

Blessed are Those Who Have Not Seen

Writing from Rome some 80 years after Christ's death, the author of First Peter addresses himself to rural Gentile Christians living in what is now northern Turkey. He sets out to strengthen their Christian lives in a pagan atmosphere. Their suffering is probably due not to a systematic persecution but to the hardships of an alienated community. They are tempted to conform to a pagan lifestyle.

The liturgical reading mentions *faith* three times and *believe* once. This baptismal exhortation recalls their initial commitment to the risen Christ in faith at baptism. Although "by the power of God" they are protected through faith, they will attain their goal of faith only in the end. In the meantime they are to endure distress, but this "tested" faith will result in the joy of Christ's Second Coming. For the author of First Peter, faith in the Resurrection means faith in action.

The selection from John's Gospel is a study in the centrality of faith. Writing for Christians who never knew the historical Jesus, the author uses the Thomas incident to emphasize a faith without the benefit of eyewitness. In the conclusion, the author applies such faith in a general way to all future believers.

Jesus' Easter appearance to the disciples links their faith-acceptance of the risen Jesus with the command to forgive. Jesus introduces his command with "peace." This *peace* is the radical overthrow of isolation and separation from God and fellow humans. It is thus the undoing of *sin*. When Christian disciples act upon Easter faith by communicating forgiveness, either to individuals or to communities, they represent the Jesus who greeted the disciples with "peace." To forgive sins and thus break the chain of alienation implies that faith in the Resurrection means faith in action.

Today's Good News

Modern Christians are often sold a bill of goods known as rank individualism. This individualism teaches that our property and our money are absolute. It also implies that the individual is beholden to no one. For Luke, the bill of goods is communal life. To share with the less fortunate is to show that faith in the Resurrection means faith in action.

Modern Christians are often pressured to conform to the ways of the self-seeking. To do otherwise is to lose friends and influence. For the author of First Peter, to accept Christ in baptism is to reject conformity. To endure hardships is to announce that faith in the Resurrection means faith in action.

Modern Christians appear foolish in the challenge to forgive and forget. Forgiveness is taken as a sign of weakness and weakness cannot be tolerated. For the author of John, to forgive is to join in the chorus of "peace" emanating from the risen Jesus. To undo the shackles of pride in forgiving is to proclaim that faith in the Resurrection means faith in action.

Points for Reflection and Discussion

1. Early Christians lived "in common." To what concrete expression of common life do you think the Spirit is guiding you?

_____

_____

_____

_____

2. An early believer once said: "I believe; help my unbelief!" (Mk 9:24). Are you ever afraid to doubt your faith?

_____

_____

_____

_____

Themes
Community, Eucharist, Forgiveness
    M1, Conversion: A Lifelong Process
    M2, The Laity: Called to Build God's Kingdom
    M3, Your Special Gifts

Reading 1, Acts 2:14,22-28

[On the day of Pentecost] Peter, standing with the eleven, raised his voice and addressed them, "Men of Judea and all who live in Jerusalem, let this be known to you, and listen to what I say. You that are Israelites, listen to what I have to say: Jesus of Nazareth, a man attested to you by God with deeds of power, wonders, and signs that God did through him among you, as you yourselves know—this man, handed over to you according to the definite plan and foreknowledge of God, you crucified and killed by the hands of those outside the law. But God raised him up, having freed him from death, because it was impossible for him to be held in its power. For David says concerning him, 'I saw the Lord always before me, for he is at my right hand so that I will not be shaken; therefore my heart was glad, and my tongue rejoiced; moreover my flesh will live in hope. For you will not abandon my soul to Hades, or let your Holy One experience corruption. You have made known to me the ways of life; you will make me full of gladness with your presence.' "

Psalm 16:1-2,5,7-8,9-10,11

Reading 2, 1 Peter 1:17-21

If you invoke as Father the one who judges all people impartially according to their deeds, live in reverent fear during the time of your exile. You know that you were ransomed from the futile ways inherited from your ancestors, not with perishable things like silver or gold, but with the precious blood of Christ, like that of a lamb without defect or blemish. He was destined before the foundation of the world, but was revealed at the end of the ages for your sake. Through him you have come to trust in God, who raised him from the dead and gave him glory, so that your faith and hope are set on God.

Gospel, Luke 24:13-35

On that same day [the first day of the week] two [disciples] were going to a village called Emmaus, about seven miles from Jerusalem, and talking with each other about all these things that had happened. While they were talking and discussing, Jesus himself came near and went with them, but their eyes were kept from recognizing him.

And he said to them, "What are you discussing with each other while you walk along?" They stood still, looking sad. Then one of them, whose name was Cleopas, answered him, "Are you the only stranger in Jerusalem who does not know the things that have taken place there in these days?"

He asked them, "What things?" They replied, "The things about Jesus of Nazareth, who was a prophet mighty in deed and word before God and all the people, and how our chief priests and leaders handed him over to be condemned to death and crucified him. But we had hoped that he was the one to redeem Israel. Yes, and besides all this, it is now the third day since these things took place. Moreover, some women of our group astounded us. They were at the tomb early this morning, and when they did not find his body there, they came back and told us that they had indeed seen a vision of angels who said that he was alive. Some of those who were with us went to the tomb and found it just as the women had said; but they did not see him."

Then he said to them, "Oh, how foolish you are, and how slow of heart to believe all that the prophets have declared! Was it not necessary that the Messiah should suffer these things and then enter into his glory?"

Then beginning with Moses and all the prophets, he interpreted to them the things about himself in all the scriptures. As they came near the village to which they were going, he walked ahead as if he were going on. But they urged him strongly, saying, "Stay with us, because it is almost evening and the day is now nearly over." So he went in to stay with them.

When he was at the table with them, he took bread, blessed and broke it, and gave it to them. Then their eyes were opened, and they recognized him; and he vanished from their sight. They said to each other, "Were not our hearts burning within us while he was talking to us on the road, while he was opening the scriptures to us?" That same hour they got up and returned to Jerusalem; and they found the eleven and their companions gathered together. They were saying, "The Lord has risen indeed, and he has appeared to Simon!"

Then they told what had happened on the road, and how he had been made known to them in the breaking of the bread.

Divine Providence

JOHN F. CRAGHAN

How often we view events in our lives as the result of blind fate. We conclude that our spouse, our friends, our problems—yes, even our faith—are random chance happenings. We cannot begin to imagine that there may be some divine plan at work. We seem so reluctant to accept a provident God.

Today's readings endorse a God who is intimately involved in the fabric of our lives. They speak of a God who is able to transform failure into success, tragedy into bliss. They reveal a God whose plans bring about cosmos, not chaos. They staunchly maintain: not chance but providence.

Peter's Pentecost discourse mentions those credentials which stamped Jesus as God's emissary: miracles, wonders, signs. The people, however, chose to reject such credentials and went so far as to use pagans to crucify and kill him. Nonetheless, the discourse does not see this death as mere chance. It speaks of God's plan at work, a plan that included death as the necessary condition for new birth in the Resurrection.

To make his point, Peter cites Psalm 16:8-11 (today's responsorial psalm). According to a Christian reinterpretation, David, the reputed author of the original psalm, was referring to Jesus. Although the original psalm does not speak of an afterlife, the Christian rereading sees a link between Jesus' pain/death and his joy/Resurrection. Thus the events of Good Friday were not a classic example of a good man's untimely demise. They were part of "the definite plan and foreknowledge of God."

Divine Life

Today the author of First Peter continues to exhort his audience to live lives worthy of their baptism. Recalling the biblical tradition of Israel's desert wandering, he speaks of the Christian life as a period of exile, yet one sustained by Christian hope. In the Exodus, the blood of the Passover lamb spared Israel from the tenth plague. But "you were ransomed...with the precious blood of Christ, like that of a lamb without defect or blemish."

The author quickly notes that this Christian liberation is not a chance occurrence. Christ was "destined before the foundation of the world, but was revealed at the end of the ages for your sake." Because God raised him from the dead and gave him glory, Christians enjoy confidence and hope.

The body of Luke's Emmaus story moves from nonrecognition to recognition. It consists of two elements: a dialogue narrative (verses 17-27) and a meal narrative (verses 28-30). The structure probably reflects early Christian assemblies where the meal followed upon the discourse.

The two disciples speak of Jesus as a great prophet who was ultimately put to death. They also express their own hopes about Jesus as the great liberator of Israel. In verses 25-27, Jesus responds to their tale of woe by explaining the Scriptures, especially the connection between tragedy and glory: "Was it not necessary that the Messiah should suffer these things and then enter into his glory?" In Luke's presentation, the Scriptures reveal God's plan for Jesus and hence for humankind.

Today's Good News

The modern Christian faces a variety of reverses. It may be a serious illness, the death of a loved one, betrayal by a friend or confidant, the loss of employment. To be sure, they are not happy events. They are tragic, but can they be more? Can they become the raw material for growth and thus a springboard for a new type of life?

Behind the maze of tragedy a divine plan is at work. It is a plan that directs the believer's attention from the abandoned figure on the cross to the transformed Lord of Easter. The plan urges us to attempt to detect the positive in the negative, to try to discover a God who will enter, intimately though mysteriously, into the fabric of our lives.

Points for Reflection and Discussion

1. The travelers to Emmaus recognized Christ in the breaking of bread. When and where has Christ revealed himself to you?

_____

_____

_____

_____

_____

2. Do you believe in divine providence? How does this differ from predestination?

_____

_____

_____

_____

Themes
God's Plan
    M1, Conversion: A Lifelong Process
    M2, The Laity: Called to Build God's Kingdom
Salvation
    M7, Holiness
    M8, Evangelization

Reading 1, Acts 2:14,36-41

[On the day of Pentecost] Peter, standing with the eleven, raised his voice and addressed them. "Let the entire house of Israel know with certainty that God has made him both Lord and Messiah, this Jesus whom you crucified."

Now when they heard this, they were cut to the heart and said to Peter and to the other apostles, "Brothers, what should we do?" Peter said to them, "Repent, and be baptized every one of you in the name of Jesus Christ so that your sins may be forgiven; and you will receive the gift of the Holy Spirit. For the promise is for you, for your children, and for all who are far away, everyone whom the Lord our God calls to him."

And he testified with many other arguments and exhorted them, saying, "Save yourselves from this corrupt generation." So those who welcomed his message were baptized, and that day about three thousand persons were added.

Psalm 23:1-3,3-4,5,6

Reading 2, 1 Peter 2:20-25

If you endure when you do right and suffer for it, you have God's approval. For to this you have been called, because Christ also suffered for you, leaving you an example, so that you should follow in his steps. "He committed no sin, and no deceit was found in his mouth." When he was abused, he did not return abuse; when he suffered, he did not threaten; but he entrusted himself to the one who judges justly. He himself bore our sins in his body on the cross, so that, free from sins, we might live for righteousness; by his wounds you have been healed. For you were going astray like sheep, but now you have returned to the shepherd and guardian of your souls.

Gospel, John 10:1-10

[Jesus said:] "Very truly, I tell you, anyone who does not enter the sheepfold by the gate but climbs in by another way is a thief and a bandit. The one who enters by the gate is the shepherd of the sheep. The gatekeeper opens the gate for him, and the sheep hear his voice. He calls his own sheep by name and leads them out. When he has brought out all his own, he goes ahead of them, and the sheep follow him because they know his voice. They will not follow a stranger, but they will run from him because they do not know the voice of strangers."

Jesus used this figure of speech with them, but they did not understand what he was saying to them. So again

Jesus said to them, "Very truly, I tell you, I am the gate for the sheep. All who came before me are thieves and bandits; but the sheep did not listen to them. I am the gate. Whoever enters by me will be saved, and will come in and go out and find pasture. The thief comes only to steal and kill and destroy. I came that they may have life, and have it abundantly."

Like a Shepherd

JOHN F. CRAGHAN

Some of us are leaders, and others are followers. In some cases, it seems that the followers are expected to put the needs of the leader first. This attitude can even extend to the point where some people think others exist merely for their own pleasure. The pursuit of self can lead to that impasse where we wholeheartedly support the concept: shepherds first, sheep last.

Today's readings focus on the relationship between shepherd and sheep. They are a radical departure from our myopic world of ends and means. Here the emphasis is on the end—the sheep and their welfare. The shepherd is thereby the means to ensure the well-being of the flock. In this world the slogan is clearly: sheep first, shepherds last. In the Ancient Near East, *shepherd* was a political title that stressed the obligation of kings to provide for their subjects. The title conjured up total concern for and dedication to others (see Jer 23:1-4; Ez 34:1-31). In today's famous psalm of confidence, the author speaks of Yahweh as his shepherd. The title connoted Yahweh's loyalty to his sheep, the people of Israel.

Besides the image of the shepherd, there is also the image of the host. Both images are set against the background of the desert where the protector of the sheep is also the protector of the desert traveler, offering hospitality and safety from enemies. The *rod* is a defensive weapon against wild animals, while the *staff* is a supportive instrument. Both rod and staff, therefore, symbolize that the sheep do not experience fear. Here, it is sheep first, shepherds last.

The Stray

In today's reading from the Acts of the Apostles, Luke offers advice to Christian slaves who, because of the economic system, suffer more than anyone else. To encourage them, he draws upon the example of the suffering Christ. Borrowing heavily from the Suffering Servant Song of Isaiah 53, the author speaks of Jesus as one who did no wrong, who returned no insult and did not counter with threats, and who brought healing through his wounds.

In 1 Peter 2:25, that author takes up the image of shepherd and sheep. Though they strayed like sheep (see Is 53:6), they returned to "the shepherd and guardian of your souls." *Guardian* (overseer) reinforces the shepherd's role of concern. Sheep first, shepherds last.

The gospel passage from John consists of: two parables (10:1-3,3-5); reaction at the failure to comprehend (10:6); and explanation of the parables (10:7-8,9-10).

In the first parable, the proper way to approach the sheep is by way of the gate. It is possible that "a thief and a bandit" refer to the Pharisees in chapter nine of John's Gospel, who do not approach the sheep properly but care only for themselves. In the second parable, "leads them out" may borrow from Ezekiel 34:13, where Yahweh the true shepherd, unlike Israel's kings, provides for his sheep. In the first explanation, only Jesus is the sheep gate, that is, the means by which the sheep can be approached. "All who came before me" may have in mind Jewish leaders of the last two centuries B.C., who looked to themselves, not the sheep. In the second explanation, Jesus is the gate that benefits the sheep, not the shepherds. Whereas the thief brings death, Jesus offers life, indeed life to the full. For John, it is sheep first, shepherds last.

Today's Good News

Shepherd may not have an immediate impact on many of us. Its underlying reality, however, is calculated to make us reflect on our relationships. *Our* sheep may be found in our homes, in our places of employment, in our social setting, in our faith community. Do we see ourselves primarily as the beneficiary of the care and concern that these relationships provide? Or do we view ourselves essentially as the conveyor of understanding and empathy that these relationships imply?

Are our rod and staff the symbols of dedication or are they the means of oppression? Are our titles the results of services rendered or are they the stimulus for rendering further service? For the psalmist, the author of First Peter, and John, the only acceptable slogan is: sheep first, shepherds last.

Points for Reflection and Discussion

1. How well do you "shepherd" the sheep entrusted to you?

_____

_____

_____

_____

2. Do you identify yourself primarily as a leader or as a follower? Why?

_____

_____

_____

_____

Themes

Good Shepherd
    M5, Your Prayer Life
Relationships
    M3, Your Special Gifts
    M4, Family Life
    M8, Evangelization
Repentance
    M1, Conversion: A Lifelong Process

Reading 1, Acts 6:1-7

During those days, when the disciples were increasing in number, the Hellenists complained against the Hebrews because their widows were being neglected in the daily distribution of food. And the twelve called together the whole community of the disciples and said, "It is not right that we should neglect the word of God in order to wait on tables. Therefore, friends, select from among yourselves seven men of good standing, full of the Spirit and of wisdom, whom we may appoint to this task, while we, for our part, will devote ourselves to prayer and to serving the word."

What they said pleased the whole community, and they chose Stephen, a man full of faith and the Holy Spirit, together with Philip, Prochorus, Nicanor, Timon, Parmenas, and Nicolaus, a proselyte of Antioch. They had these men stand before the apostles, who prayed and laid their hands on them. The word of God continued to spread; the number of the disciples increased greatly in Jerusalem, and a great many of the priests became obedient to the faith.

Psalm 33:1-2,4-5,18-19

Reading 2, 1 Peter 2:4-9

Come to [the Lord], a living stone, though rejected by mortals yet chosen and precious in God's sight, and like living stones, let yourselves be built into a spiritual house, to be a holy priesthood, to offer spiritual sacrifices acceptable to God through Jesus Christ.

For it stands in scripture: "See, I am laying in Zion a stone, a cornerstone chosen and precious; and whoever believes in him will not be put to shame." To you then who believe, he is precious; but for those who do not believe, "The stone that the builders rejected has become the very head of the corner," and "A stone that makes them stumble, and a rock that makes them fall." They stumble because they disobey the word, as they were destined to do.

But you are a chosen race, a royal priesthood, a holy nation, God's own people, in order that you may proclaim the mighty acts of him who called you out of darkness into his marvelous light.

Gospel, John 14:1-12

[Jesus said to his disciples:] "Do not let your hearts be troubled. Believe in God, believe also in me. In my Father's house there are many dwelling places. If it were not so, would I have told you that I go to prepare a place for you? And if I go and prepare a place for you, I will come again

and will take you to myself, so that where I am, there you may be also. And you know the way to the place where I am going." Thomas said to him, "Lord, we do not know where you are going. How can we know the way?"

Jesus said to him, "I am the way, and the truth, and the life. No one comes to the Father except through me. If you know me, you will know my Father also. From now on you do know him and have seen him."

Philip said to him, "Lord, show us the Father, and we will be satisfied."

Jesus said to him, "Have I been with you all this time, Philip, and you still do not know me? Whoever has seen me has seen the Father. How can you say, 'Show us the Father'? Do you not believe that I am in the Father and the Father is in me? The words that I say to you I do not speak on my own; but the Father who dwells in me does his works. Believe me that I am in the Father and the Father is in me; but if you do not, then believe me because of the works themselves. Very truly, I tell you, the one who believes in me will also do the works that I do and, in fact, will do greater works than these, because I am going to the Father."

Louder Than Words

JOHN F. CRAGHAN

How often we suffer from "promises, promises." We meet people who promise us everything but then deliver absolutely nothing. Moreover, we too have been guilty at times of merely talking a good game. We give assurance, but do we always back up our assurances with deeds?

Today's readings are a call to Christian action. They are intended to awaken us from our lethargy and make our baptismal commitment something more than just pious words. They are the upsetting reminder that to accept Christ is to accept a Christian way of life. They make the point that actions speak louder than words.

Luke offers an example of how a painful reality of discrimination can become the occasion for community growth. This discrimination resulted from the unfair distribution of food between the Hellenist widows (who spoke only Greek) and the Hebrew widows (who spoke a Semitic language besides Greek). It should be noted that not only languages but also cultural and religious differences separated the two groups. To resolve the problem, the Twelve gather the community, who accept the proposal to choose seven assistants to alleviate the need.

While the seven are intended to be relief workers, they are nowhere presented in Acts as actually carrying out that function. At least two from the group, however, are conspicuous for other forms of Christian service. The stories about Philip (8:4-40) and Stephen (6:8—7:60) illustrate their participation in preaching, debating, expounding the Scriptures, and evangelization. Luke carefully places the story of the seven between two statements about the growth of the community (6:1,7). Thus the Word of God is spread as a result of Christian commitment in action. Here, actions speak louder than words.

Living Stones

In this section of First Peter, the author opens with the invitation to come to the Lord, a living stone. He follows up on this image by calling these Christians "living stones." The community is indeed a Temple and, as such, is required to lead a life of service, namely, by offering spiritual sacrifices. The result of their holiness must not be their departure to a sacred place but their involvement in action.

In verse 9 the writer speaks of the community as a chosen race (see Is 43:20), a royal priesthood and a holy nation (see Ex 19:6), and a people claimed by God (see Is 43:21). Their royal and priestly status implies the call to action. They must reflect God's holiness by worship and service.

The Way

John speaks of Jesus as the way, the truth, and the life. As the way, Jesus is the unique means of salvation. As the truth, he is the revelation of the Father. As the life, he is the communication of that common life with the Father. In turn, these images have implications for the disciple of Jesus. The way includes Jesus' return to the Father via his earthly activity, death, and Resurrection. The follower is thus called to share in Jesus' ministry and death, and ultimately in his Resurrection. The truth involves God's faithful undertakings in history on behalf of his people. Similarly the disciple of Jesus must actively emulate that truth. The disciple is called to communicate that transcendent reality to others. For John, therefore, Jesus' self-identification as the way, the truth, and the life has clear implications for Christian discipleship.

Today's Good News

Maturing in a religious sense is no simple process. It is relatively easy to make our baptismal promises. It is much more difficult to act upon them. Do we really reject Satan and all his works and all his empty promises? If we do, then our family life and our business practices will show that. Do we really believe in the forgiveness of sins and life everlasting? If we do, then our reconciliation with those who have hurt us will show that. Our readings imply that Christianity is more than registration in our local parish. They clearly endorse the consequences of that registration, namely, that actions speak louder than words.

Points for Reflection and Discussion

1. "How can we know the way?" Thomas asks Jesus. The question looms before us still. What does Jesus' answer mean for you?

_____

_____

_____

_____

2. Today's readings present many analogies for Jesus: cornerstone, word, way, truth, and so forth. What are some of your own (or your favorite) analogies, and why?

_____

_____

_____

_____

Themes
Chosen, Deacons
   M2, The Laity: Called to Build God's Kingdom
   M3, Your Special Gifts
   M6, Discernment

Reading 1, Acts 8:5-8,14-17

Philip went down to the city of Samaria and proclaimed the Messiah to them. The crowds with one accord listened eagerly to what was said by Philip, hearing and seeing the signs that he did, for unclean spirits, crying with loud shrieks, came out of many who were possessed; and many others who were paralyzed or lame were cured. So there was great joy in that city.

Now when the apostles at Jerusalem heard that Samaria had accepted the word of God, they sent Peter and John to them. The two went down and prayed for them that they might receive the Holy Spirit (for as yet the Spirit had not come upon any of them; they had only been baptized in the name of the Lord Jesus). Then Peter and John laid their hands on them, and they received the Holy Spirit.

Psalm 66:1-3,4-5,6-7,16,20

Reading 2, 1 Peter 3:15-18

In your hearts sanctify Christ as Lord. Always be ready to make your defense to anyone who demands from you an accounting for the hope that is in you; yet do it with gentleness and reverence. Keep your conscience clear, so that, when you are maligned, those who abuse you for your good conduct in Christ may be put to shame. For it is better to suffer for doing good, if suffering should be God's will, than to suffer for doing evil.

For Christ also suffered for sins once for all, the righteous for the unrighteous, in order to bring you to God. He was put to death in the flesh, but made alive in the spirit.

Gospel, John 14:15-21

[Jesus said to his disciples:] "If you love me, you will keep my commandments. And I will ask the Father, and he will give you another Advocate, to be with you forever. This is the Spirit of truth, whom the world cannot receive, because it neither sees him nor knows him. You know him, because he abides with you, and he will be in you.

"I will not leave you orphaned; I am coming to you. In a little while the world will no longer see me, but you will see me; because I live, you also will live. On that day you will know that I am in my Father, and you in me, and I in you. They who have my commandments and keep them are those who love me; and those who love me will be loved by my Father, and I will love them and reveal myself to them."

A Splendid Spirit

JOHN F. CRAGHAN

Christianity is a many-splendored presence, but we can get caught up in the dues-paying and worship syndrome. We can equate Christianity with our weekly financial contribution and our one-hour attendance at liturgy. While these are commendable, we may be tempted to limit Christian presence to these two forms. It may prove difficult to look at the larger spectrum and embrace some more challenging ways of Christian presence.

Today's readings reflect different forms of presence. They powerfully suggest that the Christian life can make considerable demands on the believer. They urge us to accept the reality that Christianity is a many-splendored presence.

Good Samaritans

At this juncture in his Acts of the Apostles, Luke narrates how the Christian message spreads from the confines of Jerusalem to Judea and Samaria. It is noteworthy that persecution becomes the catalyst for this onward march "in all Judea and Samaria, and even to the ends of the earth" (Acts 1:8).

It is no accident that Luke speaks about Samaria. Although the Samaritans accepted the first five books of the Hebrew Scriptures and believed in a Messiah, they were nonetheless regarded as non-Jews. Luke tells us that Philip proclaimed the coming of the Messiah and performed miracles for these outsiders. Since missionary expansion must be rooted in the Church of Jerusalem, Peter and John incorporated the Samaritans into that community by conferring the Spirit. For Luke, such missionary activity attests that Christianity is a many-splendored presence.

The author of First Peter takes up the issue of persecution, although he does not necessarily envision being hauled before judges. Christians should be willing and able to explain their manner of presence. If they must suffer, then it should be because of good deeds, not evil ones. Indeed, their conduct should be such that their persecutors will be ashamed. At the same time, their Christian presence should be marked by gentleness and respect. The issue of brute force will only weaken that presence.

By way of encouragement, the author proposes Jesus' reaction to persecution. Perhaps borrowing from an early hymn or creed, he depicts Jesus as the just person who suffers on behalf of the unjust (see Is 53:11). His death meant that humans could experience a new relationship with God ("in order to bring you to God").

Although Jesus was put to death, he was empowered to communicate the Spirit he received in the Resurrection. For this writer, bearing up under persecution shows that Christianity is a many-splendored presence.

The Spirit Moves

The author of John is very much concerned with the question of presence and absence. Since Jesus has gone home to the Father, the Christian naturally wonders about his or her relationship to the Lord. In this passage, the author insists that keeping Jesus' commands binds the believer to him. These commands are not mere external prescriptions. Rather, they are a way of life that manifest the ongoing link between believer and Lord.

The author also develops the question of presence by speaking about the role of the Spirit. Jesus is the first Advocate (see 1 Jn 2:1) whose work the Spirit ("another Advocate") must complement. Indeed this Advocate will be not only *with* the disciple, but also *within* the disciple. It is significant that the believer must release the Spirit so that this Advocate can console, teach (see Jn 14:26), and witness (see Jn 15:26-27). For this writer too, the reality of life is that Christianity is a many-splendored presence.

Today's Good News

We can all point to others in the Christian community who bring the Good News to unbelievers, who are the victims of violence, who are the professional communicators of the Spirit. We react to the disturbing message of Acts, First Peter, and John by urging that we are ordinary, pew-abiding people who are not called upon to enter into this fray.

In our daily lives, however, we *do* meet those who need to hear Good News about themselves and their basic human dignity. Hence, we are missionaries. We *do* know of those who are the victims of prejudice and discrimination. By sustaining them, we are also the victims of such oppression. We *do* come across those who have to be consoled, taught, and directed. By providing for them, we are the releasers of the Spirit. Christian presence takes a variety of forms. Our contribution according to our gifts and opportunities is a many-splendored presence.

Points for Reflection and Discussion

1. How have you experienced the Spirit working in you or through you recently?

_____

_____

_____

_____

2. What gifts of the Spirit do you feel particularly graced with?

_____

_____

_____

_____

Themes

Gifts of the Spirit, Holy Spirit
   M3, Your Special Gifts
   M6, Discernment

Reading 1, Acts 1:12-14

[After Jesus was taken up to heaven, the apostles] returned to Jerusalem from the mount called Olivet, which is near Jerusalem, a sabbath day's journey away. When they had entered the city, they went to the room upstairs where they were staying, Peter, and John, and James, and Andrew, Philip and Thomas, Bartholomew and Matthew, James son of Alphaeus, and Simon the Zealot, and Judas son of James. All these were constantly devoting themselves to prayer, together with certain women, including Mary the mother of Jesus, as well as his brothers.

Psalm 27:1,4,7-8

Reading 2, 1 Peter 4:13-16

Rejoice insofar as you are sharing Christ's sufferings, so that you may also be glad and shout for joy when his glory is revealed. If you are reviled for the name of Christ, you are blessed, because the spirit of glory, which is the Spirit of God, is resting on you.

But let none of you suffer as a murderer, a thief, a criminal, or even as a mischief maker. Yet if any of you suffers as a Christian, do not consider it a disgrace, but glorify God because you bear this name.

Gospel, John 17:1-11

[Jesus] looked up to heaven and said, "Father, the hour has come; glorify your Son so that the Son may glorify you, since you have given him authority over all people, to give eternal life to all whom you have given him. And this is eternal life, that they may know you, the only true God, and Jesus Christ whom you have sent. I glorified you on earth by finishing the work that you gave me to do. So now, Father, glorify me in your own presence with the glory that I had in your presence before the world existed.

"I have made your name known to those whom you gave me from the world. They were yours, and you gave them to me, and they have kept your word. Now they know that everything you have given me is from you; for the words that you gave to me I have given to them, and they have received them and know in truth that I came from you; and they have believed that you sent me. I am asking on their behalf; I am not asking on behalf of the world, but on behalf of those whom you gave me, because they are yours. All mine are yours, and yours are mine; and I have been glorified in them. And now I am no longer in the world, but they are in the world, and I am coming to you."

A New World

JOHN F. CRAGHAN

To pray is to see the world in a new way. How often we look upon prayer as an exercise to be endured at all costs. We are told to pray and so we go through the motions of trying to communicate with the *Omnipotent One*. We bring our agenda to this deity and program ourselves to survive the session. We assume that this *Other* will get the message and make the proper response.

Today's readings address the vital issue of prayer. We are introduced to the prayer of the psalmist, the early Church, and Jesus himself. Actually, we are admitted into a realm where we are to put aside our total fascination with self and focus on *Another*. To pray is to see the world in a new way.

In Acts, Luke narrates the apostles' return from Mount Olivet to Jerusalem. It is hardly surprising that Luke pictures them and the others in constant prayer, since this evangelist stresses the absolute need for prayer (see Lk 3:21;6:12;11:1 for examples). In order to prepare for Judas' replacement and, more importantly, the coming of the Spirit, the group must seclude itself. Prayer provides an atmosphere where one can think the thoughts of God.

Luke notes especially the presence of Mary, the mother of Jesus. While the Eleven are the link with the public ministry of Jesus, Mary is the sole link with the early years of Jesus. Luke has depicted her as the perfect disciple, the model of faith (see Lk 1:45;8:19-21; 11:27-28). What is also significant is that Luke has twice pictured her at prayer. At the birth of Jesus she "treasured all these words and pondered them in her heart" (Lk 2:19). At the time of the loss in the Temple she "treasured all these things in her heart" (Lk 2:51). These were puzzling events that Mary sought to interpret. But in the light of Jesus' exaltation she sees how he is Savior, Messiah, and Lord (Lk 2:11). Here, to pray is to see the world in a new way.

Letting Go

Psalm 27 is the lament of an individual that combines both complaint and confidence. Accordingly, the psalmist implores God to hear, pity, and answer. His problem has now become God's problem.

In the midst of such overwhelming grief, the psalmist elects to gaze on God's loveliness. He seeks God's presence. By his unshakable trust (see 27:10), he yearns to see his plight as bound up with the concerns of a loving God. His pain is not an accident of history. It has become the raw material for a fresh understanding of life. For him, to pray is to see the world in a new way.

Letting God

In the gospel, the author of John presents Jesus' high-priestly prayer (Jn 17:1-26). Jesus, the sacrificial victim, offers the prayer of consecration for his approaching death. Like Moses (see Dt 33), Jesus speaks a final blessing over his community. Today's reading may be divided into Jesus' prayer for his own glorification (verses 1-8) and his prayer for the disciples (verses 9-11).

The author captures the intimacy of this prayer by the frequent use of the title *Father* (verses 1,5; see also verses 11,21,24,25). He shows the ministry of Jesus against the background of the Father's will. The disciples thus realize that everything Jesus has comes from the Father. Indeed, through their own work God's name will be glorified. In this realm of prayer—in the very face of death—Jesus invites the disciples to see his work and theirs in a new and challenging way. To pray is to see the world in a new way.

Today's Good News

The Jewish philosopher, Abraham Heschel, has written: "To pray is to bring God back into the world." At prayer we are invited not to dismiss our problems and worries but to view them as related to Another. Like Luke's Mary, we are urged to ponder our puzzles in the company of this God. Like the psalmist, we are challenged to reflect on our pain in the presence of this God. Like the Johannine Jesus, we are called to link our manner of ministry with the will of the Father of Jesus. Prayer is never a retreat to illusion. It is the realistic decision to see other realities at work in our personal life and the life of our community. Our biblical authors insist that to pray is to see the world in a new way.

Points for Reflection and Discussion

1. Do you make time for daily prayer?

_____

_____

_____

_____

2. Relate an experience of prayer that definitively and permanently changed your worldview.

_____

_____

_____

_____

Themes
Faith, Trust
   M1, Conversion: A Lifelong Process
Prayer
   M5, Your Prayer Life

Reading 1, Acts 2:1-11

When the day of Pentecost had come, they were all together in one place. And suddenly from heaven there came a sound like the rush of a violent wind, and it filled the entire house where they were sitting. Divided tongues, as of fire, appeared among them, and a tongue rested on each of them. All of them were filled with the Holy Spirit and began to speak in other languages, as the Spirit gave them ability.

Now there were devout Jews from every nation under heaven living in Jerusalem. And at this sound the crowd gathered and was bewildered, because each one heard them speaking in the native language of each. Amazed and astonished, they asked, "Are not all these who are speaking Galilean? And how is it that we hear, each of us, in our own native language? Parthians, Medes, Elamites, and residents of Mesopotamia, Judea and Cappadocia, Pontus and Asia, Phrygia and Pamphylia, Egypt and the parts of Libya belonging to Cyrene, and visitors from Rome, both Jews and proselytes, Cretans and Arabs—in our own languages we hear them speaking about God's deeds of power."

Psalm 104:1,24,29-30,31,34

Reading 2, 1 Corinthians 12:3-7,12-13

No one speaking by the Spirit of God ever says "Let Jesus be cursed!" and no one can say "Jesus is Lord" except by the Holy Spirit.

Now there are varieties of gifts, but the same Spirit; and there are varieties of services, but the same Lord; and there are varieties of activities, but it is the same God who activates all of them in everyone. To each is given the manifestation of the Spirit for the common good.

For just as the body is one and has many members, and all the members of the body, though many, are one body, so it is with Christ. For in the one Spirit we were all baptized into one body—Jews or Greeks, slaves or free— and we were all made to drink of one Spirit.

Gospel, John 20:19-23

When it was evening on that day, the first day of the week, and the doors of the house where the disciples had met were locked for fear of the Jews, Jesus came and stood among them and said, "Peace be with you." After he said this, he showed them his hands and his side. Then the disciples rejoiced when they saw the Lord.

Jesus said to them again, "Peace be with you. As the Father has sent me, so I send you." When he had said this, he breathed on them and said to them, "Receive the Holy Spirit. If you forgive the sins of any, they are forgiven them; if you retain the sins of any, they are retained."

Sharing the Spirit

JOHN F. CRAGHAN

To receive the Spirit is to share in the Spirit. We Christians take pride in the fact that we are temples of the Holy Spirit. We glory in the fact that we are, thereby, a privileged dwelling place for the Spirit. Unfortunately, we are also tempted to see this privilege as a personal monopoly. We may curtail our gifts and talents, namely, manifestations of the Spirit, to cater to our own personal needs. It is indeed difficult to accept the view that to receive the Spirit is to share the Spirit.

Today's readings violently denounce a purely private appropriation of the Spirit. They see individual Christians as community members who are empowered to release the Spirit for the common good. Salvation is never single file but always arm in arm. These authors staunchly maintain that to receive the Spirit is to share the Spirit.

Luke, the author of Acts, understands Pentecost as the start of the Church's universal mission, which has the Spirit as its driving force. The Spirit is that power which utterly destroys all those walls that keep people apart. Fittingly, Luke provides an international list of Jews and proselytes. He links the Pentecost event with the Tower of Babel story (Gn 11:7-9). The outcome, however, is vastly different. Here there is unity, not division.

It is likely that Luke has changed the original charismatic speaking in tongues *(glossolalia)* into a speaking in foreign languages. He then sees the reception of the Spirit in terms of a sharing with those assembled, noting their linguistic achievements happened "as the Spirit gave them ability." For Luke, to receive the Spirit is to share the Spirit.

Paul's Corinthian community included some who flaunted their gifts of the Spirit in an excessively individualistic manner. Thus, they understood the manifestations of the Spirit in purely personal terms. Paul had to educate his new Christians about unity and diversity. To be sure, there are *many* gifts but they are all manifestations of *one* Spirit. "To each is given the manifestation of the Spirit for the common good."

Paul buttresses his argument by appealing to the analogy of the human body. Each member does not exist in splendid isolation. Rather, each organ contributes to the overall good of the body. It is such a view of community that levels all ethnic (Jew and Greek) and social (slave and free) differences. Paul strongly insists that gifts are never purely personal acquisitions. For him, to receive the Spirit is to share the Spirit.

Peace Be With You

For John, Pentecost occurs on Easter Sunday. On that occasion the glorified Jesus, who has already ascended to the Father, communicates the Spirit to the disciples. The word *peace*, far from being a harmless greeting, suggests God's presence (see Jgs 6:23). By showing the disciples his wounds, the exalted Lord links the crucifixion and the Resurrection. The sharing of the Spirit is thereby grounded in a life of service.

The Johannine commission is in terms of forgiving/binding sins (contrast Mt 28:16-20). The reception of the Spirit empowers the disciples to force people to make a decision about Jesus. In John's Gospel, *sin* is basically the refusal to accept Jesus. By breathing on them, Jesus symbolizes the new creation (see Gn 2:7). The task, therefore, of the Spirit-empowered disciples, is to breathe upon others so that they may opt for the message of Jesus. In this way, John also asserts that to receive the Spirit is to share the Spirit.

Today's Good News

Pentecost was never intended to be an isolated experience in the history of the Christian community. We are not entitled to look back nostalgically on a great event and limit it within the narrow confines of the early days of the Church. By its very nature, the reception of the Spirit is always dynamic, never static.

Today's biblical authors challenge us to confront the divisions that continue to exist in our family, our government, and our Church. We are asked to heal the ostracism of members of our family. We are urged to denounce our government's insufficient care of the poor. We are called upon to protest our Church's misuse of power. Having received the Spirit, we must not be content to keep our gifts of healing to ourselves. Luke, Paul, and John are clearly in agreement: to receive the Spirit is to share the Spirit.

Points for Reflection and Discussion

1. Have you ever experienced the Spirit working through you for the common good?

_____

_____

_____

_____

2. Being only a "part" of the "whole" forces a sense of responsibility that is lacking in the "every one for himself or herself" society. Do you find this responsibility limiting or freeing? Why?

_____

_____

_____

_____

Themes

Confirmation
   M8, Evangelization
Corporate Ministry
   M2, The Laity: Called to Build God's Kingdom
   M3, Your Special Gifts
Pentecost
   M6, Discernment
   M7, Holiness

Reading 1, Exodus 34:4-6,8-9

[Moses] rose early in the morning and went up on Mount Sinai, as the Lord had commanded him, and took in his hand the two tablets of stone. The Lord descended in the cloud and stood with him there, and proclaimed the name, "The Lord."

The Lord passed before him, and proclaimed, "The Lord, the Lord, a God merciful and gracious, slow to anger, and abounding in steadfast love and faithfulness."

And Moses quickly bowed his head toward the earth, and worshiped. He said, "If now I have found favor in your sight, O Lord, I pray, let the Lord go with us. Although this is a stiff-necked people, pardon our iniquity and our sin, and take us for your inheritance."

Daniel 3:52,53,54,55,56

Reading 2, 2 Corinthians 13:11-13

Brothers and sisters, put things in order, listen to my appeal, agree with one another, live in peace; and the God of love and peace will be with you. Greet one another with a holy kiss. All the saints greet you. The grace of the Lord Jesus Christ, the love of God, and the communion of the Holy Spirit be with all of you.

Gospel, John 3:16-18

[Jesus said to Nicodemus:] "God so loved the world that he gave his only Son, so that everyone who believes in him may not perish but may have eternal life.

"Indeed, God did not send the Son into the world to condemn the world, but in order that the world might be saved through him. Those who believe in him are not condemned; but those who do not believe are condemned already, because they have not believed in the name of the only Son of God."

The Way of the Trinity

JOHN F. CRAGHAN

Giving is the Trinity's way. On Trinity Sunday we celebrate the Christian mystery that God is one, yet three. We may somehow think of that truth as a head trip, as a reality that we are to admire but not imitate. As a result, belief in the Trinity is a phrase to be piously recited, not a pattern of life to be vigorously pursued. We can't really imagine that giving is the Trinity's way.

Today's readings offer a dynamic view of the Trinity. They urge us not to be mere theological bystanders, but dynamic participants in the mystery of our God. They assert that the Trinity's lifestyle is to become the Christian lifestyle.

Renewal

The scene in Exodus captures the renewal of Israel's covenant with God after the people had sinned in the Golden Calf incident (see Ex 32). It is interesting that this renewal is grounded in Moses' personal relationship with God. The intimacy of that relationship is reflected in the use of God's personal name, "Lord," and in the radiance of Moses' face (see 34:27-35).

The author employs a traditional formula in speaking of the Lord: "merciful and gracious, slow to anger; and abounding in steadfast love and faithfulness." Whereas the Israelites have been unfaithful, God is always faithful. Thus the traditional formula is not an empty cliché. It is an urgent request to have the God of Israel demonstrate the reality of that creedal expression in the following way: "Pardon our iniquity and our sin, and take us for your inheritance." The Lord's forgiving demonstrates that giving is the Trinity's way.

The second reading, the conclusion to Paul's Letter to the Corinthians, is not a pious platitude. It is an energetic appeal, on Paul's part, to this divided community, to make mutual peace a reality. He exhorts them to return to the gospel and put an end to all their factions. If they act upon these urgings, then the God of love and peace will be truly in their midst.

In his concluding blessing, Paul usually refers only to Jesus (see Rom 16:20; 1 Cor 16:23). Here, however, Paul mentions God and the Spirit as well. By this formula, he is calling upon his community to appropriate the Trinity's way of life: Jesus' self-giving in death, the Father's loving surrender of the Son, and the Spirit's creation of communion between Christ and the Christian, are all to characterize the behavior of the Corinthians.

God So Loved the World

Today's gospel passage is part of Jesus' dialogue with Nicodemus. Earlier (Jn 3:5-8), Jesus noted that entrance into God's kingdom was linked to the outpouring of the Spirit, a reality that humans could not attain through their own efforts. Here (3:15-21) Jesus points out that faith is necessary in order to benefit from the gift of the Spirit.

The author shows that, like Abraham, the Father so loves his only Son that he gives him for the benefit of all nations of the earth (see Gn 22:2,12,18). It is the Father's sending of the Son that brings salvation to the world. Jesus, therefore, is the expression par excellence of the Father's concern for humanity. To accept the message of Jesus, who provokes people to make a final decision, is to be caught up in the pattern of giving, sending, and loving. For the author of John, giving is the Trinity's way.

Today's Good News

The modern Christian is really not removed from these scenes in Exodus, Second Corinthians, and the Gospel of John. In the face of hurt and betrayal, we are asked to reflect a God who reaches out and forgives. In the midst of community disruption and factionalism, we are called upon to create an atmosphere of peace. Before a world that is ego-choked, we are exhorted to demonstrate giving, sending, and loving.

While all of the above may seem to be isolated acts of kindness, they are basically the Christian's attempt to reflect the implication of belief in the Trinity. "In the name of the Father, and of the Son, and of the Holy Spirit" is not the sterile recollection of Christian doctrine. That expression is the challenge to reach out to our world and so share the world of our God. The legacy and responsibility of the Christian is to offer a way of life that demonstrates giving is the Trinity's way.

Points for Reflection and Discussion

1. How do you view the "three-in-one" analogy of the Divine? Can you discern a "three-in-one"-ness in your own life?

_____

_____

_____

_____

2. What has the Trinity meant in your life? Do you find it easier to relate to one or another of the Trinitarian signs: Father, Son, Spirit? Why?

_____

_____

_____

_____

Themes

Blessing
    Q3, What is the Meaning of the Mass?
    Q10, Catholics and Prayer
    M3, Your Special Gifts
    M5, Your Prayer Life
Love
    Q1, Journey of Faith
    M4, Family Life
    M7, Holiness
Trinity
    Q2, What Do Catholics Believe?
    Q4, The Bible
    M6, Discernment
    M8, Evangelization

Reading 1, Deuteronomy 8:2-3,14-16

[Moses said to the people:] "Remember the long way that the Lord your God has led you these forty years in the wilderness, in order to humble you, testing you to know what was in your heart, whether or not you would keep his commandments. He humbled you by letting you hunger, then by feeding you with manna, with which neither you nor your ancestors were acquainted, in order to make you understand that one does not live by bread alone, but by every word that comes from the mouth of the Lord.

"Do not exalt yourself, forgetting the Lord your God, who brought you out of the land of Egypt, out of the house of slavery, who led you through the great and terrible wilderness, an arid wasteland with poisonous snakes and scorpions. He made water flow for you from flint rock, and fed you in the wilderness with manna that your ancestors did not know."

Psalm 147:12-13,14-15,19-20

Reading 2, 1 Corinthians 10:16-17

The cup of blessing that we bless, is it not a sharing in the blood of Christ? The bread that we break, is it not a sharing in the body of Christ? Because there is one bread, we who are many are one body, for we all partake of the one bread.

Gospel, John 6:51-58

[Jesus said to the crowds:] "I am the living bread that came down from heaven. Whoever eats of this bread will live forever; and the bread that I will give for the life of the world is my flesh."

The Jews then disputed among themselves, saying, "How can this man give us his flesh to eat?"

So Jesus said to them, "Very truly, I tell you, unless you eat the flesh of the Son of Man and drink his blood, you have no life in you. Those who eat my flesh and drink my blood have eternal life, and I will raise them up on the last day; for my flesh is true food and my blood is true drink. Those who eat my flesh and drink my blood abide in me, and I in them. Just as the living Father sent me, and I live because of the Father, so whoever eats me will live because of me. This is the bread that came down from heaven, not like that which your ancestors ate, and they died. But the one who eats this bread will live forever."

Celebrate Life!

JOHN F. CRAGHAN

Sunday Eucharist brings its own set of problems and concerns. We suffer from the lingering disease of legalism. We go to Mass because we are commanded to. In addition, we run the risk of meeting those community members whom we prefer not to meet. We would rather encounter Christ, not some neighbors. Finally, there is the ever-present danger of boredom. We have done this Mass thing so many times before that we are now weary. In such circumstances, we cannot accept the idea that to celebrate Eucharist is to celebrate life.

The readings for this celebration of the Body and Blood of Christ are upsetting invitations to reassess our eucharistic values. They are the challenge to ask: Do we celebrate life or do we tolerate life? Do we appropriate the self-giving of Jesus or do we merely focus on self? Do we share in the bread and wine with our neighbor or do we go it alone? We are forced to examine whether to celebrate Eucharist is to celebrate life.

Not By Bread Alone

The sermon from Deuteronomy pictures Moses giving last minute instructions to the Israelites as they get ready to enter the Promised Land. It envisions, specifically, the way Israel, once settled down and beginning to prosper, must hear God's Word. Life in the land, therefore, is the author's concentration. Indeed, the author knows only too well that the temptation in the midst of prosperity is to forget and, to that extent, to cease to live: "When you have eaten your fill and you have built fine houses (v 12)...do not exalt yourself, forgetting the Lord your God."

To offset the danger of forgetting, the author recalls the Lord's special provisions during the wilderness years, that is, in an extremely hostile environment. The Lord fed Israel miraculously with manna. The Lord also brought forth water from the flinty rock. Now that they enjoy the fertile land and its prosperity, they are reminded that one does not live by bread alone. Commitment to God's Word ensures life.

In writing to the Corinthians, Paul addressed a Christian community that was divided and celebrated only a sham Eucharist (see 1 Cor 11:17-34). In today's reading, Paul vividly points out that to participate in both the Eucharist and in pagan rituals involves a contradiction and a blatant disservice to other members of the community (10:14-22). To eat the bread and drink the wine are a genuine participation in the body and blood of Christ. As such, Eucharist is diametrically opposed to pagan rituals.

It is likely that today's gospel passage was originally part of John's narrative of the Last Supper. Indeed, verse 51 sounds very much like John's form of the words of institution: "The bread that I will give for the life of the world is my flesh." An editor has removed the passage from its Last Supper setting and reshaped it to conform to the Bread of Life discourse in John (6:22-71). The focus is now on the Eucharist, that is, Jesus as the source of life and nourishment.

The author uses "life/live" no less than eight times, placing more emphasis on the personal than the communal dimension of the Eucharist. By participating in the Eucharist, the believer participates in the life of Father, Son, and Spirit (see Jn 15:26). The result of this participation is the establishment of an eternal relationship with God.

Today's Good News

To celebrate sacrifice is a paradox of life. Truly, every time we celebrate the sacrifice of the Mass we receive the Real Presence, the very body and life-blood of our Savior. Eucharist strengthens us for the journey and sustains us on our way. "The one who eats this bread will live forever."

As we attend Mass, do the words of Deuteronomy have an impact so that we celebrate life by remembering the Author of life? As we rub elbows with our neighbors, does the message of Paul have an effect so that we realize we must be food and drink to those neighbors? As we receive the body and blood of Christ, does the teaching of John make us aware that we are indeed caught up in God's life? Today's feast is that special celebration which patently proclaims: To celebrate Eucharist is to celebrate life.

Points for Reflection and Discussion

1. Eucharist is at the very heart of our Catholic Christian faith. What does Eucharist mean to you?

participation with christ's family in one belief

2. Reflect on how God feeds the hungry, from manna in the desert to the very body of Christ at the eucharistic table. If we are to live in imitation of our Creator, what are we doing to feed the hungry? What, specifically, are you doing?

what sacrifice are we making

Themes
Celebration
    Q11, Catholic Practices
    Q12, Catholics and Church
    M5, Your Prayer Life
Eucharist
    Q9, Who's Who in the Church
    M8, Evangelization
Life
    Q1, Journey of Faith
    M1, Conversion: A Lifelong Process
    M4, Family Life
    M7, Holiness

Reading 1, Deuteronomy 11:18,26-28

[Moses told the people:] "You shall put these words of mine in your heart and soul, and you shall bind them as a sign on your hand, and fix them as an emblem on your forehead.

"See, I am setting before you today a blessing and a curse: the blessing, if you obey the commandments of the Lord your God that I am commanding you today; and the curse, if you do not obey the commandments of the Lord your God, but turn from the way that I am commanding you today, to follow other gods that you have not known."

Psalm 31:1-2,2-3,16,24 (NRSV)

Reading 2, Romans 3:21-25,28

Now, apart from law, the righteousness of God has been disclosed, and is attested by the law and the prophets, the righteousness of God through faith in Jesus Christ for all who believe. For there is no distinction, since all have sinned and fall short of the glory of God; they are now justified by his grace as a gift, through the redemption that is in Christ Jesus, whom God put forward as a sacrifice of atonement by his blood, effective through faith. He did this to show his righteousness, because in his divine forbearance he had passed over the sins previously committed.

For we hold that a person is justified by faith apart from works prescribed by the law.

Gospel, Matthew 7:21-27

[Jesus said to his disciples:] "Not everyone who says to me, 'Lord, Lord,' will enter the kingdom of heaven, but only the one who does the will of my Father in heaven. On that day many will say to me, 'Lord, Lord, did we not prophesy in your name, and cast out demons in your name, and do many deeds of power in your name?' Then I will declare to them, 'I never knew you; go away from me, you evildoers.'

"Everyone then who hears these words of mine and acts on them will be like a wise man who built his house on rock. The rain fell, the floods came, and the winds blew and beat on that house, but it did not fall, because it had been founded on rock. And everyone who hears these words of mine and does not act on them will be like a foolish man who built his house on sand. The rain fell, and the floods came, and the winds blew and beat against that house, and it fell—and great was its fall!"

Blessings and Curses

ELSIE HAINZ McGRATH

From the time of Moses, it has clearly been our choice: Follow God's way and be blessed; follow "other gods that [we] have not known" and be cursed. Holding circumstances, other people, even God, responsible for our bad choices may seem to rationally exonerate us, but ultimately we have nothing and no one to blame but ourselves. Those "other gods" may be very enticing, offering power or wealth or whatever, but they can never supplant the effective Presence of God and life's true blessings.

A renewal of the covenant between God and the people of Israel begins in the tenth chapter of Deuteronomy. Blessing and curse became the form of the covenant taken on by the contracting partners. The existential nature of this covenantal encounter is emphasized in the need of people to choose between the two. God is the initiator of the covenant; the people's response determines their faithfulness to it.

Today's gospel picks up the theme: "Not everyone who says to me, 'Lord, Lord,' will enter the kingdom of heaven, but only the one who does the will of my Father in heaven." The will of the Father is our keeping the covenant. Doing good deeds, even in the name of the Lord, doesn't earn our place in heaven. God is faithful and Jesus saves, but *we* must decide yea or nay, the straight path or the crooked, the blessing or the curse.

Today's gospel always brings to mind the story of the three little pigs and the big bad wolf. Likely, the weaver of that tale read the Gospel of Matthew for literary inspiration. But Matthew doesn't present us with a big bad wolf, who can shoulder at least some of the blame when a great fall is our fate. The blame is wholly ours: we took the easy way out, not willing to invest ourselves in the time and the toil required to build on the solid rock of faith.

Justification by Faith

Paul writes to the Romans in anticipation of his coming to visit them. One of the most important parts of the letter is that portion we hear today because it explicates his theology of universal salvation through Jesus Christ. Jesus was a manifestation of God, proving God's righteous faithfulness, "the power of God for salvation to everyone who has faith..." (1:16).

This universal salvation comes to us "apart from law," but was foretold "by the law and the prophets." Thus Paul tells the Romans that the Christian charter of salvation stands on its own, destined to supersede the Mosaic Law that prophesied its coming. This is not to say, however, that the faith God gifts Christians with either excludes the Jews or overthrows the Mosaic Law. That is made obvious by those verses omitted from today's lectionary (29-31), which conclude this portion of Paul's letter.

Further, "a person is justified by faith apart from works prescribed by the law" is not to say that good works are not necessary, or that all are "saved" regardless of how they live their lives. This became a major Reformation issue, but a quick look at key verses omitted from today's lectionary (26-27) makes it obvious that Paul doesn't grant God's salvation, *carte blanche*. Our obedience to God's Law is our grateful and freeing response to God's gift of salvation. Faith initiates good works; one cannot *not* do good works if one has faith. (See also, for example, Gal 5:6; 1 Cor 15:10.)

Justification by "faith apart from works" means, quite simply, that we cannot earn heaven. Justification is not our doing. The credit belongs solely to God, "by his grace as a gift." God loves us unconditionally, in spite of our sins and heedless of our acts of mercy.

Today's Good News

We may sometimes wonder how the good we do fails to chalk up points for us in God's eyes. We question, even judge, others' sinful acts. Is it truly possible, we wonder, for a person who isn't about the Lord's work (like we are!) to merit heaven? If salvation belongs to everyone, why are we knocking ourselves out to serve others? Where's our reward for missing out on all the "fun"; for deliberately stifling self-centered interests and conquering hateful prejudices?

Today we can rest in the words of the covenant, conveyed by Moses so very long ago. The Word of God is in our hearts, in our souls, in our hands, and in our heads. Blessing! To turn our back on what is inherently *us* is to call down curses upon ourself. It is to choose alienation from life and damnation in death.

Ah, but the blessings! Good News, indeed!

Points for Reflection and Discussion

1. What do Paul's words, "a person is justified by faith," mean to you?

_____

_____

_____

_____

2. Do you believe there is a hell? If so, who is there? If not, what happens to murderers and plunderers and all those who wreck havoc in the lives of others when they die?

_____

_____

_____

_____

Themes

Covenant
   Q3, What is the Meaning of the Mass?
   Q4, The Bible
   Q12, Catholics and Church
   M8, Evangelization
Faith
   Q1, Journey of Faith
   M1, Conversion: A Lifelong Process
   M2, The Laity: Called to Build God's Kingdom
   M3, Your Special Gifts
Justification, Salvation
   Q2, What Do Catholics Believe?

Reading 1, Hosea 6:3-6

"Let us know, let us press on to know the Lord; his appearing is as sure as the dawn; he will come to us like the showers, like the spring rains that water the earth."

What shall I do with you, O Ephraim? What shall I do with you, O Judah? Your love is like a morning cloud, like the dew that goes away early. Therefore I have hewn them by the prophets, I have killed them by the words of my mouth, and my judgment goes forth as the light. For I desire steadfast love and not sacrifice, the knowledge of God rather than burnt offerings.

Psalm 50:1,8,12-13,14-15

Reading 2, Romans 4:18-25

Hoping against hope, [Abraham] believed that he would become "the father of many nations," according to what was said, "So numerous shall your descendants be." He did not weaken in faith when he considered his own body, which was already as good as dead (for he was about a hundred years old), or when he considered the barrenness of Sarah's womb. No distrust made him waver concerning the promise of God, but he grew strong in his faith as he gave glory to God, being fully convinced that God was able to do what he had promised. Therefore his faith "was reckoned to him as righteousness."

Now the words, "it was reckoned to him," were written not for his sake alone, but for ours also. It will be reckoned to us who believe in him who raised Jesus our Lord from the dead, who was handed over to death for our trespasses and was raised for our justification.

Gospel, Matthew 9:9-13

As Jesus was walking along, he saw a man called Matthew sitting at the tax booth; and he said to him, "Follow me." And he got up and followed him. And as he sat at dinner in the house, many tax collectors and sinners came and were sitting with him and his disciples. When the Pharisees saw this, they said to his disciples, "Why does your teacher eat with tax collectors and sinners?" But when he heard this, he said, "Those who are well have no need of a physician, but those who are sick. Go and learn what this means, 'I desire mercy, not sacrifice.' For I have come to call not the righteous but sinners."

The Desires of God

ELSIE HAINZ MCGRATH

How often do we go to God when we have "nowhere else to turn"? How often do we attempt to bribe the Omnipotent One with empty promises of what we will or won't do if only we get what we're after at present? How often do we presume that *our* will is divine will? How often—and how well—do we hear what today's readings are saying to us?

The reading from Hosea begins with the prayer of the people who, finding themselves in dire need, resort to a rhetoric of repentance that they hope Yahweh will buy. Hosea presents his interpretation of Yahweh's thoughts upon hearing this plea: "What shall I do with you?" Yahweh wants to save these stubborn people, but they do not deserve it. They simply cannot get into their heads that Yahweh does not want their simpering, ritualistic prayers and sacrifices; all Yahweh wants is faithfulness. Why can't they come to know and love the God who fashioned them?

Nothing is Impossible with God

Paul tells the citizens of Rome today that Abraham, "hoping against hope," believed in the creative power of God to do what was humanly impossible; Abraham had the kind of steadfast faith that God so desired of the people in Hosea's time. And, because of his utter trust "concerning the promise of God," God credited Abraham as a righteous man.

But not only Abraham, Paul says. Abraham's trust in a God who could bring to life Abraham's "own body, which was already as good as dead," prefigures the faith of Christians "who believe in him who raised Jesus our Lord from the dead." We need only have the faith of Abraham!

The gospel continues to tell us the true desires of God, as we hear again the story of the call of Matthew. The story is short. Matthew was collecting taxes; Jesus walked by and said, "Follow me"; Matthew followed. It is up to us to fill in the missing pieces. Why did Matthew follow Jesus? Were there any questions? Was there any resistance? What happened to all the money? (We recall the story of the tax collector, Zacchaeus [Lk 19:1-10], who gave away half his possessions and paid back four times what he had extorted from clients.)

The supposition, based upon Paul's theology, is that Matthew was a righteous man, despite being a tax collector. Tax collectors were despised because they extorted the people's money; but their government wages were so meager that they justified the sin as necessary for their own livelihood. Maybe Matthew didn't defraud the poor, or maybe he didn't extort so much that he lived lavishly, like most tax collectors did.

Our questions aren't answered. But after Matthew follows Jesus (to whose house?), "many tax collectors and sinners came and were sitting with [Jesus] and his disciples." Once again, the Pharisees try to trap Jesus with a question designed to elicit an answer that can be used against him. His answer is one that is heard a lot in our own times: "Those who are well have no need of a physician, but those who are sick." He continues, "Go and learn what this means, 'I desire mercy, not sacrifice'." *Déjà vous!* God's thoughts in the reading from Hosea.

Finally, Jesus says, "I have come to call not the righteous but sinners." So Matthew wasn't already righteous, as Abraham had been. Neither were the Pharisees righteous, who still had not learned to faithfully know and love God.

Today's Good News

We, of course, still have to deal with "learn[ing] what this means…". Taxes bleed the poor while the rich get richer, our health "care" industry aborts babies and turns its back on the indigent, and hoards of today's sinners self-righteously deny the very existence of God. In a world that is dominated by bad news, it becomes increasingly difficult to hear and believe in the Good News.

Despite Matthew's unrighteousness, he followed Jesus. Ultimately, he was steadfastly faithful as he came to know and love God through his Lord. Thus he inherited the promise of Abraham: "His faith 'was reckoned to him as righteousness'."

So we are obligated to continue to learn mercy and love and faithfulness. We have a responsibility, one to the other, to spread the Good News. This doesn't mean ringing doorbells and quoting Scripture verses. It does mean taking a pro-life stance—fullness of life for *all* God's people: the poor and the rich, the unborn and the elderly, the victims and the abusers, the heterosexuals and the homosexuals, the citizens and the immigrants, the powerful and the powerless, the fundamentalists and the feminists, the white and the black and the red and the yellow…*all* God's people.

When we "learn what this means," when we come to "the knowledge of God rather than burnt offerings," then "it will be reckoned to us who believe in him who raised Jesus our Lord from the dead, who was handed over to death for our trespasses and was raised for our justification."

Points for Reflection and Discussion

1. When you pray that God's will be done, do you presume to tell God what that will is? Have you ever had a prayer answered in the "wrong" way, and later realized it was God's way because all worked out for the best?

_____

_____

_____

_____

2. The people in Jesus' day "labeled" sinners: tax collectors, shepherds, grave diggers, prostitutes. Are there any groups of people you "label" sinners? If so, who? Why?

_____

_____

_____

_____

_____

Themes
Faith, Sin
   Q1, Journey of Faith
   Q3, What is the Meaning of the Mass?
   Q6, The Saints
   Q7, Mary
   M1, Conversion: A Lifelong Process
   M2, The Laity: Called to Build God's Kingdom
   M3, Your Special Gifts
   M6, Discernment
   M7, Holiness
   M8, Evangelization

Reading 1, Exodus 19:2-6 (NRSV)

[The Israelites] had journeyed from Rephidim, entered the wilderness of Sinai, and camped in the wilderness; Israel camped there in front of the mountain.

Then Moses went up to God; the Lord called to him from the mountain, saying, "Thus you shall say to the house of Jacob, and tell the Israelites: You have seen what I did to the Egyptians, and how I bore you on eagles' wings and brought you to myself. Now therefore, if you obey my voice and keep my covenant, you shall be my treasured possession out of all the peoples. Indeed, the whole earth is mine, but you shall be for me a priestly kingdom and a holy nation."

Psalm 100:1-2,3,5

Reading 2, Romans 5:6-11

While we were still weak, at the right time Christ died for the ungodly. Indeed, rarely will anyone die for a righteous person—though perhaps for a good person someone might actually dare to die. But God proves his love for us in that while we still were sinners Christ died for us. Much more surely then, now that we have been justified by his blood, will we be saved through him from the wrath of God.

For if while we were enemies, we were reconciled to God through the death of his Son, much more surely, having been reconciled, will we be saved by his life. But more than that, we even boast in God through our Lord Jesus Christ, through whom we have now received reconciliation.

Gospel, Matthew 9:36—10:8

When [Jesus] saw the crowds, he had compassion for them, because they were harassed and helpless, like sheep without a shepherd. Then he said to his disciples, "The harvest is plentiful, but the laborers are few; therefore ask the Lord of the harvest to send out laborers into his harvest."

Then Jesus summoned his twelve disciples and gave them authority over unclean spirits, to cast them out, and to cure every disease and every sickness. These are the names of the twelve apostles: first, Simon, also known as Peter, and his brother Andrew; James son of Zebedee, and his brother John; Philip and Bartholomew; Thomas and Matthew the tax collector; James son of Alphaeus, and Thaddaeus; Simon the Cananaean, and Judas Iscariot, the one who betrayed him.

These twelve Jesus sent out with the following instructions: "Go nowhere among the Gentiles, and enter no town of the Samaritans, but go rather to the lost sheep of the house of Israel. As you go, proclaim the good news, 'The kingdom of heaven has come near.' Cure the sick, raise the dead, cleanse the lepers, cast out demons. You received without payment; give without payment."

Gifted

ELSIE HAINZ MCGRATH

Through Moses, we hear God calling us "my treasured possession...a priestly kingdom and a holy nation." Matthew says that Jesus has "compassion" for us. Paul tells us: "God proves his love for us in that while we still were sinners Christ died for us." Even the psalmist declares: "The Lord is good; his steadfast love endures forever, and his faithfulness to all generations." God gifts us throughout the ages.

But, wait. What do those designations God assigns the people mean: "a priestly kingdom, a holy nation"? And what's this big IF all about: "IF you obey my voice and keep my covenant"? Whoops! Are there conditions on these gifts?

In the Wilderness

God's admonition, through Moses to the Israelites, let the people know their privileged position demanded accountability. They were asked to ratify the covenant God offered by obeying its precepts. From those to whom much is given, more will be asked. The Israelites were asked to be holy, to be priestly—to be God-like. It was their choice, of course. If they chose not to accept the offer, not to ratify the covenant...well...who knew what might happen?

One thing that happened was that Jesus saw the uncovenanted as "the lost sheep of the house of Israel." He sent apostles to perform his own works of mercy: "cure the sick, raise the dead, cleanse the lepers, cast out demons." In the process, the apostles were to "proclaim the good news, 'The kingdom of heaven has come near'. " And they were to do these things, as Jesus did, without recompense. The reason they were expected to "give without payment" was because they had "received without payment." Be holy, be priestly—be God-like.

Among the Gentiles

Paul identified himself, at the start of his Letter to the Romans, as "called to be an apostle...to bring about the obedience of faith among all the Gentiles" (1:1,5), and the lead-in to today's second reading, which is omitted from the lectionary, provides important background for Paul's conclusion that we have been justified through the death of Christ: "We boast in our hope of sharing the glory of God. And not only that, but we also boast in our sufferings, knowing that suffering produces endurance, and endurance produces character, and character produces hope, and hope does not disappoint us, because God's love has been poured into our hearts through the Holy Spirit that has been given to us" (5:2b-5).

Paul made clear, in other words, that the covenant first offered to the people of Israel had expanded. Even Jesus, in today's gospel reading, instructed his disciples to minister only among the people of Israel. These were the people of the covenant, Yahweh's "treasured possession out of all the peoples." It was only right that they be the first ones offered the *new* covenant. But Jesus' death definitively changed all that, because "while we were enemies, we were reconciled to God through the death of his Son."

Today's Good News

So the people of Israel and we Gentiles too—via the justification brought about by Jesus' death—are God's "treasured possession...a priestly kingdom and a holy nation." Do we act like it? How do the words "treasured" and "priestly" and "holy" impact our lives? What would we answer if God suddenly appeared before us and asked if we obey the voice of God and keep the holy covenant?

Jesus had compassion on the people who were "like sheep without a shepherd." One of the most abiding images we have of Jesus is that of the Good Shepherd. He went out among the people and did what needed to be done, whether it was curing the sick or forgiving the sinner. Everywhere he went, Jesus proclaimed the Good News: "The kingdom of heaven has come near."

He traveled light, but he never traveled alone. As he moved from town to town, he taught his disciples to do as he did, even sending them out to minister in his name while he was himself still ministering. And he prayed to his Abba for the strength and the courage to fulfill the divine will—no matter what.

As Jesus' present-day disciples, we are sent, and asked to pray for more companions on the Way, as we preach the Word: "Ask the Lord of the harvest to send out laborers into his harvest...[and] as you go, proclaim the good news...". Do we do either? What things do we most pray for? Do we ever pray without asking for anything? Do we boldly proclaim the faith? What would we answer if Jesus suddenly appeared before us and asked if we minister willingly to those who need us, and without expecting anything in return?

Points for Reflection and Discussion

1. The apostle to the Gentiles stressed that God's magnanimous love was proved by the death of Jesus because he died for us "while we were still sinners." Though his death was once, for all, we are still sinners. How do we reconcile this ignoble fact?

_____

_____

_____

_____

2. The gift of faith is truly a great gift, given unconditionally by our very own Creator. Reflect on your faith. When were you first aware of it? How have you embraced it and made it your own?

_____

_____

_____

_____

Themes

Covenant
  Q3, What is the Meaning of the Mass?
  Q4, The Bible
Faith
  Q1, Journey of Faith
  M1, Conversion: A Lifelong Process
Kingdom of God, Witness
  Q12, Catholics and Church
  M2, The Laity: Called to Build God's Kingdom
  M8, Evangelization

Reading 1, Jeremiah 20:10-13

[Jeremiah said:] I hear many whispering: "Terror is all around! Denounce him! Let us denounce him!" All my close friends are watching for me to stumble. "Perhaps he can be enticed, and we can prevail against him, and take our revenge on him."

But the Lord is with me like a dread warrior; therefore my persecutors will stumble, and they will not prevail. They will be greatly shamed, for they will not succeed. Their eternal dishonor will never be forgotten.

O Lord of hosts, you test the righteous, you see the heart and the mind; let me see your retribution upon them, for to you I have committed my cause. Sing to the Lord; praise the Lord! For he has delivered the life of the needy from the hands of evildoers.

Psalm 69:7-9,13,16,32-33,35,36 (NRSV)

Reading 2, Romans 5:12-15

Just as sin came into the world through one man, and death came through sin, and so death spread to all because all have sinned—sin was indeed in the world before the law, but sin is not reckoned when there is no law. Yet death exercised dominion from Adam to Moses, even over those whose sins were not like the transgression of Adam, who is a type of the one who was to come.

But the free gift is not like the trespass. For if the many died through the one man's trespass, much more surely have the grace of God and the free gift in the grace of the one man, Jesus Christ, abounded for the many.

Gospel, Matthew 10:26-33

[Jesus said to his apostles:] "Have no fear; for nothing is covered up that will not be uncovered, and nothing secret that will not become known. What I say to you in the dark, tell in the light; and what you hear whispered, proclaim from the housetops. Do not fear those who kill the body but cannot kill the soul; rather fear him who can destroy both soul and body in hell. Are not two sparrows sold for a penny? Yet not one of them will fall to the ground apart from your Father. And even the hairs of your head are all counted. So do not be afraid; you are of more value than many sparrows.

"Everyone therefore who acknowledges me before others, I also will acknowledge before my Father in heaven; but whoever denies me before others, I also will deny before my Father in heaven."

Answering the Call

ELSIE HAINZ MCGRATH

The prophet, Jeremiah, was confident in the face of persecution. "The Lord is with me," he said, perhaps remembering the promise made to him earlier: "They will fight against you; but they shall not prevail against you, for I am with you, says the Lord, to deliver you" (1:19).

The apostle, Paul, was confident in the face of sin. "...the grace of God and the free gift in the grace of...Jesus Christ, abounded for the many," he wrote. "Many" means "all," as is evidenced by his earlier comment concerning sin and grace: "All have sinned and fall short of the glory of God; they are now justified by his grace as a gift, through the redemption that is in Christ Jesus" (3:23-24).

Jesus instilled confidence in his apostles, even in the face of death. "Do not fear those who kill the body but cannot kill the soul," he urged. Persecution...sin...death...*nothing* can separate us from the love of God.

Trust

It took more than confidence to face the trials of prophets and apostles, however. It is one thing to be confident in what we hold as truth. It is quite another to proclaim that truth in the face of persecution and sin and death. Working for the Lord requires perseverance and courage. And trust. Maybe trust most of all.

The gospel message today stresses radical trust: "What I say to you in the dark, tell in the light; and what you hear whispered, proclaim from the housetops...". Trust your dreams, trust your intuitions, trust your insights. Or, as the psalmist said so long ago (Ps 95:7-8): "O that today you would listen to his voice! Do not harden your hearts." And don't *only* trust, but also proclaim. "[And] do not be afraid...[because] everyone...who acknowledges me before others, I also will acknowledge before my Father in heaven."

Jeremiah's profile is contained at the beginning of the Book of Jeremiah (1:1-3). Called and fortified by God, Jeremiah prophesied for forty turbulent years of anarchy, war, and exile. Throughout his years of prophesying, everyone turned against him—family, friends, priests, kings, even fellow prophets. But Jeremiah never faltered in his convictions, nor in speaking them. He criticized both politics and religion, and generally prophesied soundly. In the end, Jeremiah was exiled into Egypt and disappeared from the pages of history.

Paul suffered numerous imprisonments and physical abuses throughout his Christian ministry which ultimately ended in martyrdom, just as Jesus' own ministry ended. He described his faithful and courageous witness this way: "Though I am free with respect to all, I have made myself a slave to all, so that I might win more of them. To the Jews I became as a Jew, in order to win Jews. To those under the law I became as one under the law (though I myself am not under the law) so that I might win those under the law. To those outside the law I became as one outside the law (though I am not free from God's law but am under Christ's law) so that I might win those outside the law. To the weak I became weak, so that I might win the weak. I have become all things to all people, that I might by all means save some. I do it all for the sake of the gospel, so that I may share in its blessings" (1 Cor 9:19-23).

Today's Good News

Today's world is saturated by ungodliness. In the name of "separation of church and state," we have made a mockery of organized religion and spawned generations of atheistic humanists. Those who profess to have faith, more often than not, are completely intolerant of others' faith. The word has become a political football, an object to be drop kicked over "goal" lines. Devoid of life blood, "faith" means less than "conservative" or "liberal," or "white" or "black."

There are still prophets, visionaries who courageously speak the truth they find in their hearts. Pope John XXIII was one. But how many others have stilled—or killed—their prophetic voices? How many are too afraid of those who can "kill the body" to speak what they hear in the dark?

And there are still apostles, ministers who confidently proclaim the risen Lord they have witnessed. Mother Teresa was one. But how many are blind to the very Son of God? How many out-and-out deny their Savior before others?

Do *we* have to face the trials and tribulations that were faced by Jeremiah, or by Paul and the other apostles? Do we have to risk *everything*—family and friends, health and home—for the sake of the gospel? Do we have exile and/or martyrdom in our future? Maybe...maybe not. But, if we do...*if* we do...*will* we?

Points for Reflection and Discussion

1. Do you know anyone you would consider a prophet? If so, why?

_____

_____

_____

_____

_____

2. Are there any things that frighten you about coming into full communion with the Catholic Church? If so, what are they? Why?

_____

_____

_____

_____

_____

Themes

Apostle, Disciple
   Q7, Mary
   Q9, Who's Who in the Church
   M2, The Laity: Called to Build God's Kingdom
   M3, Your Special Gifts
   M8, Evangelization
Prophet
   Q6, The Saints
   Q12, Catholics and Church
   M6, Discernment
Trust
   Q1, Journey of Faith
   M1, Conversion: A Lifelong Process
   M5, Your Prayer Life
   M7, Holiness

Reading 1, 2 Kings 4:8-11,14-16

One day Elisha was passing through Shunem, where a wealthy woman lived, who urged him to have a meal. So whenever he passed that way, he would stop there for a meal. She said to her husband, "Look, I am sure that this man who regularly passes our way is a holy man of God. Let us make a small roof chamber with walls, and put there for him a bed, a table, a chair, and a lamp, so that he can stay there whenever he comes to us." One day when he came there, he went up to the chamber and lay down there.

[Elisha] said [to his servant], "What then may be done for her?" Gehazi answered, "Well, she has no son, and her husband is old." He said, "Call her." When he had called her, she stood at the door. He said, "At this season, in due time, you shall embrace a son."

Psalm 89:1-2,15-16,17-18 (NRSV)

Reading 2, Romans 6:3-4,8-11

Do you not know that all of us who have been baptized into Christ Jesus were baptized into his death? Therefore we have been buried with him by baptism into death, so that, just as Christ was raised from the dead by the glory of the Father, so we too might walk in newness of life.

But if we have died with Christ, we believe that we will also live with him. We know that Christ, being raised from the dead, will never die again; death no longer has dominion over him. The death he died, he died to sin, once for all; but the life he lives, he lives to God. So you also must consider yourselves dead to sin and alive to God in Christ Jesus.

Gospel, Matthew 10:37-42

[Jesus said to his apostles:] "Whoever loves father or mother more than me is not worthy of me; and whoever loves son or daughter more than me is not worthy of me; and whoever does not take up the cross and follow me is not worthy of me. Those who find their life will lose it, and those who lose their life for my sake will find it.

"Whoever welcomes you welcomes me, and whoever welcomes me welcomes the one who sent me. Whoever welcomes a prophet in the name of a prophet will receive a prophet's reward; and whoever welcomes a righteous person in the name of a righteous person will receive the reward of the righteous; and whoever gives even a cup of cold water to one of these little ones in the name of a disciple—truly I tell you, none of these will lose their reward."

The Measure of Values

JOHN F. CRAGHAN

We often exclude people—and for a variety of reasons. A person is worth what he or she can do for me. A person is worth what he or she earns. The criterion of utilitarianism makes it very difficult for us to accept that God is the measure of values.

Today's readings offer an entirely different approach to this question of values. They perceive people from a whole other vantage point. They challenge us to adopt a perspective whereby God's priorities determine the status of a person. They endorse the principle that God is the measure of values.

The story from the Elisha cycle testifies to the great impression made by this ninth-century prophet. The wealthy woman from the town of Shunem, in the northern kingdom of Israel, discovers more than a great personality in Elisha. This is evident in her remark to her husband that Elisha is surely "a holy man of God." She is able to pierce the externals of this colorful and extravagant spokesperson and detect the presence of the God of Israel. The guest room, while it provides privacy and ensures ritual purity, symbolizes this perception. Elisha is God's emissary and, as such, is worthy of respect and charity.

Death to Life

Paul emphasizes the transformation experience of death and resurrection. Through baptism, the Christian dies with Christ and is buried with Christ. The Christian also shares in Jesus' Resurrection since he or she is called upon to live a new life as a result. At the same time, the Christian also looks forward to the Parousia, that is, the Second Coming.

For Paul, this transformation has a profound effect on the Christian. He or she is nothing less than a new creation. "If anyone is in Christ, there is a new creation: everything old has passed away; see, everything has become new!" (2 Cor 5:17). For Paul, this transformation means the leveling of all distinctions based on race, social status, and sex (see Gal 3:27-28). To appraise a Christian is to recall his or her overwhelming dignity. Here there is no question but that God is the measure of values.

Welcoming the Lord

In this conclusion of his missionary discourse, Matthew lines up the members in his community: apostles, prophets, holy men, and lowly ones. The principle is that to accept any one of these members is to accept Jesus, and to accept Jesus is to accept the Father. Here the values of each class derive from Jesus and ultimately from the one who sent him, namely, the Father. "Whoever welcomes you welcomes me, and whoever welcomes me welcomes the one who sent me."

It is significant that Matthew does not focus solely on the important people in the community, namely, the apostles, prophets, and holy men. He also includes the lowly ones (see Mt 18:10). Even a glass of cold water has great value because the giver recognizes the dignity of the person as a disciple of Jesus. Accordingly, such seemingly minimal generosity will not go unrewarded.

Today's Good News

The modern Christian is tempted to confuse subjects with objects, persons with things. Unwittingly, perhaps, we immediately put a price tag on a person. The final price then determines how we shall treat him or her. If the price tag is sufficiently high, we may resort to flattery and deception. If the price is strikingly low, we may give way to manipulation and harshness.

We are naturally upset at the emancipation proclamation of Paul. We are prone to make evaluations about people on the basis of ethnic background, social status, and sex. We are overwhelmed by these differences in daily life. How difficult it is to adopt Paul's view that the Christian—yes, every Christian—is a new creation.

We are equally perturbed with the non-discriminatory message of the Matthean Jesus. We prefer to cater to the "nice people," who in turn can benefit us. The ones who really hurt—our modern version of the "lowly ones"—tend to be pushed aside so that we can direct our attention to the apostles and prophets. After all, we surmise, rank has its privilege.

In these and similar instances, today's readings are no less than revolutionary. God and God's criteria are to take the place of our pragmatic business practices and social conventions. They are the disturbing summons to adopt new perceptions so that God is the measure of values.

Points for Reflection and Discussion

1. Discuss what it means for you to be baptized into Christ's death.

_____

_____

_____

_____

2. In this age of treachery and violence, how do you go about welcoming strangers in your house?

_____

_____

_____

_____

Themes

Death, Life
   M1, Conversion: A Lifelong Process
Discipleship
   Q9, Who's Who in the Church
   Q12, Catholics and Church
   M2, The Laity: Called to Build God's Kingdom
   M3, Your Special Gifts
   M8, Evangelization

Reading 1, Zechariah 9:9-10

Rejoice greatly, O daughter Zion! Shout aloud, O daughter Jerusalem! Lo, your king comes to you; triumphant and victorious is he, humble and riding on a donkey, on a colt, the foal of a donkey. He will cut off the chariot from Ephraim and the war horse from Jerusalem; and the battle bow shall be cut off, and he shall command peace to the nations; his dominion shall be from sea to sea, and from the River to the ends of the earth.

Psalm 145:1-2,8-9,10-11,13-14

Reading 2, Romans 8:9,11-13

You are not in the flesh; you are in the Spirit, since the Spirit of God dwells in you. Anyone who does not have the Spirit of Christ does not belong to him. If the Spirit of him who raised Jesus from the dead dwells in you, he who raised Christ from the dead will give life to your mortal bodies also through his Spirit that dwells in you. So then, brothers and sisters, we are debtors, not to the flesh, to live according to the flesh—for if you live according to the flesh, you will die; but if by the Spirit you put to death the deeds of the body, you will live.

Gospel, Matthew 11:25-30

At that time Jesus said, "I thank you, Father, Lord of heaven and earth, because you have hidden these things from the wise and the intelligent and have revealed them to infants; yes, Father, for such was your gracious will. All things have been handed over to me by my Father; and no one knows the Son except the Father, and no one knows the Father except the Son and anyone to whom the Son chooses to reveal him.

"Come to me, all you that are weary and are carrying heavy burdens, and I will give you rest. Take my yoke upon you, and learn from me; for I am gentle and humble in heart, and you will find rest for your souls. For my yoke is easy, and my burden is light."

Compassion

JOHN F. CRAGHAN

How often we live by "production is the name of the game" and "business is business." We thereby assume that only those who meet our standards, goals, and expectations are worth our time and energy. All those who fail to meet the above are insignificant and expendable. We are thus tied to an immutable set of criteria that allows for no transgressions. In this mind-set, it is almost impossible to maintain that compassion is our most important product.

Today's readings urge us to take a long look at our purely pragmatic business practices. They rivet our attention on the down-and-out, the rejects of society who are incapable of meeting our absolute norms. These biblical selections vividly bring to mind that we are to reach out to the unfortunate and provide for them.

Merciful Peace

Second Zechariah, that is, chapters 9 through 11 of the Book of Zechariah, is often dated after the arrival of Alexander the Great in Palestine in 332 B.C. The author seeks to offer a message of consolation now that Israel is subject to yet another conqueror. Fittingly, he invites Jerusalem to break forth into shouts of joy because of God's involvement. This author longs for a return of the Davidic kingdom, but in a manner vastly different from the past.

Like Israel, the king has suffered a setback but he also enjoys God's special care (see Is 45:17). He is humble and rides the animal linked to the anointing of kings (see 1 Kgs 1:33). Significantly, he does not mount a horse, which would suggest a time of warfare. "A colt, the foal of an ass" recalls the eminence of the Davidic kings (see Gn 49:11). The Davidic king will effect a period of peace, unifying the north (Ephraim) and the south (Jerusalem) and extending Israel's borders to include all the civilized world (see Ps 72:8).

Today's response is a psalm of descriptive praise, that is, it extols the Lord for ongoing care. Borrowing a traditional expression of the Lord's qualities (see Ex 34:6), the psalmist announces that this God "is gracious and merciful, slow to anger and abounding in steadfast love" (145:8).

It is significant that the word "merciful" derives from the Hebrew word for "womb." Thus the Lord has the same compassion that a mother shows the child of her womb. This divine maternal compassion lifts up the bowed down.

Peaceful Rest

Matthew develops the image of Jesus after the manner of Lady Wisdom (see Prv 8-9). Like Lady Wisdom, Jesus invites the disciple to learn his message by accepting his person. He directs that invitation to the religious outcasts of his day. They are the "people of the land" whom the Pharisees despise for not observing the yoke of the Mosaic Law. As such, these people are weary and find life burdensome.

Jesus speaks of "rest," that is, the peace associated with the Messiah in the final days. Jesus also refers to himself as "gentle" and "humble." These are the qualities not of the heavy-handed bill collector but of the concerned, outgoing Son of God. Jesus, therefore, invites the disciple to assume not the Mosaic Law but his own attitudes and, ultimately, his very person. This is a yoke that the "people of the land" can find light.

Today's Good News

The opportunity for compassion is everywhere. We realize that local, state, and federal agencies offer some care for our poor. Zechariah, however, would suggest that we can only break out into joy when we give over and above the minimum to the indigent. We realize that various organizations provide to some extent for the disabled. The psalmist, however, would recommend that we show maternal concern by not counting the extra cost. We realize also that different groups reach out to the chemically dependent. The Matthean Jesus, however, would urge that we make their yoke easier and their burden lighter by becoming involved. Compassion is still our most important product.

Points for Reflection and Discussion

1. Compassion has come to be identified with feelings of sympathy and concern, but at its root the word means "with passion." A compassionate friend does not necessarily sympathize with our problems, but is willing to take them on with gusto. What are you compassionate about?

_____

_____

_____

_____

2. Do you ever wonder how some people can "bear" the crosses they seem saddled with? Have you ever prayed for a lighter cross for yourself?

_____

_____

_____

_____

Themes
Holy Spirit
    Q2, What Do Catholics Believe?
    M3, Your Special Gifts
    M8, Evangelization
Resurrection
    M2, The Laity: Called to Build God's Kingdom
Wisdom
    Q1, Journey of Faith
    M1, Conversion: A Lifelong Process
    M6, Discernment
    M7, Holiness

Reading 1, Isaiah 55:10-11

[The Lord said:] "As the rain and the snow come down from heaven, and do not return there until they have watered the earth, making it bring forth and sprout, giving seed to the sower and bread to the eater, so shall my word be that goes out from my mouth; it shall not return to me empty, but it shall accomplish that which I purpose, and succeed in the thing for which I sent it."

Psalm 65:9,9-10,11-12,13 (NRSV)

Reading 2, Romans 8:18-23

I consider that the sufferings of this present time are not worth comparing with the glory about to be revealed to us. For the creation waits with eager longing for the revealing of the children of God; for the creation was subjected to futility, not of its own will but by the will of the one who subjected it, in hope that the creation itself will be set free from its bondage to decay and will obtain the freedom of the glory of the children of God. We know that the whole creation has been groaning in labor pains until now; and not only the creation, but we ourselves, who have the first fruits of the Spirit, groan inwardly while we wait for adoption, the redemption of our bodies.

Gospel, Matthew 13:1-23

Jesus went out of the house and sat beside the sea. Such great crowds gathered around him that he got into a boat and sat there, while the whole crowd stood on the beach. And he told them many things in parables, saying: "Listen! A sower went out to sow. And as he sowed, some seeds fell on the path, and the birds came and ate them up. Other seeds fell on rocky ground, where they did not have much soil, and they sprang up quickly, since they had no depth of soil. But when the sun rose, they were scorched; and since they had no root, they withered away. Other seeds fell among thorns, and the thorns grew up and choked them. Other seeds fell on good soil and brought forth grain, some a hundredfold, some sixty, some thirty. Let anyone with ears listen!"

Then the disciples came and asked him, "Why do you speak to them in parables?" He answered, "To you it has been given to know the secrets of the kingdom of heaven, but to them it has not been given. For to those who have, more will be given, and they will have an abundance; but from those who have nothing, even what they have will be taken away. The reason I speak to them in parables is that 'seeing they do not perceive, and hearing they do not listen, nor do they understand.' With them indeed is fulfilled the prophecy of Isaiah that says: 'You will indeed listen, but never understand, and you will indeed look, but never perceive. For this people's heart has grown dull, and their ears are hard of hearing, and they have shut their eyes; so that they might not look with their eyes, and listen with their ears, and understand with their heart and turn—and I would heal them.' But blessed are your eyes, for they see, and your ears, for they hear. Truly I tell you, many prophets and righteous people longed to see what you see, but did not see it, and to hear what you hear, but did not hear it.

"Hear then the parable of the sower. When anyone hears the word of the kingdom and does not understand it, the evil one comes and snatches away what is sown in the heart; this is what was sown on the path. As for what was sown on rocky ground, this is the one who hears the word and immediately receives it with joy; yet such a person has no root, but endures only for a while, and when trouble or persecution arises on account of the word, that person immediately falls away. As for what was sown among thorns, this is the one who hears the word, but the cares of the world and the lure of wealth choke the word, and it yields nothing. But as for what was sown on good soil, this is the one who hears the word and understands it, who indeed bears fruit and yields, in one case a hundredfold, in another sixty, and in another thirty."

Farmer God

JOHN F. CRAGHAN

We may prefer to speak of our God as awesome and omnipotent. We may choose to focus on the titles of Creator and Redeemer. But have we ever really considered ourselves as the daughters and sons of God the farmer?

Today's readings present God as a farmer. The image, far from being neutral, is one that challenges us to exhibit the qualities of fidelity, involvement, and perseverance. They hold before our eyes a God who is concerned and interested.

Concluding his message of consolation to the despairing exiles, Second Isaiah takes up the theme of God's Word with which he began. To demonstrate the fidelity of God to his Word, Second Isaiah in effect describes God as a farmer, the giver of fertility par excellence. God sends the rain and the snow from the heavens that ultimately soak the earth. Thereafter they return to the heavens in the form of bushes, trees, and food. This is a God who is faithful to his Word, even in the face of Israel's infidelity.

Psalm 65, a psalm of descriptive praise, presents three images of the God of Israel. God is the God of Zion, the one who resides in the Jerusalem Temple (verses 2-5). God is the Lord of the universe and history (verses 6-9). Finally, God is God the farmer (verses 10-14). The God who conquers kingdoms, restrains oceans, and accepts praise in the Temple is also the God who shows involvement by farming the land. Yahweh drenches the furrows, breaks up the clods, and softens the land with showers. The valleys blanketed with grain eloquently testify to the concern of this farmer for day-to-day needs. The God of cult and history is the one who muddies his hands.

Speaking in Parables

The gospel parable suggests a period in the ministry of Jesus when he has met with resistance and lack of response from his audience. The impasse raises the delicate question of determining loss and gain in the kingdom. Jesus' reply is to adopt the stance of the farmer in assessing pluses and minuses. Like the farmer, he too will be persevering.

The parable is the parable of the seed and of the natural inevitability of failure and loss in sowing. Jesus offers three states of loss: immediate ("the path"), gradual ("rocky ground"), and ultimate ("thorns"). He also offers three stages of growth: "some a hundredfold, some sixty, some thirty." Like the farmer, Jesus is persevering in the accomplishment of his mission. He acknowledges that God's mysterious plan is at work.

Today's Good News

God is faithful to his Word. This image challenges our sense of fidelity. Do we continue to speak the words of comfort and support that we promised on our wedding day or similar occasions?

God does not hesitate to become involved in farming the land and assuring the crop. This image challenges our sense of involvement. Do we continue to be involved by looking to the needs of family and community, or do we prefer the ministry of being aloof?

God perseveres even in the face of significant loss. This image challenges our sense of perseverance. Do we continue to persevere in our commitment to our faith and our values by not dwelling on our mistakes but by continuing to hope in God's mysterious plan for us?

Today's agricultural images offer a new vantage point for assessing our relationship with our God and our sisters and brothers. We are indeed the daughters and sons of God the farmer.

Points for Reflection and Discussion

1. Think about the plight of farmers over the years: blight and famine, flood and fire, injustice and disrespect. Imagine that the farmer who is suffering at the hands of governments and big business is God.

_____

_____

_____

_____

2. Reflect again on the parable. Where has God's Word taken root in your own life: on the path, or on rocky ground, or among the thorns, or on good soil?

_____

_____

_____

_____

_____

Themes
Fidelity
    Q1, Journey of Faith
    Q7, Mary
    M4, Family Life
    M7, Holiness
Growth, Productivity
    Q2, What Do Catholics Believe?
    Q6, The Saints
    M2, The Laity: Called to Build God's Kingdom
    M8, Evangelization
Perseverance
    Q10, Catholics and Prayer
    M1, Conversion: A Lifelong Process
    M5, Your Prayer Life

Reading 1, Wisdom 12:13,16-19

There is no god besides you, Lord, whose care is for all people, to whom you should prove that you have not judged unjustly. For your strength is the source of righteousness, and your sovereignty over all causes you to spare all. For you show your strength when people doubt the completeness of your power, and you rebuke any insolence among those who know it. Although you are sovereign in strength, you judge with mildness, and with great forbearance you govern us; for you have power to act whenever you choose.

Through such works you have taught your people that the righteous must be kind, and you have filled your children with good hope, because you give repentance for sins.

Psalm 86:5-6,9-10,15-16

Reading 2, Romans 8:26-27

The Spirit helps us in our weakness; for we do not know how to pray as we ought, but that very Spirit intercedes with sighs too deep for words. And God, who searches the heart, knows what is the mind of the Spirit, because the Spirit intercedes for the saints according to the will of God.

Gospel, Matthew 13:24-43

[Jesus] put before [the crowd] another parable: "The kingdom of heaven may be compared to someone who sowed good seed in his field; but while everybody was asleep, an enemy came and sowed weeds among the wheat, and then went away. So when the plants came up and bore grain, then the weeds appeared as well. And the slaves of the householder came and said to him, 'Master, did you not sow good seed in your field? Where, then, did these weeds come from?' He answered, 'An enemy has done this.' The slaves said to him, 'Then do you want us to go and gather them?' But he replied, 'No; for in gathering the weeds you would uproot the wheat along with them. Let both of them grow together until the harvest; and at harvest time I will tell the reapers, Collect the weeds first and bind them in bundles to be burned, but gather the wheat into my barn'."

He put before them another parable: "The kingdom of heaven is like a mustard seed that someone took and sowed in his field; it is the smallest of all the seeds, but when it has grown it is the greatest of shrubs and becomes a tree, so that the birds of the air come and make nests in its branches."

He told them another parable: "The kingdom of heaven is like yeast that a woman took and mixed in with three measures of flour until all of it was leavened."

Jesus told the crowds all these things in parables; without a parable he told them nothing. This was to fulfill what had been spoken through the prophet: "I will open my mouth to speak in parables; I will proclaim what has been hidden from the foundation of the world."

Then he left the crowds and went into the house. And his disciples approached him, saying, "Explain to us the parable of the weeds of the field." He answered, "The one who sows the good seed is the Son of Man; the field is the world, and the good seed are the children of the kingdom; the weeds are the children of the evil one, and the enemy who sowed them is the devil; the harvest is the end of the age, and the reapers are angels. Just as the weeds are collected and burned up with fire, so will it be at the end of the age. The Son of Man will send his angels, and they will collect out of his kingdom all causes of sin and all evildoers, and they will throw them into the furnace of fire, where there will be weeping and gnashing of teeth. Then the righteous will shine like the sun in the kingdom of their Father. Let anyone with ears listen!"

Strength Through Leniency

John F. Craghan

We associate power with force. Not to employ it in our relationships seems to imply weakness. Today's readings consider the theme of leniency. They unfold the image of a God who chooses to demonstrate control by means of kindness and patience. This is a God who governs by showing compassion.

Writing for Alexandrian Jews in the first century B.C., the author of the Book of Wisdom emphasizes God's special care of Israel during the Exodus. Keeping in mind the needs of his audience, he also takes up the special problem of the treatment of the just and the unjust. The author of Wisdom digresses on God's power and mercy.

God does not act unjustly, since power is the very basis of his justice. Instead of leading to blind rage, God's power results in clemency. In this way God manages a balance between justice and mercy. It is this balance that the audience should imitate by way of kindness and forgiveness. For this writer, the proper approach is to show strength by being lenient.

Like a Mother

In today's psalm of lament, an individual has suffered from persecution. The persecutors are intent upon taking the life of the psalmist—indeed they are people who neglect to consider the God of Israel. Though the bleak situation of the victim is described in rather general terms, it is still a situation that demands God's immediate action. "Show me a sign of your favor, so that those who hate me may see it and be put to shame, because you, Lord, have helped me and comforted me" (86:17).

The psalm is significant in that it does not detail a plan of havoc to be wreaked on the persecutor. Rather, it describes God's power in terms of leniency toward the psalmist. Verse 5 speaks of God's goodness, forgiveness, and covenantal loyalty. Verse 15 addresses God as a tender mother ("merciful" derives from the Hebrew word for "womb"). Maternal concern is the answer to the psalmist's plight.

The Means to the End

The parable of the wheat and the weeds (darnel, that is, poisonous weeds) exemplifies Jesus' understanding of the kingdom. It is a kingdom that embraces both wheat and weeds, both good and evil. The owner confronts two problems: how to save the wheat, and how to outwit the enemy. He resolves the first by permitting the wheat and weeds to grow together until harvest time. He resolves the second by using the weeds as fuel.

To be sure, the emergency faced by the owner calls for firm and swift action. The owner, however, realizes that violence (killing the weeds) will only endanger the common good (the wheat may also be destroyed). So too in the kingdom, the common good demands both patience and forgiveness. By combining swift action with a sense of compassion, the owner becomes Jesus' expression of a basic attitude in the kingdom: strength through leniency.

Today's Good News

In today's world we constantly experience the tension between mercy and justice. Our first reading raises the question: Will our power lead to blind rage or will it promote justice? Our responsorial psalm asks: Will we be motherly in our exercise of power? While being firm, will we also demonstrate a tenderness that can win over the subject? Our gospel implies: Will we hurt the common good by hasty and ill-advised use of power?

Power is given to help others. If we find that our use of power is more destructive than constructive, then we must be challenged by these readings. They powerfully endorse the stance: show strength—be merciful.

Points for Reflection and Discussion

1. Have you ever watched something grow big from a tiny seed? Have you ever watched bread dough rise? How do these compare with the "kingdom of heaven"?

_____

_____

_____

_____

2. Reread the second reading. Have you ever persevered in prayer when you felt "prayerless"? Has your prayer ever led you into areas where you never intended to go?

_____

_____

_____

_____

_____

Themes

Kingdom of God
    Q2, What Do Catholics Believe?
    Q12, Catholics and Church
Mercy
    M3, Your Special Gifts

Reading 1, 1 Kings 3:5,7-12

The Lord appeared to Solomon in a dream by night; and God said, "Ask what I should give you." [Solomon answered:] "O Lord my God, you have made your servant king in place of my father David, although I am only a little child; I do not know how to go out or come in. And your servant is in the midst of the people whom you have chosen, a great people, so numerous they cannot be numbered or counted. Give your servant therefore an understanding mind to govern your people, able to discern between good and evil; for who can govern this your great people?"

It pleased the Lord that Solomon had asked this. God said to him, "Because you have asked this, and have not asked for yourself long life or riches, or for the life of your enemies, but have asked for yourself understanding to discern what is right, I now do according to your word. Indeed I give you a wise and discerning mind; no one like you has been before you and no one like you shall arise after you."

Psalm 119:57,72,76-77,127-128,129-130

Reading 2, Romans 8:28-30

We know that all things work together for good for those who love God, who are called according to his purpose. For those whom he foreknew he also predestined to be conformed to the image of his Son, in order that he might be the firstborn within a large family. And those whom he predestined he also called; and those whom he called he also justified; and those whom he justified he also glorified.

Gospel, Matthew 13:44-52

[Jesus said:] "The kingdom of heaven is like treasure hidden in a field, which someone found and hid; then in his joy he goes and sells all that he has and buys that field.

"Again, the kingdom of heaven is like a merchant in search of fine pearls; on finding one pearl of great value, he went and sold all that he had and bought it.

"Again, the kingdom of heaven is like a net that was thrown into the sea and caught fish of every kind; when it was full, they drew it ashore, sat down, and put the good into baskets but threw out the bad. So it will be at the end of the age. The angels will come out and separate the evil from the righteous and throw them into the furnace of fire, where there will be weeping and gnashing of teeth.

"Have you understood all this?" [The disciples] answered, "Yes." And he said to them, "Therefore every scribe who has been trained for the kingdom of heaven is like the master of a household who brings out of his treasure what is new and what is old."

Role Models

JOHN F. CRAGHAN

We adopt role models for planning and managing our lives. If interested in glamour and beauty, we may extrapolate role models from the world of Hollywood. If caught up in power, we may select role models from the world of big business. If anxious to become a superstar, we may borrow role models from the world of the NBA, NFL, NHL, and so forth. It is worth our while to think about whom we have chosen as our role models.

In the Hebrew Scriptures, the wise person par excellence is Solomon. Employing a dream as a mode of divine revelation, the author depicts Solomon's wisdom as one that derives from God. Eschewing long life, wealth, and victory over enemies, Solomon asks for "an understanding mind to govern your people, able to discern between good and evil." Fundamentally, this is a request to rule well and hence provide for the people, especially the disenfranchised (see Ps 72:1-4; Is 11:3-5). God's granting of the request initially suggests Solomon as a role model for rulers and politicians.

The Bible is quick to add that Solomon did not live up to the expectations of today's reading. As a matter of fact, he bled the people with taxes to finance his building projects. He even went so far as to impose forced labor on them (see 1 Kgs 11:28). The final verdict of First Kings is that Solomon is not the role model for just government and proper political behavior.

God's Will

In the second reading, Paul speaks of that plan for humans whereby they can arrive at the destiny God intended from the beginning. He uses five verbs (foreknew, predestined, called, justified, glorified) that capture God's benefits on behalf of Israel. But now humans who respond in faith can also share in those benefits.

After the verb "predestined," Paul adds a qualification, namely, "to be conformed to the image of his Son." By "image," Paul understands a role model. The risen Lord is the exemplar of God's design for humanity. To be fully human is to appropriate to oneself the lifestyle and death-style of the Lord. The latter implies a manner of living whereby one thinks consistently in terms of others. Paul obviously has no hesitation when he answers the question: "Who is my role model?"

A New World

In the parable of the buried treasure (as well as that of the pearl), Matthew offers a role model for how growth in the kingdom takes place. The first stage is normalcy, that is, the monotonous life of the farmer in his day-to-day activities. The second stage is the discovery of the treasure that opens up a vastly new world. The third stage is the overturning of the past—hence the farmer sells all he possesses to buy the field. The fourth stage is that new world that Jesus offers the disciple.

In this parable, Matthew presents a disciple who looks at this new possibility with significantly different eyes. His is a world grounded in the person of Jesus, which demands a radical commitment. The total reversal of one's life for the sake of the kingdom is the challenge that Matthew holds out to his community.

Today's Good News

The Solomon role model of First Kings asks us relevant questions about our position and our job. No matter how great or how small our power and influence, do we use it to benefit others? Or in the seemingly trivial actions of daily life will we employ our authority to oppress others? Is Solomon our role model?

The true disciple role model of Matthew possesses timely questions about our sense of commitment. Are we really willing to turn our lives around and make the kingdom a reality in our lives? Or are we content to let our gifts and talents lie buried in the field? Is the true disciple our role model?

The Jesus role model of Paul poses nagging questions about our lifestyles. Do we really see ourselves as persons for others and hence concerned about living/dying for others? Or do we view ourselves as egocentrics caught up in the private world of concerns and pleasures? Is the risen Lord our role model?

Points for Reflection and Discussion

1. Who is your role model today? Why? Who was your role model when you were growing up? Why?

_____

_____

_____

_____

2. How would you define "predestination"? How is it different from "the will of God"? How is it the same?

_____

_____

_____

_____

Themes

Kingdom of God
    Q2, What Do Catholics Believe?
    Q12, Catholics and Church
    M2, The Laity: Called to Build God's Kingdom
    M8, Evangelization
Role Models
    Q6, The Saints
    Q7, Mary
    Q9, Who's Who in the Church

Reading 1, Isaiah 55:1-3

Everyone who thirsts, come to the waters; and you that have no money, come, buy and eat! Come, buy wine and milk without money and without price. Why do you spend your money for that which is not bread, and your labor for that which does not satisfy? Listen carefully to me, and eat what is good, and delight yourselves in rich food. Incline your ear, and come to me; listen, so that you may live. I will make with you an everlasting covenant, my steadfast, sure love for David.

Psalm 145:8-9,15-16,17-18

Reading 2, Romans 8:35,37-39

Who will separate us from the love of Christ? Will hardship, or distress, or persecution, or famine, or nakedness, or peril, or sword? No, in all these things we are more than conquerors through him who loved us. For I am convinced that neither death, nor life, nor angels, nor rulers, nor things present, nor things to come, nor powers, nor height, nor depth, nor anything else in all creation, will be able to separate us from the love of God in Christ Jesus our Lord.

Gospel, Matthew 14:13-21

When Jesus heard [about the death of John the Baptist], he withdrew from there in a boat to a deserted place by himself. But when the crowds heard it, they followed him on foot from the towns. When he went ashore, he saw a great crowd; and he had compassion for them and cured their sick.

When it was evening, the disciples came to him and said, "This is a deserted place, and the hour is now late; send the crowds away so that they may go into the villages and buy food for themselves." Jesus said to them, "They need not go away; you give them something to eat." They replied, "We have nothing here but five loaves and two fish." And he said, "Bring them here to me."

Then he ordered the crowds to sit down on the grass. Taking the five loaves and the two fish, he looked up to heaven, and blessed and broke the loaves, and gave them to the disciples, and the disciples gave them to the crowds. And all ate and were filled; and they took up what was left over of the broken pieces, twelve baskets full. And those who ate were about five thousand men, besides women and children.

Nourishment

JOHN F. CRAGHAN

How often we hear the expression: "I'm sorry, but that's your problem." Not infrequently we insulate ourselves from the shocks of others and isolate ourselves from their concerns. We even keep others out of our relationship with God. In that way, God's not a problem; God doesn't get in our way. But is this gospel living?

Today's first reading, responsorial psalm, and gospel deal with the implications of relationships. They presuppose that to reach our God is to reach out to others. They do not view humans as obstacles to our union with God but the very condition for that union. People, therefore, are the barometer of our standing with our God, and "your problem is my problem."

Problem-Solving

Around 540 BC, Second Isaiah preached to the despondent exiles at Babylon. Doubting whether God was interested in them and, if interested, whether God could do anything, they despaired of divine intervention. In response to this dire situation, Second Isaiah speaks of Yahweh as a concerned, life-giving God who seeks to renew the covenant with them. He graphically develops this intent through the symbols of water/grain (the essentials of life) and wine/milk (the superfluous items of the good life). As the condition for this demonstration of involvement, he adds: "Come to me; listen, so that you may live."

A further example of God's care is the application of the Davidic promise to all believers. This implies God's promise of abiding fidelity to the Davidic dynasty (see 2 Sm 7:13-16,24-29) and is offered to all people. The languishing exiles are now sharers in that dynasty and hence participants in the divine promise. Indeed, Israel as a nation is now God's king (see Is 41:9).

Today's psalm is a hymn or psalm of descriptive praise, that is, it speaks of God's ongoing providence for the people. Significantly, in verse 11 the author mentions God's kingdom: "They shall speak of the glory of your kingdom…". In the ancient Near East—ideally, at least—the king sought to alleviate the welfare cases, such as the widowed and the fatherless. In part, this psalm praises God for taking this regal charge very seriously.

At first the psalmist states Yahweh's commitment in general terms (see verses 8-9). Then he offers specific examples. Thus Yahweh gives his people their food at the right time (v 15). His hand is not closed but open (v 16). He lifts up the falling and raises up the bowed down (v 14). This is not a king who has limited office hours. Rather, he is near to all who seek his time and influence (v 18). In effect, this psalm sings of a God who maintains that "your problem is my problem."

Miracle Meal

In this scene Matthew underlines Jesus' sense of involvement. He is a new Moses since he provides bread in the desert (see Ex 16). He is a new messianic king since he hosts a banquet that looks to the final banquet in the kingdom (see Mt 26:29). He is the Jewish father presiding over the family meal, since he praises and thanks God for the food that he shares with the family members. The people's concern is his concern.

In relating this incident, Matthew has adapted his source, Mark. Matthew chooses to emphasize Jesus' compassion (see also Mt 9:36; 15:32). Whereas Mark has Jesus teach the people (Mk 6:34), Matthew has Jesus cure the sick. By dropping the disciples' question and Jesus' counter-question (Mk 6:37-38), Matthew reveals a Jesus who is very much in command of the situation. In addition, Matthew heightens the effect of the miracle by noting that the five thousand did not include women and children (see Mk 6:44). Matthew's touches enhance the picture of a Jesus who believes that "your problem is my problem."

Today's Good News

Once we realize that we love our God in and through loving fellow humans, we would do well to ask ourselves if we are loving well. Are our appointment books and office hours inexorably limited or, like the psalmist, can we be near to all petitioners? Are the down-and-out the remote objects of our pity or, like the Matthean Jesus, can we invite them to our table? The abiding question is, therefore: How far will we go when we say, "your problem is my problem"?

Points for Reflection and Discussion

1. What does "your problem is my problem" mean to you? Can we really solve other people's problems? How can we make them our own without relieving others of their responsibility?

_____

_____

_____

_____

2. Have you ever found yourself as Jesus is today—caught up in ministering to (an)other(s) instead of solitarily grieving a personal loss? What were the results?

_____

_____

_____

_____

_____

Themes
Ministry
   Q1, Journey of Faith
   Q9, Who's Who in the Church
   M2, The Laity: Called to Build God's Kingdom
Responsibility
   Q12, Catholics and Church
   M3, Your Special Gifts
   M6, Discernment
   M8, Evangelization

Reading 1, 1 Kings 19:9,11-13

[When Elijah reached Horeb, the mountain of God], he came to a cave, and spent the night there. Then the word of the Lord came to him, saying, "Go out and stand on the mountain before the Lord, for the Lord is about to pass by."

Now there was a great wind, so strong that it was splitting mountains and breaking rocks in pieces before the Lord, but the Lord was not in the wind; and after the wind an earthquake, but the Lord was not in the earthquake; and after the earthquake a fire, but the Lord was not in the fire; and after the fire a sound of sheer silence.

When Elijah heard it, he wrapped his face in his mantle and went out and stood at the entrance of the cave.

Psalm 85:8,9,10-11,12-13 (NRSV)

Reading 2, Romans 9:1-5

I am speaking the truth in Christ—I am not lying; my conscience confirms it by the Holy Spirit—I have great sorrow and unceasing anguish in my heart. For I could wish that I myself were accursed and cut off from Christ for the sake of my own people, my kindred according to the flesh. They are Israelites, and to them belong the adoption, the glory, the covenants, the giving of the law, the worship, and the promises; to them belong the patriarchs, and from them, according to the flesh, comes the Messiah, who is over all, God blessed forever. Amen.

Gospel, Matthew 14:22-33

Immediately [after feeding the crowd, Jesus] made the disciples get into the boat and go on ahead to the other side, while he dismissed the crowds. And after he had dismissed the crowds, he went up the mountain by himself to pray. When evening came, he was there alone, but by this time the boat, battered by the waves, was far from the land, for the wind was against them.

And early in the morning he came walking toward them on the sea. But when the disciples saw him walking on the sea, they were terrified, saying, "It is a ghost!" And they cried out in fear. But immediately Jesus spoke to them and said, "Take heart, it is I; do not be afraid."

Peter answered him, "Lord, if it is you, command me to come to you on the water." He said, "Come." So Peter got out of the boat, started walking on the water, and came toward Jesus. But when he noticed the strong wind, he became frightened, and beginning to sink, he cried out, "Lord, save me!"

Jesus immediately reached out his hand and caught him, saying to him, "You of little faith, why did you doubt?" When they got into the boat, the wind ceased. And those in the boat worshiped him, saying, "Truly you are the Son of God."

God's Presence

JOHN F. CRAGHAN

Presence fights fear. We all experience anxiety and frustration. They seem to be part and parcel of our human existence. The crucial question, however, appears to be: How do we overcome these bouts with fear? Are we helped by a friend who listens or a neighbor who has time for us? When we analyze life-threatening experiences and their resolutions, would it not be true to say that it is presence (however variable) that fights fear?

Today's first two readings and gospel focus on fear-filled people. Their pain is indeed acute and their plight all too real. To these encounters with fear the liturgical readings offer a common antidote, namely, divine presence. It is the healing presence of God that routs despair and dispels discouragement. Here presence fights fear.

Silent Presence

Around the middle of the ninth century BC, the prophet Elijah experienced excruciating fear. After defeating the pagan prophets at Carmel and thus incurring the wrath of Queen Jezebel, he is forced to flee. In his fear, he searches for his religious roots; hence he travels to Sinai (Horeb), where Yahweh shared his covenant presence with Israel. Like Moses, Elijah experiences that presence in a special manifestation (see Ex 33:21-23).

Wind, earthquake, and fire were traditional elements of God's presence. At Sinai, the Israelites felt that presence in both the fire and earthquake (see Ex 19:16-19). At this very spot, Elijah learns that God will be present in a new way, namely, through the prophetic word (a tiny whispering sound). Elijah, therefore, is commissioned to resume his prophetic career by the fearless proclamation of God's Word. It is this Word that will make God present to his people and thus overcome their fear. For both Elijah and the community, presence fights fear.

Promised Presence

In the second passage, the reader senses Paul's anguish. The lamentable fact is that Israel as a body did not enter the Christian community. In dealing with this problem, Paul notes Israel's privileges, for example, covenants, lawgiving, worship, and so forth. This culminates in the human origin of the Messiah. Sadly, Israel did not recognize the Christ who sprang from its midst. Ironically, the Gentiles did recognize him and thus share in the destiny originally set aside for Israel.

God's presence resolves Paul's fears and anxieties. In chapter 11 of Romans, he observes that God's gifts and call are irrevocable (v 29). Though Paul cannot reconcile human failure and divine purpose, he knows that God is intimately involved in human events. Hence God does not stand removed from Israel's plight but is really present despite the failure and the tragedy. It is God's mysterious presence that fights fear (see Rom 11:33).

Saving Presence

Matthew's scene borrows from Hebrew traditions. There Yahweh walks on the waters of chaos (see Jb 38:16), rescues humans captured in the flood waters of death (see Ps 18:16-17), and indicates his presence and willingness to save (see Is 45:18). Consequently, when chaos threatens the Church, Jesus is there. When anxiety grips the community, Jesus says: "Do not be afraid!" When faith yields to doubt, Jesus is willing to stretch out his saving hand. For Matthew (contrast Mk 6:52), Jesus is present not simply as another wonder-worker but as the Son of God.

Peter is symptomatic of the fearful Christian hovering between faith and doubt, presence and absence. "Little faith" sums up his wavering. Nonetheless, Jesus reacts to Peter's request by offering his hand, and to the other disciples' need by entering the boat. Even in the bleakest situations Jesus does not neglect his community. His response to that community's concerns is the gift of presence.

Today's Good News

It is believers who make God present and who thus serve as agents of hope and courage. It is the biblical conviction that the omnipotent God chooses to depend on weak humans in order to realize the divine plan for the world. Hence believers are challenged to radiate God's comforting presence and offset the fear and disillusionment that plague the world.

People who seek to improve the status of the under-privileged make God present. Those who attempt to comfort the terminally ill and the dying make God present. Those who help to reconstruct the shattered lives of the divorced make God present. Those who lobby to make peace and justice a reality make God present. In these and similar situations, believers react to the specter of fear that pervades our society. In these instances, presence fights fear.

Points for Reflection and Discussion

1. Have you ever unexpectedly felt the presence of God in your life?

_____

_____

_____

_____

2. While Peter kept his eyes on the Lord, he walked on water; when he let his gaze fall, he began to sink. Can you identify with Peter's experience in your own faith life?

_____

_____

_____

_____

Themes
Faith
    Q1, Journey of Faith
    Q12, Catholics and Church
    M1, Conversion: A Lifelong Process
Presence
    Q3, What is the Meaning of the Mass?
    Q4, The Bible
    M7, Holiness

Reading 1, Isaiah 56:1,6-7

Thus says the Lord: Maintain justice, and do what is right, for soon my salvation will come, and my deliverance be revealed. And the foreigners who join themselves to the Lord, to minister to him, to love the name of the Lord, and to be his servants, all who keep the sabbath, and do not profane it, and hold fast my covenant—these I will bring to my holy mountain, and make them joyful in my house of prayer; their burnt offerings and their sacrifices will be accepted on my altar; for my house shall be called a house of prayer for all peoples.

Psalm 67:1-2,4-5,6-7 (NRSV)

Reading 2, Romans 11:13-15,29-32

I am speaking to you Gentiles. Inasmuch then as I am an apostle to the Gentiles, I glorify my ministry in order to make my own people jealous, and thus save some of them. For if their rejection is the reconciliation of the world, what will their acceptance be but life from the dead! For the gifts and the calling of God are irrevocable. Just as you were once disobedient to God but have now received mercy because of their disobedience, so they have now been disobedient in order that, by the mercy shown to you, they too may now receive mercy. For God has imprisoned all in disobedience so that he may be merciful to all.

Gospel, Matthew 15:21-28

Jesus went away to the district of Tyre and Sidon. Just then a Canaanite woman from that region came out and started shouting, "Have mercy on me, Lord, Son of David; my daughter is tormented by a demon." But he did not answer her at all. And his disciples came and urged him, saying, "Send her away, for she keeps shouting after us." He answered, "I was sent only to the lost sheep of the house of Israel."

But she came and knelt before him, saying, "Lord, help me." He answered, "It is not fair to take the children's food and throw it to the dogs." She said, "Yes, Lord, yet even the dogs eat the crumbs that fall from their masters' table."

Then Jesus answered her, "Woman, great is your faith! Let it be done for you as you wish." And her daughter was healed instantly.

Building Bridges

JOHN F. CRAGHAN

At times we suffer from the debilitating disease of triumphalism. We take pride in the fact that we belong to the Church. As a result, we may be tempted to look down on non-members. We may consider them second-class citizens of the kingdom. We may even condemn them to the outer limits of God's love and care.

Today's readings provoke us to expand, not contract, the possibilities of the kingdom. They are a timely reminder to set aside our preoccupation with ourselves and focus on others. They are the upsetting news that we must reject our myopic vision and adopt the limitless horizons of our God. They all subscribe to this view: Build bridges, don't burn them.

The author of today's first reading is Third Isaiah (chapters 56-66). Writing around 500 BC, he endeavored to adapt the joyful message of his predecessor (Second Isaiah, chapters 40-55), to the despair of the people of Judah and Jerusalem. He begins by urging his audience to do what is just because of the nearness of God's salvation (v 1). He also directs his message to non-Jews (v 3).

In verses 6-7, the prophet responds to the lament of these outsiders. He notes the implications of loving Yahweh and being his servant, namely, honoring the Sabbath and obeying the covenant. He also depicts their joy as they come to God's dwelling place and offer their sacrifices. The former rejects become full-fledged members of God's community.

Divine Paradox

In the second reading, Paul revels in divine paradox. The Jewish rejection of the Christian message has meant salvation for the Gentiles. Paul, however, cautions his Roman audience against deriding the Jews. Indeed, awareness of this paradox will lead some fellow Jews to accept Christ. Such acceptance is nothing less than a trek from death to life (see Rom 6:4).

In verses 29-32, Paul develops this divine paradox by insisting that God shows mercy to all. Israel's disobedience is mercy for the Gentiles. Despite the infidelity of both Jew and Gentile, God displays mercy toward all. Catching up this paradox of mercy, Paul, who glories in his mission as the apostle of the Gentiles (v 13), "could wish that I myself were accursed and cut off from Christ for the sake of my own people, my kindred according to the flesh" (Rom 9:3-4). Paul certainly maintains: Build bridges, don't burn them.

Crumbs From the Table

In the gospel episode, Matthew shows Jesus in contact with a Gentile for a second time (see also 8:5-13). The evangelist elaborates the good news that the basis for discipleship is not ethnic origin but persistent faith in Jesus. Matthew is foreshadowing that moment at the very end of his gospel when the risen Jesus will command the Eleven: "Go, therefore, and make disciples of all nations" (28:19). Matthew's end is much like his beginning, where the story of the Magi anticipates the Gentile mission of the Church (2:1-12).

Matthew's use of "Canaanite" (contrast Mk 7:26) may underline the chasm that existed between Israel and the Gentiles since the conquest/settlement in the time of Joshua. By calling Jesus "Lord, Son of David," the Gentile woman accepts what Israel rejects, namely, Jesus' messianic identity. Even after learning of the originally intended limits of Jesus' mission to the house of Israel, and even after hearing his comparison of Gentiles to dogs, she pursues her goal inexorably. Her perseverance is Matthew's way of insisting that more than crumbs will fall from the table of Judaism. Faith of this caliber obliterates all distinctions between Jew and Gentile.

Today's Good News

Through baptism, Christians are commissioned to share the message of Jesus of Nazareth. Instead of assuming an elitist attitude, Christians are called upon to reflect the presence of Jesus through word and action. Among other things, Christians must applaud the goodness and kindness of non-members. To recognize such qualities is to acknowledge that our God is already present and active. Christians must heal the pain and the sorrow that festers in the division of denominationalism. Every act of love is the nonviolent rejection of all such obstacles. In this kind of attitude, modern Christians follow the tradition of Third Isaiah, Paul, and Matthew: Build bridges, don't burn them.

Points for Reflection and Discussion

1. Think about a time when you experienced prejudice from (an)other(s). How did you feel? How did you react?

_____

_____

_____

_____

2. Think about a person or group of persons you are prejudiced against. What caused that prejudice? What have you done about it? What do you intend to do about it?

_____

_____

_____

_____

Themes

Acceptance, Prejudice
   Q1, Journey of Faith
   M1, Conversion: A Lifelong Process
   M2, The Laity: Called to Build God's Kingdom
   M7, Holiness
Reconciliation
   Q3, What is the Meaning of the Mass?
   Q12, Catholics and Church
   M8, Evangelization

Reading 1, Isaiah 22:15,19-23

Thus says the Lord God of hosts: Come, go to this steward, to Shebna, who is master of the household, and say to him: "I will thrust you from your office, and you will be pulled down from your post. On that day I will call my servant Eliakim son of Hilkiah, and will clothe him with your robe and bind your sash on him. I will commit your authority to his hand, and he shall be a father to the inhabitants of Jerusalem and to the house of Judah. I will place on his shoulder the key of the house of David; he shall open, and no one shall shut; he shall shut, and no one shall open. I will fasten him like a peg in a secure place, and he will become a throne of honor to his ancestral house."

Psalm 138:1-2,2-3,6,8

Reading 2, Romans 11:33-36

O the depth of the riches and wisdom and knowledge of God! How unsearchable are his judgments and how inscrutable his ways! "For who has known the mind of the Lord? Or who has been his counselor?"

"Or who has given a gift to him, to receive a gift in return?" For from him and through him and to him are all things. To him be the glory forever. Amen.

Gospel, Matthew 16:13-20

When Jesus came into the district of Caesarea Philippi, he asked his disciples, "Who do people say that the Son of Man is?" And they said, "Some say John the Baptist, but others Elijah, and still others Jeremiah or one of the prophets."

He said to them, "But who do you say that I am?" Simon Peter answered, "You are the Messiah, the Son of the living God."

And Jesus answered him, "Blessed are you, Simon son of Jonah! For flesh and blood has not revealed this to you, but my Father in heaven. And I tell you, you are Peter, and on this rock I will build my church, and the gates of Hades will not prevail against it. I will give you the keys of the kingdom of heaven, and whatever you bind on earth will be bound in heaven, and whatever you loose on earth will be loosed in heaven."

Then he sternly ordered the disciples not to tell anyone that he was the Messiah.

Who's in Charge?

JOHN F. CRAGHAN

We relish positions with a heady sense of importance and prestige. We value titles because they cater to our sense of self-esteem and significance. The ever-lurking danger in this attitude is that we may see our power and status in terms of our own advantage. As we climb up the corporate ladder, it is all the harder to admit that to be in charge means to protect our charges.

Today's readings reflect on the meaning of power and the subsequent care of those under our authority. They are a reminder that power exists for the good of the powerless. In effect, they demand that we strive for office only if we intend "to preserve, protect, and defend" our sense of duty to the people we serve. They wholeheartedly endorse this platform: To be in charge means to protect our charges.

The passage from Isaiah provides a pointed contrast in the use and abuse of power. Toward the end of the eighth century BC, Isaiah of Jerusalem was sent to inform Shebna, the prime minister, of his removal from office (but see 2 Kgs 18:18,26,37). The prophet accuses him of show and pretentiousness in carving out a fine tomb and providing ceremonial chariots for himself (see Is 22:16,18). In addition, the prophet labels him a "disgrace to your master's house!" (22:18). This may imply Shebna's foolhardy advice to King Hezekiah to revolt against Assyria, the superpower of the day.

The prophet also speaks of Eliakim as one truly worthy of high office who will receive signs of authority (the key with the exclusive power of opening and closing the palace) that Shebna once enjoyed—because Eliakim will discharge the duty of office as a "father." The term "father" expresses the loving yet firm care he will show by meeting the needs of the people (see Gn 45:8). Just as the tent peg supports the entire tent, so Eliakim will support King Hezekiah and his kingdom by paternal service. To be in charge means to protect our charges.

Divine Works

Psalm 138 is a thanksgiving psalm, that is, a psalm of declarative praise. It announces the radical change in the life of the suppliant who suffered from sickness (v 3). In effect, the psalm praises Yahweh for living up to his name and his covenant loyalty (v 2). "On the day I called, you answered me" captures this sense of divine commitment. Though Yahweh's station is a lofty one, still the Lord responds to the needs of the lowly (v 6). Indeed, God will not abandon the work of God's hands (v 8). Yahweh's abiding fidelity states that to be in charge means to protect our charges.

Matthew combines the scene of Peter's confession (see Mk 8:27-30) with a post-resurrectional appearance of Jesus to this unique disciple (see Jn 21:15-17). Jesus calls Peter blessed because of his perception: "You are the Messiah, the Son of the living God." This perception is rooted in a revelation from Jesus' Father, not in personal research. Thus Jesus confers on Peter the grace of leadership.

Peter's new position is not a purely personal attainment. He is called "rock" because he will provide that dimension of stability for Jesus' Church (see Mt 7:24-27). Against the background of Isaiah 22, "the keys" suggest the power of a prime minister—he will teach the way to the kingdom (see Mt 23:13). The power of binding and loosing conjures up authoritative teaching and disciplinary power (see also Mt 18:18). As leader, Peter must focus on the community of Jesus, not on himself. For Matthew, to be in charge means to protect our charges.

Today's Good News

Our first reaction to power is to think of those in exalted positions who determine the lives of many. While admitting the necessity of the right use of power by the mighty, we should also look to our discharge of authority. Parents, spouses, teachers, and so forth all possess power of one type or another. The haunting question is: Who comes first, the powerful or their charges? Are we more Shebna or Eliakim? Are we intent upon making our power felt or are we concerned with the obligations of that power? Is our use of authority more self-serving or parental? Isaiah of Jerusalem, the psalmist, and Matthew all speak in unison: To be in charge means to protect our charges.

Points for Reflection and Discussion

1. Abuses of power may be the cause of every evil in our world. What kinds of power abuse have you suffered in your life? What kinds of power abuse have you committed?

_____

_____

_____

_____

2. Have you ever felt called (obligated) to be a lone voice in opposition to an abuse of some kind? Did you speak? What happened?

_____

_____

_____

_____

Themes

Authority, Power, Responsibility
  Q8, Places in the Catholic Church
  Q9, Who's Who in the Church
  Q11, Catholic Practices
  Q12, Catholics and Church
  M2, The Laity: Called to Build God's Kingdom
  M3, Your Special Gifts
  M4, Family Life
  M6, Discernment
  M7, Holiness
  M8, Evangelization

Reading 1, Jeremiah 20:7-9

O Lord, you have enticed me, and I was enticed; you have overpowered me, and you have prevailed. I have become a laughingstock all day long; everyone mocks me. For whenever I speak, I must cry out, I must shout, "Violence and destruction!" For the word of the Lord has become for me a reproach and derision all day long. If I say, "I will not mention him, or speak any more in his name," then within me there is something like a burning fire shut up in my bones; I am weary with holding it in, and I cannot.

Psalm 63:1,2-3,4-5,7-8 (NRSV)

Reading 2, Romans 12:1-2

I appeal to you, brothers and sisters, by the mercies of God, to present your bodies as a living sacrifice, holy and acceptable to God, which is your spiritual worship. Do not be conformed to this world, but be transformed by the renewing of your minds, so that you may discern what is the will of God—what is good and acceptable and perfect.

Gospel, Matthew 16:21-27

Jesus began to show his disciples that he must go to Jerusalem and undergo great suffering at the hands of the elders and chief priests and scribes, and be killed, and on the third day be raised. And Peter took him aside and began to rebuke him, saying, "God forbid it, Lord! This must never happen to you." But he turned and said to Peter, "Get behind me, Satan! You are a stumbling block to me; for you are setting your mind not on divine things but on human things."

Then Jesus told his disciples, "If any want to become my followers, let them deny themselves and take up their cross and follow me. For those who want to save their life will lose it, and those who lose their life for my sake will find it. For what will it profit them if they gain the whole world but forfeit their life? Or what will they give in return for their life?

"For the Son of Man is to come with his angels in the glory of his Father, and then he will repay everyone for what has been done."

What Does God Think?

JOHN F. CRAGHAN

What does God think? This question is not often asked in our media, in the surveys of pollsters, or from the platforms of politicians. It is difficult to open up to the demands of a greater reality to say: What does God think?

Today's readings have to do with God's frame of reference. Far from disparaging human investigation, they challenge believers to consider all the alternatives. They suggest that we act in accord with God's will insofar as we can discern it.

Unquenchable Fire

The passage from the Book of Jeremiah is one of the so-called confessions. It is likely that, while they do not necessarily provide biographical information, they do interpret the prophet's career for a later audience. They depict Jeremiah as one who courageously preached God's Word in the late seventh and early sixth century BC. Attentive to that Word, he warned the kings of Judah and its citizens to surrender to the neo-Babylonians rather than resist. His countrymen reacted violently to such warnings.

In this confession Jeremiah vents his anger against Yahweh. Jeremiah fears that God has seduced (see Ex 22:15) and deceived him (see 1 Kgs 22:20-22). His message is only bad news. Hence he has "become a laughingstock" of Judah and Jerusalem. In his frustration, he is tempted to abandon his prophetic career. But the Word of God is "like a burning fire" (see Jer 5:14). Thus he will continue to preach.

Paul exhorts his readers to reflect God's mercy in their relationships (see Rom 11:30-32). "Spiritual worship" implies that they are to let these relationships become a way of praising God. Their offering must reflect Christ's offering, perhaps even unto death. Paul urges the Romans to adopt a way of thinking and acting that goes beyond the world's pragmatic policies: "Do not be conformed to this world, but be transformed by the renewing of your minds." Their task, therefore, is to discern God's will. In other words they must attempt to ask what God thinks.

The Way to Glory

Through the revelation of the Father, Peter perceives that Jesus is the Messiah, the Son of the living God (Mt 16:16). Peter, however, cannot understand Jesus' mission of being a suffering Messiah. For Peter, it makes no sense to say that suffering and death are the way to glory. Like the devil in the temptation account (see Mt 4:1-11), Peter suggests an easier, more manipulative way of carrying out the will of God. Peter thus became an obstacle to that mission. Jesus discloses the falseness of this thinking: "You are setting your mind not on divine things but on human things."

Jesus follows God's standards. To lose oneself for God's sake means to find oneself. To win the entire world but to destroy oneself in doing so is not to turn a profit. To sacrifice oneself now is to assure oneself of more than survival on the Last Day. Peter is slow to understand God's way.

Today's Good News

We are eminently practical people. We seek the advice of physicians, solicit the opinion of lawyers, and search out the counsel of friends. We rightly conclude that this is a perfectly reasonable way to proceed. Without neglecting these and similar sources, today's readings urge us to consider a larger canvas and to see with a greater depth. We are bidden to make God one of our circle of counselors.

The will of God is not always clear. To be sure, God speaks through our friends and professional people. God also speaks through the Christian community. God speaks in and through our consciences. It is a question, therefore, of discerning God's will in its many-splendored presence. Negatively, we are encouraged not to be like Peter in assuming that there is only one way to act—our way. Positively, we are urged to be like Jesus by presuming that God may have a bigger and better way to accomplish the divine plan. It is Jesus, in the company of both Jeremiah and Paul, who would have us ask: What does God think?

Points for Reflection and Discussion

1. We sometimes talk about bearing our cross without giving any thought to what we're really saying. What do you believe is meant by bearing one's cross?

_____

_____

_____

_____

_____

2. Discerning God's will for us is a lifelong process. Reflect on your own processes of discernment throughout the years. If you are willing, share a personal experience of discernment with the group.

_____

_____

_____

_____

_____

Themes

Discernment

    Q1, Journey of Faith

    M1, Conversion: A Lifelong Process

    M3, Your Special Gifts

    M5, Your Prayer Life

    M6, Discernment

    M7, Holinessf

Reading 1, Ezekiel 33:7-9

You, mortal, I have made a sentinel for the house of Israel; whenever you hear a word from my mouth, you shall give them warning from me. If I say to the wicked, "O wicked ones, you shall surely die," and you do not speak to warn the wicked to turn from their ways, the wicked shall die in their iniquity, but their blood I will require at your hand. But if you warn the wicked to turn from their ways, and they do not turn from their ways, the wicked shall die in their iniquity, but you will have saved your life.

Psalm 95:1-2,6-7,7-9 (NRSV)

Reading 2, Romans 13:8-10

Owe no one anything, except to love one another; for the one who loves another has fulfilled the law. The commandments, "You shall not commit adultery; You shall not murder; You shall not steal; You shall not covet"; and any other commandment, are summed up in this word, "Love your neighbor as yourself." Love does no wrong to a neighbor; therefore, love is the fulfilling of the law.

Gospel, Matthew 18:15-20

[Jesus said to his disciples:] "If another member of the church sins against you, go and point out the fault when the two of you are alone. If the member listens to you, you have regained that one. But if you are not listened to, take one or two others along with you, so that every word may be confirmed by the evidence of two or three witnesses. If the member refuses to listen to them, tell it to the church; and if the offender refuses to listen even to the church, let such a one be to you as a Gentile and a tax collector. Truly I tell you, whatever you bind on earth will be bound in heaven, and whatever you loose on earth will be loosed in heaven.

"Again, truly I tell you, if two of you agree on earth about anything you ask, it will be done for you by my Father in heaven. For where two or three are gathered in my name, I am there among them."

People Keeping

JOHN F. CRAGHAN

Although we might at times like to isolate ourselves from community, we are our brother's and sister's keeper. Today's readings paint this picture of believers relating to one another and to their God. The lessons from the Bible do not reduce fellow humans to the categories of "nonexistent" or "obtrusive." They subscribe to a plan of salvation in which we are our brother's and sister's keeper.

In 585 BC, Ezekiel entered upon a new phase in his prophetic career. Instead of being a scolder, as he had been earlier in the book (see 3:26), he became a sentry for God's exiled people. Although Ezekiel clearly recognized individual retribution (see 18; 33:10-20), he also emphasized the interaction of individual and community. In today's passage, he dramatizes that tension.

The task of the sentry is to stay alert and warn the people of the approach of the enemy so that they can take refuge within the city walls. The sentry is essential to the well-being of the community. God made that Ezekiel's area of responsibility. When the prophet became aware of God's course of action, he was to inform the people so that they could be won over. Not to communicate God's decision to the people was to incur guilt for endangering the common good. Ezekiel clearly held that he was his brother's and sister's keeper.

Paul considered the obligation of charity. It is interesting to note that he focused on duties, not rights. Charity is the very center of Christian life. For Paul, love is the fulfillment of the Mosaic law (see also Mk 12:28-34). Paul cited some of the Ten Commandments that deal with inter-human relationships. He subsumed all commandments under the one commandment: "Love your neighbor as yourself." In quoting this text from Leviticus 19:18, Paul (like others) extended its meaning to embrace not only every Israelite but also all Gentile people. By loving our neighbor, we are paying our debt of love. For Paul, there was no doubt that we are our brother's and sister's keepers.

Chapter 18 in the Gospel of Matthew is one of Matthew's five great sermons. In this chapter, he dealt with problems affecting the local Christian community. He brought together independent sayings to focus on those problems.

Matthew did not conceive of Christians as isolated entities. He demonstrated the course of Christian action in community toward sinful members. To begin, there was to be a private correction of the person in question. If this failed, a few more witnesses were called upon to help make the point to the sinner. If this likewise failed, the entire local community was summoned to prevail upon the sinner. If the process was still unsuccessful, the person was excommunicated and God ratified the decision of the community. Verses 19-20 of today's gospel pertain to community action under the rubric of prayer. For Matthew, it was abundantly clear that we are our brother's and sister's keeper.

Today's Good News

How do we react to public news, especially bad news? Do we anesthetize ourselves to become oblivious of hurting people or do we energize ourselves to become involved? Ezekiel would maintain that we have no choice but to participate in the healing of pain.

How do we react to the people we don't like? Do we excommunicate them from our world of concern or do we incorporate them into our arena of responsibility? Paul would hold that we cannot exclude them.

How do we react to sinners? Do we allow them to continue in their sin or do we endeavor to turn their lives around? Matthew would believe that we and other members of the community must reach out to them.

These are but a few examples of our link with one another. They suggest that we must reject the isolated "me and Jesus" approach to God. They demand that we see our relationship to God in our relationship to all God's family. After all, we are our brother's and sister's keeper.

Points for Reflection and Discussion

1. How do you try to live up to your responsibility as "people keeper"?

_____

_____

_____

_____

2. Why do you suppose Jesus says, in today's gospel, that those who refuse to listen to the Church should "be to you as a Gentile and a tax collector"? These terms would translate, for Jesus, into analogies for "sinner." If Jesus came "to save sinners" and we are called to imitate him, doesn't this mean our obligation to and responsibility for these "sinners" increases?

_____

_____

_____

_____

_____

Themes
Community
    Q1, Journey of Faith
    Q12, Catholics and Church
    M2, The Laity: Called to Build God's Kingdom
Love
    Q3, What is the Meaning of the Mass?
    M7, Holiness
    M8, Evangelization
Responsibility
    Q9, Who's Who in the Church
    Q11, Catholic Practices
    M3, Your Special Gifts

Reading 1, Sirach 27:30—28:7

Anger and wrath, these are abominations, yet a sinner holds on to them. The vengeful will face the Lord's vengeance, for he keeps a strict account of their sins. Forgive your neighbor the wrong that is done, and then your sins will be pardoned when you pray.

Does anyone harbor anger against another, and expect healing from the Lord? If one has no mercy toward another like oneself, can one then seek pardon for one's own sins? If a mere mortal harbors wrath, who will make an atoning sacrifice for that one's sins?

Remember the end of your life, and set enmity aside; remember corruption and death, and be true to the commandments. Remember the commandments, and do not be angry with your neighbor; remember the covenant of the Most High, and overlook faults.

Psalm 103:1-2,3-4,9-10,11-12

Reading 2, Romans 14:7-9

We do not live to ourselves, and we do not die to ourselves. If we live, we live to the Lord, and if we die, we die to the Lord; so then, whether we live or whether we die, we are the Lord's. For to this end Christ died and lived again, so that he might be Lord of both the dead and the living.

Gospel, Matthew 18:21-35

Peter came and said to [Jesus], "Lord, if another member of the church sins against me, how often should I forgive? As many as seven times?" Jesus said to him, "Not seven times, but, I tell you, seventy-seven times.

"For this reason the kingdom of heaven may be compared to a king who wished to settle accounts with his slaves. When he began the reckoning, one who owed him ten thousand talents was brought to him; and, as he could not pay, his lord ordered him to be sold, together with his wife and children and all his possessions, and payment to be made. So the slave fell on his knees before him, saying, 'Have patience with me, and I will pay you everything.' And out of pity for him, the lord of that slave released him and forgave him the debt. But that same slave, as he went out, came upon one of his fellow slaves who owed him a hundred denarii; and seizing him by the throat, he said, 'Pay what you owe.' Then his fellow slave fell down and pleaded with him, 'Have patience with me, and I will pay you.' But he refused; then he went and threw him into prison until he would pay the debt. When his fellow slaves saw what had happened, they were greatly distressed, and

they went and reported to their lord all that had taken place. Then his lord summoned him and said to him, 'You wicked slave! I forgave you all that debt because you pleaded with me. Should you not have had mercy on your fellow slave, as I had mercy on you?' And in anger his lord handed him over to be tortured until he would pay his entire debt. So my heavenly Father will also do to every one of you, if you do not forgive your brother or sister from your heart."

Forgiveness

JOHN F. CRAGHAN

People hurt us, injure us, disparage us. Our natural reaction is retaliation. After all, so we reason, an eye for an eye and a tooth for a tooth. Even when we suppress our urge for vengeance, we may resort to a more subtle type of vindictiveness. We may choose not to forgive the guilty party. We thereby retaliate by not communicating pardon.

Today's readings deal with the theme of forgiveness. As used in the Church's liturgy, they suggest God's norm as our own measure of forgiving one another. They demand that we emulate our God's capacity to deal with pain and frustration by forgiving. They challenge us to look beyond ourselves and our hurt to a God who never ceases to say: "I love you and, therefore, I forgive you." Forgive as God forgives!

Around the beginning of the second century BC, Ben Sira compiled a compendium of Israel's wisdom. In this section, especially 28:2-7, he considers the theme of forgiveness. One of his arguments for mutual pardon is the avoidance of God's punishment. To forgive our neighbor is to be assured of forgiveness of our own sins at prayer. On the contrary, to refuse to forgive is to eliminate God's healing from our own failings. Toward the end, the saga proposes two more motives for forgiveness: the thought of death and God's covenant.

Ben Sira parallels the commandments with Yahweh's covenant with Israel. According to the covenant, to be related to God is to be related to one another. The norm for morality is not caprice or personal aggrandizement but the love of a God who makes former slaves Chosen People. In this sense, Ben Sira advocates: Forgive as God forgives.

The Lord is Kind and Merciful

Although the classification of today's psalm is not clear, what is evident is that the author considers the God of Israel as one who responds to pain and rebellion with healing and forgiveness. In verse 3, the psalmist concretely depicts God as one who regularly pardons iniquities. According to verse 9, God is one who refuses to hold grudges. More specifically, according to verse 10, Yahweh is one who rejects human norms for forgiveness: "He does not deal with us according to our sins."

A few lines later, the poet powerfully reveals a God who bypasses human calculations for pardon. God puts the transgressions of Israel as far from the divine self as the east is from the west. Against the background of Israel's worship, this psalm seeks to nurture the community's emulation of Yahweh: Forgive as God forgives.

The gospel is part of Matthew's discourse on church order. It presupposes that there are problems in the community that need attention. Specifically, it considers the issue of whether or not there are limits to forgiveness. Although Peter's offer of the number of times the Christian should forgive appears generous, it is short of Jesus' view of the kingdom. Peter tries to limit the exercise of mutual forgiveness. For Jesus, forgiveness must not only be generous it must also be boundless.

The parable contrasts the huge sum owed by one official and the paltry amount owed by another. It is all too clear that the first official learned absolutely nothing about the obligation of mutual pardon. In the midst of a troubled community, Matthew demands that Christians follow the lead of the king who was moved to pity and forgave the debt. Forgive as God forgives.

Today's Good News

We all recognize that there are times when we must be assertive. Once we acknowledge the need for firmness, however, what model or norm shall we adopt in trying to handle the guilty party? Ben Sira reminds us that the wrongdoer is our brother or sister; hence, vindictiveness is unacceptable. The psalmist calls to mind the fact that the God of Israel rejects human estimates for pardon; therefore, a less than genuine forgiveness is wrong. Jesus teaches that strictures are not part of the kingdom's operation, and that a less than boundless pardon is inadequate. Shall we imitate the king and forgive, or the first official and refuse to forgive? The challenge is always: Forgive as God forgives.

Points for Reflection and Discussion

1. If I repeatedly tell my teenager I don't trust him to keep the house rules curfew, and next Saturday night he comes home late, my tendency is to say, "I told you so," not, "I forgive you." Why? Can it be that forgiveness is radically akin to love, insofar as it is virtually impossible to forgive another if we have not first forgiven ourself for our part in the other's transgression?

_____

_____

_____

_____

2. With forgiveness comes love that borders on unconditional, and with unconditional love comes reconciliation, and with reconciliation comes peace. Reflect on such experiences of forgiveness in your own life. If you feel comfortable with doing so, share one such experience with the group.

_____

_____

_____

_____

_____

Themes

Forgiveness, Reconciliation
    Q1, Journey of Faith
    Q3, What is the Meaning of the Mass?
    Q10, Catholics and Prayer
    Q12, Catholics and Church
    M1, Conversion: A Lifelong Process
    M6, Discernment
    M7, Holiness
    M8, Evangelization

Reading 1, Isaiah 55:6-9

Seek the Lord while he may be found, call upon him while he is near; let the wicked forsake their way, and the unrighteous their thoughts; let them return to the Lord, that he may have mercy on them, and to our God, for he will abundantly pardon. For my thoughts are not your thoughts, nor are your ways my ways, says the Lord. For as the heavens are higher than the earth, so are my ways higher than your ways and my thoughts than your thoughts.

Psalm 145:2-3,8-9,17-18

Reading 2, Philippians 1:20-24,27

Christ will be exalted now as always in my body, whether by life or by death. For to me, living is Christ and dying is gain. If I am to live in the flesh, that means fruitful labor for me; and I do not know which I prefer. I am hard pressed between the two: my desire is to depart and be with Christ, for that is far better; but to remain in the flesh is more necessary for you.

Only, live your life in a manner worthy of the gospel of Christ, so that, whether I come and see you or am absent and hear about you, I will know that you are standing firm in one spirit, striving side by side with one mind for the faith of the gospel.

Gospel, Matthew 20:1-16

[Jesus spoke this parable to his disciples:] "The kingdom of heaven is like a landowner who went out early in the morning to hire laborers for his vineyard. After agreeing with the laborers for the usual daily wage, he sent them into his vineyard. When he went out about nine o'clock, he saw others standing idle in the marketplace; and he said to them, 'You also go into the vineyard, and I will pay you whatever is right.' So they went. When he went out again about noon and about three o'clock, he did the same. And about five o'clock he went out and found others standing around; and he said to them, 'Why are you standing here idle all day?' They said to him, 'Because no one has hired us.' He said to them, 'You also go into the vineyard.' When evening came, the owner of the vineyard said to his manager, 'Call the laborers and give them their pay, beginning with the last and then going to the first.' When those hired about five o'clock came, each of them received the usual daily wage. Now when the first came, they thought they would receive more; but each of them also received the usual daily wage. And when they received it, they grumbled against the landowner, saying, 'These last worked only one hour, and you have made them equal to us who have borne the burden of the day and the scorching heat.' But he replied to one of them, 'Friend, I am doing you no wrong; did you not agree with me for the usual daily wage? Take what belongs to you and go; I choose to give to this last the same as I give to you. Am I not allowed to do what I choose with what belongs to me? Or are you envious because I am generous?' So the last will be first, and the first will be last."

The Generosity of God

JOHN F. CRAGHAN

Usually we think of freedom as the ability to provide for ourselves, to move about at will, to enjoy the good life. It means we are able to pay off all our creditors, receive the proper receipts, and meet all our obligations. Freedom is the condition in which we bask in our self-sufficiency. Secure in this environment, we'd rather not be disturbed by the notion that freedom might mean something different.

Today's readings consider the theme of God's generosity. They reflect a God who cannot and will not be constrained by the human canons of propriety and reasonableness. They reveal a God who chooses to give to the most unlikely and undeserving because that is the nature of God.

The first reading is part of the conclusion of Second Isaiah, who spoke to a despairing audience in Babylon as they doubted whether God could or would do anything to help them (see Is 40:12-31). Isaiah urged the people to repent, to have a change of heart, and to return to Yahweh and God's mysterious plan.

God's Way

Israel was slow to accept God's plan, which is like the distance separating the heavens and the earth. It seemed so unlikely that Yahweh could create something new out of the chaos of exile. It seemed so unbelievable that the depressed could yet break out into song. Isaiah, therefore, had to underline Yahweh's paradoxical ways. God does not respect the human categories of success and failure.

The seemingly artificial composition of Psalm 145 pulls together many of the principal themes of praise of God. Of particular interest in this hymn is the emphasis on God's freedom and compassion. The author demands an appreciation of the mystery of God's freedom (v 3), and indicates the exercise of that freedom without restraint. Yahweh is good and compassionate to all (v 9). This is precisely the affection of a mother ("merciful," v 8) who does not count the cost of generous love. One cannot claim that this God neglects justice (v 17). This is a God who welcomes everyone (v 18). Situated against the ups and downs of Israel's history, the psalm praises Yahweh, who shows concretely that to be free is to give surprises.

Jesus' original parable appears to have included only verses 1-13. This embraced the hiring of the five groups (1-7) and the paying of the same wage to each group, starting with the last (8-13). Verses 14-16 were perhaps the work of Matthew himself. He reminded his audience that God is free to reward merely on the basis of God's own goodness.

Today's Good News

Is it sufficient to accept God's free giving of surprises as a divine quality, or is this divine paradox a call to action directed to all believers? Our biblical passages and Christian Tradition suggest that the second position is the correct one. This demands that we put aside our checklist of "obligations to be met" and focus on those who seem to have no demand on our generosity, our compassion, and our love. Do we dare to be generous, compassionate, and loving because God is and we are the children of God? These passages conjure up the possibility of making a list of those who have the remotest claim on our freedom. The actual execution of such a list would certainly show that to be free is to give surprises.

Points for Reflection and Discussion

1. Does today's gospel bring feelings of discomfort and/or confusion within you? To your mind, is there a question of justice in its resolution? What of the "equal pay for equal work" concept?

_____

_____

_____

_____

2. Have you ever received recompense that you believe you hadn't earned? If so, how did you react?

_____

_____

_____

_____

Themes
Kingdom of God
    Q2, What Do Catholics Believe?
    Q4, The Bible
    Q12, Catholics and Church
    M2, The Laity: Called to Build God's Kingdom
    M8, Evangelization

Reading 1, Ezekiel 18:25-28

You say, "The way of the Lord is unfair." Hear now, O house of Israel: Is my way unfair? Is it not your ways that are unfair?

When the righteous turn away from their righteousness and commit iniquity, they shall die for it; for the iniquity that they have committed they shall die.

Again, when the wicked turn away from the wickedness they have committed and do what is lawful and right, they shall save their life. Because they considered and turned away from all the transgressions that they had committed, they shall surely live; they shall not die.

Psalm 25:4-5,6-7,8-9

Reading 2, Philippians 2:1-11

If there is any encouragement in Christ, any consolation from love, any sharing in the Spirit, any compassion and sympathy, make my joy complete: be of the same mind, having the same love, being in full accord and of one mind. Do nothing from selfish ambition or conceit, but in humility regard others as better than yourselves. Let each of you look not to your own interests, but to the interests of others.

Let the same mind be in you that was in Christ Jesus, who, though he was in the form of God, did not regard equality with God as something to be exploited, but emptied himself, taking the form of a slave, being born in human likeness. And being found in human form, he humbled himself and became obedient to the point of death—even death on a cross.

Therefore God also highly exalted him and gave him the name that is above every name, so that at the name of Jesus every knee should bend, in heaven and on earth and under the earth, and every tongue should confess that Jesus Christ is Lord, to the glory of God the Father.

Gospel, Matthew 21:28-32

[Jesus said to the chief priests and elders of the people:] "What do you think? A man had two sons; he went to the first and said, 'Son, go and work in the vineyard today.' He answered, 'I will not'; but later he changed his mind and went. The father went to the second and said the same; and he answered, 'I go, sir'; but he did not go. Which of the two did the will of his father?" They said, "The first."

Jesus said to them, "Truly I tell you, the tax collectors and the prostitutes are going into the kingdom of God ahead of you. For John came to you in the way of righteousness and you did not believe him, but the tax collectors and the prostitutes believed him; and even after you saw it, you did not change your minds and believe him."

Following Through

JOHN F. CRAGHAN

Most of us have the best of intentions, but how often we fail to keep them. We may be determined to do our job to the best of our ability, but actual job performance may indicate something less. We may vow to love and cherish our spouse and family, but daily living may reveal a bit of selfishness. We may agree to remove prejudice from our lives, but regular discrimination may reflect only halfhearted seriousness.

Today's readings speak of the strain between intention and performance. They offer examples of those who take their pledges seriously and those who do not. They challenge the believer to take a stance: Say and do or do not say at all. They clearly teach that doing is the name of the game.

In the aftermath of the destruction of Jerusalem, around 585 BC, Ezekiel faced a despondent exiled community. They argued that they were not personally responsible for the catastrophe. They maintained that they were merely incurring the guilt of their forefathers' sins. Hence the allegation: "The way of the Lord is unfair." To this the prophet replied that the present generation had also been unfaithful.

Walking the Walk

Paul reminds the Philippians that Christ is the model of community service and love. Paul incorporates a Jewish-Christian hymn in his letter (with some additions). Though Jesus was God's perfect image ("form of God") and should not have been subjected to death and corruption (see Wis 2:23), he chose to do otherwise. He accepted a life of suffering ("emptied himself"). He dismissed his privileges by experiencing death (here Paul adds: "even death on a cross"). But God super-exalted him and gave him the title ("Lord") and authority formerly reserved to God alone (see Is 45:23).

Jesus is authentic humanity. It is, then, the self-emptying of Jesus that Paul offers as an example to the Philippians. Positively, this means unity in spirit and ideals; negatively, it means the avoidance of rivalry and deceit. To look to the interests of others is the model Paul offers.

Talking the Talk

Verses 28-30 of the gospel, which recount the responses of the two sons, are Jesus' original parable. These lines deal with the human predicament of saying one thing but doing another. With the addition of verses 31-32, Matthew directs his attention to the Jewish leadership. The tax collectors and the prostitutes had reacted positively to the message of John the Baptist; the Jewish leaders had not. The talkers but non-doers were the Jewish community while the non-talkers but doers were the Gentiles.

The tension between saying and doing is a favorite theme in Matthew. It is not enough to cry "Lord, Lord"; one must also do the will of Jesus' Father (7:21-23). Jesus' brother and sister and mother are those who do the will of his Father (12:50; see also 23:4-5). For Matthew, viable membership in the Christian community demands much more than empty promises.

Today's Good News

Modern believers are called upon to discover those areas wherein they promised a specific course of action: marriage vows, business contracts, oaths of office, and so forth. We know when we are keeping to our word in these very obvious matters.

But other external actions should also be considered—the sign of peace at Mass is an example. How does our sign of peace motivate us upon leaving the church? Do we offer that person the right of way and the courtesy of the road?

Or consider the Pledge of Allegiance, which includes our promotion of "liberty and justice for all." How do we react to the news of discrimination in our community? Do we practice justice, no matter what the race, creed, or color of our neighbor?

Our everyday handshake expresses a regard and concern for others. How do we respond to gossip or slander about those persons? Do we focus on the good in those people because we have already extended the sign of friendship? Doing is the name of the game.

Points for Reflection and Discussion

1. In today's gospel story, Jesus might well have said those famous words, "The road to hell is paved with good intentions." Have there been times in your life when you easily related to the parable's first son? To the second son?

_____

_____

_____

_____

2. What are you doing to stand behind the words "with liberty and justice for all"? Do you merely talk the talk, or are you also walking the walk?

_____

_____

_____

_____

_____

Themes
Humility
    Q6, The Saints
    M7, Holiness
Justice
    Q12, Catholics and Church
    M2, The Laity: Called to Build God's Kingdom
    M8, Evangelization

Reading 1, Isaiah 5:1-7

Let me sing for my beloved my love-song concerning his vineyard: My beloved had a vineyard on a very fertile hill. He dug it and cleared it of stones, and planted it with choice vines; he built a watchtower in the midst of it, and hewed out a wine vat in it; he expected it to yield grapes, but it yielded wild grapes.

And now, inhabitants of Jerusalem and people of Judah, judge between me and my vineyard. What more was there to do for my vineyard that I have not done in it? When I expected it to yield grapes, why did it yield wild grapes?

And now I will tell you what I will do to my vineyard. I will remove its hedge, and it shall be devoured; I will break down its wall, and it shall be trampled down. I will make it a waste; it shall not be pruned or hoed, and it shall be overgrown with briers and thorns; I will also command the clouds that they rain no rain upon it. For the vineyard of the Lord of hosts is the house of Israel, and the people of Judah are his pleasant planting; he expected justice, but saw bloodshed; righteousness, but heard a cry!

Psalm 80:8,11,12-13,14-15,18-19 (NRSV)

Reading 2, Philippians 4:6-9

Do not worry about anything, but in everything by prayer and supplication with thanksgiving let your requests be made known to God. And the peace of God, which surpasses all understanding, will guard your hearts and your minds in Christ Jesus. Finally, beloved, whatever is true, whatever is honorable, whatever is just, whatever is pure, whatever is pleasing, whatever is commendable, if there is any excellence and if there is anything worthy of praise, think about these things. Keep on doing the things that you have learned and received and heard and seen in me, and the God of peace will be with you.

Gospel, Matthew 21:33-43

[Jesus said to the chief priests and elders of the people:] "Listen to another parable. There was a landowner who planted a vineyard, put a fence around it, dug a wine press in it, and built a watchtower. Then he leased it to tenants and went to another country. When the harvest time had come, he sent his slaves to the tenants to collect his produce. But the tenants seized his slaves and beat one, killed another, and stoned another. Again he sent other slaves, more than the first; and they treated them in the same way. Finally he sent his son to them, saying, 'They will respect my son.' But when the tenants saw the son, they said to themselves, 'This is the heir; come, let us kill him and get his inheritance.' So they seized him, threw him out of the vineyard, and killed him. Now when the owner of the vineyard comes, what will he do to those tenants?"

They said to him, "He will put those wretches to a miserable death, and lease the vineyard to other tenants who will give him the produce at the harvest time."

Jesus said to them, "Have you never read in the scriptures: 'The stone that the builders rejected has become the cornerstone; this was the Lord's doing, and it is amazing in our eyes'? Therefore I tell you, the kingdom of God will be taken away from you and given to a people that produces the fruits of the kingdom."

Obligations of the Chosen

JOHN F. CRAGHAN

"Nobility obliges" is an expression that we usually associate with royalty and crowned heads of state. Such special people must behave according to their high station. Their rank imposes constraints on their public lifestyles so that they must do "the right thing." Scandal or less than royal comportment flies in the face of their exalted positions.

Today's readings consider the moral implications of being God's people. Although the first reading and gospel offer negative examples of that status, they, along with the second reading, stress the fact that the call to high station must have repercussions in daily life. They point up the fact that believers must reflect in their lives the uniqueness of the God who calls them.

The vineyard is a traditional symbol of God's people (see, for example, Is 27:2-6; Ez 15:1-8). Posing as a ballad singer at the vintage festival, Isaiah of Jerusalem employed this symbol to get the audience to examine their consciences. He sang of his friend's unstinting efforts to make the vineyard productive, yet despite all the work, the vineyard produced nothing and needed to be destroyed.

The prophet then turned the tables on his audience. They were the vineyard, the chosen house of Israel. Although they were the special objects of God's love and attention, they had not lived out their high calling. In a Hebrew play on words, God looked for "justice" and "righteousness," but found instead only "bloodshed" and the "cry" of the oppressed poor. God's people condemned themselves for failing to meet the requirements of their noble calling.

Implications of the Faith

For Paul, faith in Christ Jesus has a radical impact on Christian living. To be called to union with Christ is to be removed from slavery to sin. Baptism implies that the Christian shares in the death and Resurrection of Christ. Such a participation means living an appropriate lifestyle (see also Rom 6:1-14).

In this section of Philippians, Paul urges the practice of virtues admired by the pagan philosophers (pursuit of what is honest, pure, admirable, and so forth). Paul, however, enfleshes these qualities by referring to himself: "Keep on doing the things that you have learned and received and heard and seen in me." To imitate Paul is to imitate Christ (see also 1 Cor 11:1), and to imitate Christ is to live out the consequences of the call to share in the death and Resurrection of Christ.

In the original gospel parable, Jesus told the story of Galilean tenant farmers who did not hand over a proper share of the harvest to the landowner. Rather, these farmers took advantage of the third emissary (the son, the heir) and killed him. Christian tradition probably supplied the reference to the vineyard in verse 33 and the question in verse 40. It also interpreted the son as Jesus whose disconcerting death gave way to exaltation (v 42 refers to Ps 118:22-23).

Matthew shapes the parable into a judgment on the people of Israel, not just its leaders (contrast Mk 12:1-10). Matthew has the tenant farmers drag the son outside the vineyard to kill him (see Mk 12:8). This is an obvious reference to the crucifixion. Finally, Matthew adds the statement that the kingdom will be taken away and given to others, namely, the Gentiles. It is this mixed group of Jews and Gentiles who will live out their high calling, and they will "produce at the harvest time."

Today's Good News

In baptism, the Christian shares in the kingship of Jesus. Baptism is the call to a royal way of life. Fundamentally, this sharing has little to do with special uniforms or other external trappings of nobility. It has everything to do with the daily living out of the gospel. Baptism is the inauguration of the Christian journey to benefit others by example and involvement.

Justice in business dealings means that we take our call seriously. Charity in our relationships shows that we respect our station properly. Caring for the downtrodden proves that we honor our status appropriately. Time spent with those who are hurting indicates that we treat our vocation respectfully. In these and similar instances, we attempt to enflesh the consequences of "nobility obliges."

Points for Reflection and Discussion

1. What obligations are attached to you, personally, calling yourself "Christian"?

_____

_____

_____

_____

2. Read another gospel vineyard story, Jn 15:1-16, and compare the two gospels. What conclusions do you draw from your reading and reflection?

_____

_____

_____

_____

_____

Themes

Discipleship, Responsible Stewardship
  Q1, Journey of Faith
  Q6, The Saints
  Q7, Mary
  Q12, Catholics and Church
  M1, Conversion: A Lifelong Process
  M2, The Laity: Called to Build God's Kingdom
  M3, Your Special Gifts
  M7, Holiness
  M8, Evangelization

Reading 1, Isaiah 25:6-10

On this mountain the Lord of hosts will make for all peoples a feast of rich food, a feast of well-aged wines, of rich food filled with marrow, of well-aged wines strained clear. And he will destroy on this mountain the shroud that is cast over all peoples, the sheet that is spread over all nations; he will swallow up death forever. Then the Lord God will wipe away the tears from all faces, and the disgrace of his people he will take away from all the earth, for the Lord has spoken.

It will be said on that day, Lo, this is our God; we have waited for him, so that he might save us. This is the Lord for whom we have waited; let us be glad and rejoice in his salvation. For the hand of the Lord will rest on this mountain.

Psalm 23:1-3,3-4,5,6

Reading 2, Philippians 4:12-14,19-20

I know what it is to have little, and I know what it is to have plenty. In any and all circumstances I have learned the secret of being well-fed and of going hungry, of having plenty and of being in need. I can do all things through him who strengthens me.

In any case, it was kind of you to share my distress. And my God will fully satisfy every need of yours according to his riches in glory in Christ Jesus. To our God and Father be glory forever and ever. Amen.

Gospel, Matthew 22:1-14

Once more Jesus spoke to [the chief priests and elders of the people] in parables, saying: "The kingdom of heaven may be compared to a king who gave a wedding banquet for his son. He sent his slaves to call those who had been invited to the wedding banquet, but they would not come. Again he sent other slaves, saying, 'Tell those who have been invited: Look, I have prepared my dinner, my oxen and my fat calves have been slaughtered, and everything is ready; come to the wedding banquet.' But they made light of it and went away, one to his farm, another to his business, while the rest seized his slaves, mistreated them, and killed them. The king was enraged. He sent his troops, destroyed those murderers, and burned their city. Then he said to his slaves, 'The wedding is ready, but those invited were not worthy. Go therefore into the main streets, and invite everyone you find to the wedding banquet.' Those slaves went out into the streets and gathered all whom they found, both good and bad; so the wedding hall was filled with guests.

"But when the king came in to see the guests, he noticed a man there who was not wearing a wedding robe, and he said to him, 'Friend, how did you get in here without a wedding robe?' And he was speechless. Then the king said to the attendants, 'Bind him hand and foot, and throw him into the outer darkness, where there will be weeping and gnashing of teeth.' For many are called, but few are chosen."

The Heavenly Banquet

JOHN F. CRAGHAN

How often we insulate and isolate ourselves from others. We choose not to become involved. We erect barriers that keep others at a safe distance. Even our God is sometimes viewed as we ourselves act, namely, aloof, unconcerned, apathetic.

Today's readings deal with banquets/parties. They speak of a God who adamantly refuses to be left alone. This God nourishes the community with the grace of divine presence. This God reaches out to seat the chosen people at table so that union becomes communion. This God loves people to such an extent that only banquets/parties will do. In turn, those who believe in this God must do the same—throw parties.

Written perhaps in the fourth century BC, the passage from Isaiah reflects a time of confusion. God's people were subject to political upheavals. Against this background, the author depicts Yahweh as a participant in the topsy-turvy world of Israel. What would be more appropriate than to express this participation by means of a banquet? To share the grief of the community, Yahweh resorts to sharing his table.

The sumptuous repast marks the end of all suffering and pain. Yahweh defeats death and mourning, symbolized by "shroud" and "sheet." Yahweh wipes away tears and disgrace. The invited guests sing that their God has indeed saved them.

The well-known Twenty-third Psalm contains two images: shepherd and host. Set against the background of the desert, Yahweh pastures and waters the sheep, and defends them against wild animals. Yahweh offers safety from all the dangers of this hostile environment. This is a committed God.

Developing the host image, the psalmist presents Yahweh performing all the amenities. Hence Yahweh spreads the table and anoints the guest. Significantly, these gestures of hospitality occur "in the presence of my enemies" (v 5). This may suggest that the enemies of the guest register utter bewilderment at the change of fortune: from harassment to banquet.

The Invitation

In the gospel, Jesus portrays his Father as a king who gives a wedding banquet for his son. Matthew develops the parable to create a panorama of God's involvement with the people. The first group of servants who urge the invited to come to the banquet (v 3) are the prophets, the second group (v 4) are Christian missionaries to the Jews. Since Israel rejects these emissaries, the king must resort to burning their city (probably the destruction of Jerusalem in AD 70).

So who is worthy to attend the final heavenly banquet? "Go...into the main streets, and invite everyone you find...". The Gentiles are invited into the banquet. In this way, Matthew demonstrates that God does not reject this mixed group of "both good and bad." The God of the Jews is also the God of the Gentiles and, hence, extends the invitation of the Good News to them as well. The royal wedding feast that symbolizes God's union with God's communion is open to everyone.

Today's Good News

Parties are an apt image for Christian involvement. They force us to think of relationships. They move us to create an atmosphere of festivity. They remind us of the centrality of community.

But whom shall we invite to our parties? We generally think of all those "nice" people who will return the favor by inviting us to their homes. Today's liturgy suggests that we expand our vision and look especially to those who are hurting. Will we attempt to wipe away tears, as Yahweh does in the first reading? Will we try to offer protection to the harassed, as Yahweh does in the responsorial psalm? Will we seek to provide hope for apparent outsiders, as the king does in the gospel? We know people who belong in these categories. The challenge is to act upon this awareness and send out the invitations.

Points for Reflection and Discussion

1. Three different kinds of banquets are presented to us today. The first (Isaiah) is atop a mountain, overlooking all the world in glory and majesty. The second (psalmist) is in a pasture, an oasis of quiet and peace within the dark valley of life's toil and pain. The third (gospel) is at a wedding, lavish and by invitation only. How do you envision the heavenly banquet?

_____

_____

_____

_____

2. Paul is immersed in community, "content with whatever I have," whether "well-fed [or] going hungry," and he "rejoice[s] in the Lord greatly" because the community is "concerned for" him. Could this be the heavenly banquet?

_____

_____

_____

_____

Themes
Call
    Q1, Journey of Faith
    Q12, Catholics and Church
    M1, Conversion: A Lifelong Process
    M2, The Laity: Called to Build God's Kingdom
    M8, Evangelization
Celebration
    Q3, What is the Meaning of the Mass?
Eternity
    Q2, What Do Catholics Believe?

Reading 1, Isaiah 45:1,4-6

Thus says the Lord to his anointed, to Cyrus, whose right hand I have grasped to subdue nations before him and strip kings of their robes, to open doors before him— and the gates shall not be closed: For the sake of my servant Jacob, and Israel my chosen, I call you by your name, I surname you, though you do not know me. I am the Lord, and there is no other; besides me there is no god. I arm you, though you do not know me, so that they may know, from the rising of the sun and from the west, that there is no one besides me; I am the Lord, and there is no other.

Psalm 96:1,3,4-5,7-8,9-10

Reading 2, 1 Thessalonians 1:1-5

Paul, Silvanus, and Timothy, To the church of the Thessalonians in God the Father and the Lord Jesus Christ: Grace to you and peace.

We always give thanks to God for all of you and mention you in our prayers, constantly remembering before our God and Father your work of faith and labor of love and steadfastness of hope in our Lord Jesus Christ. For we know, brothers and sisters beloved by God, that he has chosen you, because our message of the gospel came to you not in word only, but also in power and in the Holy Spirit and with full conviction; just as you know what kind of persons we proved to be among you for your sake.

Gospel, Matthew 22:15-21

The Pharisees went and plotted to entrap [Jesus] in what he said. So they sent their disciples to him, along with the Herodians, saying, "Teacher, we know that you are sincere, and teach the way of God in accordance with truth, and show deference to no one; for you do not regard people with partiality. Tell us, then, what you think. Is it lawful to pay taxes to the emperor, or not?"

But Jesus, aware of their malice, said, "Why are you putting me to the test, you hypocrites? Show me the coin used for the tax." And they brought him a denarius. Then he said to them, "Whose head is this, and whose title?" They answered, "The emperor's."

Then he said to them, "Give therefore to the emperor the things that are the emperor's, and to God the things that are God's."

The Balance Sheet

JOHN F. CRAGHAN

Don't cheat—balance your loyalties. We live in a very complex world, wherein we owe allegiance to different individuals and groups as well as to ourselves. We belong to families, local churches, civic groups, governments, and so forth. The delicate art of living consists in aligning our priorities and then giving each the proper degree of attention. From experience, we know that problems arise when we do not hold our loyalties in reasonable tension.

Today's readings deal with the reality of loyalties. While they admit that life is gray, not black and white, they also contend that the believer must seek to harmonize the varied facets of life. Without providing any mathematical equation, they urge the believer to take a long hard look at this complex world and make honest assessments. They maintain: Don't cheat—balance your loyalties.

It was only a matter of time before the Persian king, Cyrus the Great, would conquer Babylon and thus claim the allegiance of Israel's exiles. Realizing this change in world rule, Second Isaiah offered his audience an interpretation of this historical event that would impact their loyalties. In a daring move, Isaiah spoke of this pagan king as God's messiah, or "anointed." He showed that, by grasping his hand, Yahweh recognized Cyrus as the legitimate ruler of his people.

Prioritize

Second Isaiah also struck a balance. Yahweh was overlord and Cyrus was his servant. Israel had to recognize that Yahweh was the only God—here there could be no compromise. Allegiance to Cyrus must not confuse the fact that Yahweh used the monarch to advance Israel's future. Though Cyrus demanded loyalty from all his subjects, Israel had to always recall Yahweh's words: "I am the Lord, and there is no other." Don't cheat—balance your loyalties.

The psalm is a hymn, possibly an enthronement psalm, extolling Yahweh's kingship in Jerusalem. Implicitly at least, this psalm is an expression of divine priority. While the gods of the pagans exist, they are really nothing and, hence, cannot claim the loyalty of Israel. While the pagans worship their gods, they must also acknowledge the kingship of Yahweh. Indeed Israel must "say among the nations, 'The Lord is king!' "

Israel continued to pray this psalm when the nation's own monarchy was gone and the people were subject to foreign rulers. In such a setting, the psalm witnesses to Israel's awareness of the rights of their God. When tempted to compromise, the singers of this psalm were bidden to recognize the demands of their King. In this sense the psalm teaches: Don't cheat—balance your loyalties.

Matthew notes the duplicity of the Pharisees and the Herodians over the matter of tribute to the emperor. Their plan is to foil Jesus, not to seek after the truth. Hence, though they address Jesus as teacher (a title Matthew reserves for non-believers in Jesus), they do not intend to become his disciples. Entrapment is obviously their purpose, and the question of tribute to the hated Roman oppressors seems well suited to that purpose.

Jesus does not enter into a detailed analysis of the percentages of loyalty due to God and Caesar. Instead, to the embarrassment of his questioners, he acknowledges the principle of loyalty to both. If he had denied tribute to Caesar, he would have appeared as a revolutionary. If he had simply accepted tribute to Caesar, he would have seemed disloyal to devout Jews and the popular crowds. In the end, the would-be foilers learn this timely lesson: Don't cheat—balance your loyalties.

Today's Good News

Home and work place significant demands on the believer. Today's liturgy suggests that the believer must assess the loyalty due to family and to career. If family concerns cease to be important and job interests absorb most of the time and energy, the moment has arrived to heed: Don't cheat—balance your loyalties.

Prayer and socializing also exact loyalties from the believer. Today's liturgy implies that the believer must confront the allegiance due to God and friends. If private and communal communication with God begins to wane and social activities command ever-increasing time and commitment, the hour has come to hear: Don't cheat—balance your loyalties.

Points for Reflection and Discussion

1. What do today's readings say to you regarding the place of government and politics in the public lives of Christians? Are non-violent protests against non-Christian policies in order? What about government lobbying?

_____

_____

_____

_____

2. What role(s) should you play in politics? What roles(s) should clergy and religious play? Why?

_____

_____

_____

_____

Themes

Church and State
  Q8, Places in the Catholic Church
Loyalty
  Q9, Who's Who in the Church
  M8, Evangelization
Priorities
  M6, Discernment

Reading 1, Exodus 22:21-27 (NRSV)

[The Lord said:] "You shall not wrong or oppress a resident alien, for you were aliens in the land of Egypt. You shall not abuse any widow or orphan. If you do abuse them, when they cry out to me, I will surely heed their cry; my wrath will burn, and I will kill you with the sword, and your wives shall become widows and your children orphans.

"If you lend money to my people, to the poor among you, you shall not deal with them as a creditor; you shall not exact interest from them. If you take your neighbor's cloak in pawn, you shall restore it before the sun goes down; for it may be your neighbor's only clothing to use as cover; in what else shall that person sleep? And if your neighbor cries out to me, I will listen, for I am compassionate."

Psalm 18:1-2,3,6,46,50 (NRSV)

Reading 2, 1 Thessalonians 1:5-10

You know what kind of persons we proved to be among you for your sake. And you became imitators of us and of the Lord, for in spite of persecution you received the word with joy inspired by the Holy Spirit, so that you became an example to all the believers in Macedonia and in Achaia. For the word of the Lord has sounded forth from you not only in Macedonia and Achaia, but in every place your faith in God has become known, so that we have no need to speak about it. For the people of those regions report about us what kind of welcome we had among you, and how you turned to God from idols, to serve a living and true God, and to wait for his Son from heaven, whom he raised from the dead—Jesus, who rescues us from the wrath that is coming.

Gospel, Matthew 22:34-40

When the Pharisees heard that [Jesus] had silenced the Sadducees, they gathered together, and one of them, a lawyer, asked him a question to test him. "Teacher, which commandment in the law is the greatest?"

He said to him, " 'You shall love the Lord your God with all your heart, and with all your soul, and with all your mind.' This is the greatest and first commandment. And a second is like it: 'You shall love your neighbor as yourself.' On these two commandments hang all the law and the prophets."

Life in Christ

JOHN F. CRAGHAN

Christian life is a triangle: God, others, and self. We might prefer to think that if we lead a good life, if we take time to love our God and ourselves, we have done our duty. The community often feels like a deliberately contrived plot to detract us from honoring God and ourselves. It is difficult to demolish this warped vision and acknowledge Christian life as triangular: God, others, and self.

Today's readings emphasize this triangle. They see neighbors, not as necessary evils but as indispensable partners in our common enterprise of loving God. In a sense, they demand that we seek to uncover our God in the problems and pains of others. Here there is no *either* God *or* neighbor; there is only *both* God *and* neighbor.

The first reading is a selection from the Covenant Code (Ex 20:22—23:19). It is part of God's communication to Israel on Mount Sinai, which emphasized the legal obligations of the covenant people. This passage exemplifies incontestable laws; thus it has Yahweh speaking directly to the people and confronting them personally about community duties.

The Code of the Covenant

Yahweh insists that to honor one's neighbor is to honor God. To make the point, the text speaks about welfare cases (widows, orphans, the poor) and those lacking full rights of citizenship (aliens). One should not wrong the widow or orphan; otherwise Yahweh will take immediate action. One should return the cloak of the poor before sunset; otherwise Yahweh will surely redress the evil. One should not molest or oppress the alien, for Israel experienced this evil as an alien in Egypt.

First Thessalonians is the first writing of the New Testament (c AD 50). In today's thanksgiving, Paul describes the interaction of the Christian missionaries and the former Greek pagans. He remarks that the missionaries acted on behalf of the Thessalonians when they shared the gospel message with them. In turn, this community imitated Paul and his companions despite significant obstacles. Specifically, the Thessalonians left their dead idols and turned to the living God.

Paul notes another dimension of this interaction. In imitating the missionaries, the Thessalonians became a model to all Greece. The Thessalonians, in believing the Good News, shared a relationship not only with God but also with the community.

Out of the 248 "thou shalt's" and the 365 "thou shalt not's" that comprised the commandments in the Torah, Jesus selected just two to answer his inquisitor in today's gospel: love of God (Dt 6:4-5) and love of neighbor (Lv 19:18). Jesus acknowledged that these commandments offer the proper spirit, which should regulate all the other laws.

Unlike his source (Mk 12:30-31), who simply states the two commandments, Matthew remarks that the first and greatest commandment is like the second. In addition, Matthew observes that these two commandments are a basic summary of all the Scriptures ("all the law and the prophets"). Although Matthew sees Jesus as the fulfillment of the Law (see 5:17-49), love of neighbor is vital (see 5:43-48). Indeed, one cannot love God without loving one's neighbor.

Today's Good News

Our God speaks to us through the needs of others. If Christian life is indeed triangular, the hurts in our community have a claim on our time and energy. The oppressed cry out to us as dramatically as they did in Moses' time. The despairing call upon us as realistically as Jesus called upon the hurting people of ancient Galilee. Only the times and the places have been changed—the needs are as real and painful as ever.

We are urged not to disparage widows and orphans, the poor and the homeless, the immigrants and the minorities—but to respect them as our sisters and brothers in Christ. We are asked not to pity them, but to enable them to lead a truly human life. We are bidden not to laugh at them, but to help them to laugh again. The only adequate, the only incontestable reason for our involvement is that Christian life is a triangle: God, others, and self. We're all in this together.

Points for Reflection and Discussion

1. Who are your neighbors? What are you doing for your neighbors? What would you be doing for your neighbors if you loved them "with all your heart, and with all your soul, and with all your mind"?

_____

_____

_____

_____

2. Have you ever been (or ever felt like you were) an alien in a foreign land? How did you feel? How did you react to kindness from strangers?

_____

_____

_____

_____

Themes
Commandments, Community, Love
   Q1, Journey of Faith
   Q3, What is the Meaning of the Mass?
   Q11, Catholic Practices
   Q12, Catholics and Church
   M2, The Laity: Called to Build God's Kingdom
   M3, Your Special Gifts
   M8, Evangelization

Reading 1, Malachi 1:14;2:2,8-10

"I am a great King," says the Lord of hosts, "and my name is reverenced among the nations. If you will not lay it to heart to give glory to my name," says the Lord of hosts, "then I will send the curse on you and I will curse your blessings; indeed I have already cursed them, because you do not lay it to heart. But you have turned aside from the way; you have caused many to stumble by your instruction; you have corrupted the covenant of Levi," says the Lord of hosts, "and so I make you despised and abased before all the people, inasmuch as you have not kept my ways but have shown partiality in your instruction."

Have we not all one father? Has not one God created us? Why then are we faithless to one another, profaning the covenant of our ancestors?

Psalm 131:1,2,3

Reading 2, 1 Thessalonians 2:7-9,13

We were gentle among you, like a nurse tenderly caring for her own children. So deeply do we care for you that we are determined to share with you not only the gospel of God but also our own selves, because you have become very dear to us. You remember our labor and toil, brothers and sisters; we worked night and day, so that we might not burden any of you while we proclaimed to you the gospel of God.

We also constantly give thanks to God for this, that when you received the word of God that you heard from us, you accepted it not as a human word but as what it really is, God's word, which is also at work in you believers.

Gospel, Matthew 23:1-12

Jesus said to the crowds and to his disciples, "The scribes and the Pharisees sit on Moses' seat; therefore, do whatever they teach you and follow it; but do not do as they do, for they do not practice what they teach. They tie up heavy burdens, hard to bear, and lay them on the shoulders of others; but they themselves are unwilling to lift a finger to move them. They do all their deeds to be seen by others; for they make their phylacteries broad and their fringes long. They love to have the place of honor at banquets and the best seats in the synagogues, and to be greeted with respect in the marketplaces, and to have people call them rabbi. But you are not to be called rabbi, for you have one teacher, and you are all students. And call no one your father on earth, for you have one Father—the one in heaven. Nor are you to be called instructors, for you have one instructor, the Messiah. The greatest among you will be your servant. All who exalt themselves will be humbled, and all who humble themselves will be exalted."

Profaning the Covenant

ELSIE HAINZ MCGRATH

The indictment that God hands down in the first reading is directed to the priests of that day (see 2:1, omitted from the lectionary reading). The indictment that Jesus hands down in the gospel is directed to the rabbis of that day. And we lean back in our pews and excuse ourselves—breath a sigh of relief, think we're off the hook. We may even become haughty and proud, denigrating those things we don't like to hear as irrelevant to *our* lives. And we have Scripture to back us up; we can proof-text, and justify turning deaf ears on the priests of our day. But the indictment stands—and a closer reading confirms that it is directed to *all* of us.

Malachi may very well not have been the proper name of the prophet we hear from today, because Malachi means "my messenger." It has also been difficult to accurately ascertain when Malachi prophesied. In short, we know nothing definitively about Malachi's life and times.

We do know, however, that this prophet recognized Temple abuses for what they were and did not excuse the faithful from *their* Temple obligations just because the priests did not practice what they preached. "Have we not all one father?" asks the prophet. "Has not one God created us?" This indictment is directed to the people, who are "profaning the covenant of our ancestors"—the "covenant of Levi," which Yahweh told the priests they had "corrupted" (see Jer 33:20-21; Lv 10:10-11).

"The scribes and the Pharisees sit in Moses' chair," Jesus told his followers, centuries after Malachi's admonishment. That makes them responsible for teaching the covenant of Levi, just as the Temple priests were in the days of Malachi. "Therefore, do whatever they teach you...but do not do as they do." These teachers of the covenant "do not practice what they teach." They expect others to bear all the burdens of life, while they flaunt their positions and exaggerate their self-importance. Jesus makes clear the ultimate reality: "All who exalt themselves will be humbled, and all who humble themselves will be exalted."

The Gospel of God

According to the Gospel of Matthew, after Jesus had chastised those who "do not practice what they teach," he said to the people: "You are not to be called rabbi....And call no one your father on earth....Nor are you to be called instructors." All these directives were explained analogously: There is only one Teacher (rabbi), one God (father), one instructor (Messiah). "The greatest among you will be your servant," the one who, according to the

Gospel of John, taught by example when he washed the feet of his students.

Today's psalmody appears to correct the excesses of the priests in the first reading. The psalmist is humble of heart (v 1), soulfully innocent (v 2), and puts all hope in the Lord (v 3). In like manner, Paul's example in the second reading corrects the excesses of the teachers in the gospel. Paul is gentle with those he teaches, cares for them, and works "night and day" in order not to burden them. Paul's letter is gracious to the Thessalonians and grateful to God, because his teaching was received "as what it really is, God's word," which continued to work in those who received it.

Today's Good News

How literally are we to take the Bible's stories? What did Jesus mean in today's gospel, for instance, when he warned against the titles "rabbi," and "father," and "instructor"? We have been taught to use these very titles as forms of address for certain authority figures in our lives. Perhaps Jesus wants to remind us who hear his words today that the authority and power of those who hold such titles comes from God, who is the only perfect title-holder. So when we call a parent or a priest "father," for example, the title should remind both him and us that he is a servant of the perfect Father.

And how valid are our age-old excuses for not doing what we are taught is right, especially if we're taught to "do as I say, not as I do"? According to Jesus—the very Word of God—the scribes and the Pharisees carried on the Mosaic Tradition even though they themselves sinned. We base the validity of our Catholic Church on an analogous plain: the Apostolic Tradition. This despite the Inquisition, despite the Crusades, despite the greed and the graft that sometimes has made its way into the *humanity* of our leaders.

"Do whatever they teach you and follow it; but do not do as they do, for they do not practice what they teach." Follow the Law of Love, hear the Word of God, and continue to "hope in the Lord from this time on and forevermore" (Ps 131:3).

Points for Reflection and Discussion

1. Reread today's Psalm (131). Try to put yourself into it, to be the psalmist who is offering this incredible prayer. How do you feel?

_____

_____

_____

_____

2. Have you ever tried to teach someone with words what you failed to teach by example? (Telling your children not to smoke as you blow smoke in their faces, for example; or to always tell the truth as you "call in sick" so you can go Christmas shopping.) What were the results?

_____

_____

_____

_____

Themes

Faith, Hope
> Q1, Journey of Faith
> Q10, Catholics and Prayer
> Q11, Catholic Practices
> Q12, Catholics and Church
> M1, Conversion: A Lifelong Process
> M2, The Laity: Called to Build God's Kingdom
> M5, Your Prayer Life
> M6, Discernment

Humility
> Q6, The Saints
> Q7, Mary
> M3, Your Special Gifts
> M7, Holiness

Teaching
> Q2, What Do Catholics Believe?
> Q3, What is the Meaning of the Mass?
> Q4, The Bible
> Q5, How Do Catholics Interpret the Bible?
> M4, Family Life
> M8, Evangelization

Reading 1, Wisdom 6:12-16

Wisdom is radiant and unfading, and she is easily discerned by those who love her, and is found by those who seek her. She hastens to make herself known to those who desire her. One who rises early to seek her will have no difficulty, for she will be found sitting at the gate.

To fix one's thought on her is perfect understanding, and one who is vigilant on her account will soon be free from care, because she goes about seeking those worthy of her, and she graciously appears to them in their paths, and meets them in every thought.

Psalm 63:1,2-3,4-5,6-7 (NRSV)

Reading 2, 1 Thessalonians 4:13-18

We do not want you to be uninformed, brothers and sisters, about those who have died, so that you may not grieve as others do who have no hope. For since we believe that Jesus died and rose again, even so, through Jesus, God will bring with him those who have died. For this we declare to you by the word of the Lord, that we who are alive, who are left until the coming of the Lord, will by no means precede those who have died. For the Lord himself, with a cry of command, with the archangel's call and with the sound of God's trumpet, will descend from heaven, and the dead in Christ will rise first. Then we who are alive, who are left, will be caught up in the clouds together with them to meet the Lord in the air; and so we will be with the Lord forever. Therefore encourage one another with these words.

Gospel, Matthew 25:1-13

[Jesus told this parable to his disciples:] "The kingdom of heaven will be like this. Ten bridesmaids took their lamps and went to meet the bridegroom. Five of them were foolish, and five were wise. When the foolish took their lamps, they took no oil with them; but the wise took flasks of oil with their lamps. As the bridegroom was delayed, all of them became drowsy and slept. But at midnight there was a shout, 'Look! Here is the bridegroom! Come out to meet him.' Then all those bridesmaids got up and trimmed their lamps. The foolish said to the wise, 'Give us some of your oil, for our lamps are going out.' But the wise replied, 'No! there will not be enough for you and for us; you had better go to the dealers and buy some for yourselves.' And while they went to buy it, the bridegroom came, and those who were ready went with him into the wedding banquet; and the door was shut. Later the other bridesmaids came also, saying, 'Lord, lord, open to us.' But he replied, 'Truly I tell you, I do not know you.' Keep awake therefore, for you know neither the day nor the hour."

Keeping Watch

JOHN F. CRAGHAN

In our highly mechanized world, we sometimes find it difficult to exercise patience. We expect instant replays. Unfortunately, we may transfer our impatience to other people, or to God. We want them to respond immediately to our needs and demands. We may even think they do not deserve our watching and waiting.

In today's readings, watching and waiting occupies center stage. These biblical passages speak of vigilance vis-à-vis our God. Since we generally approach God through others, however, these selections imply that we develop the capacity to watch and wait for our sisters and brothers. Our liturgy staunchly maintains that, as responsible people, we watch and wait.

Wisdom and Joy

In the middle of the first century BC, the author of the Book of Wisdom exhorted readers to seek Lady Wisdom. Through Lady Wisdom, while residing in Alexandria, the community would be able to remain faithful to the traditions of Abraham and Moses and, at the same time, use to advantage the sophisticated culture that surrounded them.

The author insisted upon both God's grace and human effort. Hence, the believer was to watch for Wisdom at dawn, to think about her, and to keep vigil for her. In turn, Lady Wisdom sat by the gates, made rounds, and sought and met the people. Wisdom is indeed a gift, but a gift people must actively seek.

Today's psalm is an individual lament that emphasizes an attitude of joyful thanksgiving. While the psalmist was aware of present troubles and tribulations (see vs 9-10), he still experienced the overwhelming desire to be in God's house. He was waiting and longing for such an opportunity. Hence he sought, thirsted, and fainted for God (v 1). He gazed toward this God in the sanctuary, eager to capture God's power and glory (v 2). This longing was not a momentary phenomenon—it carried over into the night watches (v 6). To know this God was to ever hunger and thirst for the divine presence.

In the midst of life's problems, the psalmist recognized that Yahweh was the means of help (v 7). The prayer of lament, however, also presumed that this problem involved the person at prayer and others surrounding him or her. In that context, the believer was asked to exhibit that same desire and longing for God, but also to be equally available to help others who waited for God, who would be revealed through the community.

Royal Wedding

The passage from Matthew concerned the Parousia, or Second Coming, of Jesus. Specifically, it warned against frivolity and urged prudence and perpetual readiness in face of the delay of that coming. The scene probably drew upon the marriage customs of that day. The bridegroom returned with his bride from the home of his in-laws. The bridesmaids were an escort of honor who awaited the arrival of the couple. Since they were unaware of the precise time of arrival, they were to exercise prudence and caution by having on hand a sufficient amount of oil. In this way, they would be able to take part in the joyful procession of the newlyweds.

For Matthew, Jesus was the bridegroom who would return at the Parousia. Since the Christian community did not know the exact time of that event, it must be prepared to wait and keep watch. Vigilance was the price of victory. For Matthew, the responsible watch and wait.

Today's Good News

We are usually more inclined to watch and wait when it is to our own advantage. We have a field of vision that focuses on our needs and pleasures. How difficult it can be to enlarge that capacity to include others.

The author of Wisdom suggests that we watch and wait for Wisdom so that we can share our insights with others. The psalmist implies that we long and pine for the presence of our God in others so that we can bind up their wounds and heal their ills. Matthew urges that we uncover the vision of the Bridegroom in the faces of his hurting sisters and brothers. In such cases the responsible watch and wait.

Points for Reflection and Discussion

1. Lady Wisdom has sometimes been identified with the Holy Spirit, sometimes identified with Jesus. How do you identify with Lady Wisdom?

_____

_____

_____

_____

_____

2. The "foolish" bridesmaids were under-prepared, but couldn't it also be said that the "wise" ones were unwilling to share their wealth? Talk about the gospel parable.

_____

_____

_____

_____

_____

Themes

Parousia
  Q2, What Do Catholics Believe?
  Q3, What is the Meaning of the Mass?
Patience, Perseverance
  Q6, The Saints
  M8, Evangelization
Wisdom
  Q5, How Do Catholics Interpret the Bible?
  M3, Your Special Gifts
  M6, Discernment

Reading 1, Proverbs 31:10-13,19-20,30-31

A capable wife who can find? She is far more precious than jewels. The heart of her husband trusts in her, and he will have no lack of gain. She does him good, and not harm, all the days of her life. She seeks wool and flax, and works with willing hands. She puts her hands to the distaff, and her hands hold the spindle. She opens her hand to the poor, and reaches out her hands to the needy.

Charm is deceitful, and beauty is vain, but a woman who fears the Lord is to be praised. Give her a share in the fruit of her hands, and let her works praise her in the city gates.

Psalm 128:1-2,3,4-5

Reading 2, 1 Thessalonians 5:1-6

Concerning the times and the seasons, brothers and sisters, you do not need to have anything written to you. For you yourselves know very well that the day of the Lord will come like a thief in the night. When they say, "There is peace and security," then sudden destruction will come upon them, as labor pains come upon a pregnant woman, and there will be no escape!

But you, beloved, are not in darkness, for that day to surprise you like a thief; for you are all children of light and children of the day; we are not of the night or of darkness. So then let us not fall asleep as others do, but let us keep awake and be sober.

Gospel, Matthew 25:14-30

[Jesus told this parable to his disciples:] "It is as if a man, going on a journey, summoned his slaves and entrusted his property to them; to one he gave five talents, to another two, to another one, to each according to his ability. Then he went away. The one who had received the five talents went off at once and traded with them, and made five more talents. In the same way, the one who had the two talents made two more talents. But the one who had received the one talent went off and dug a hole in the ground and hid his master's money. After a long time the master of those slaves came and settled accounts with them. Then the one who had received the five talents came forward, bringing five more talents, saying, 'Master, you handed over to me five talents; see, I have made five more talents.' His master said to him, 'Well done, good and trustworthy slave; you have been trustworthy in a few things, I will put you in charge of many things; enter into the joy of your master.' And the one with the two talents also came forward, saying, 'Master, you handed over to me two talents; see, I have made two more talents.' His master
said to him, 'Well done, good and trustworthy slave; you have been trustworthy in a few things, I will put you in charge of many things; enter into the joy of your master.' Then the one who had received the one talent also came forward, saying, 'Master, I knew that you were a harsh man, reaping where you did not sow, and gathering where you did not scatter seed; so I was afraid, and I went and hid your talent in the ground. Here you have what is yours.' But his master replied, 'You wicked and lazy slave! You knew, did you, that I reap where I did not sow, and gather where I did not scatter? Then you ought to have invested my money with the bankers, and on my return I would have received what was my own with interest. So take the talent from him, and give it to the one with the ten talents. For to all those who have, more will be given, and they will have an abundance; but from those who have nothing, even what they have will be taken away. As for this worthless slave, throw him into the outer darkness, where there will be weeping and gnashing of teeth'. "*

Gifts and Talents

JOHN F. CRAGHAN

In our individualism, we tend to view our talents and abilities in splendid isolation. We see them as attached to our self-fulfillment. Any infringement on our gifts by others constitutes a serious crime. We live and we die for ourselves.

Today's readings address the tension between self and community. They understand individuals only within the context of the common good. To live a full human life is to make the lives of others more human. Hence, talents and graces, by definition, embrace the needs of others. In the liturgy, personal gifts are common property.

The classical passage from Proverbs, while written from the decidedly male perspective, takes up the question of the truly beautiful woman. Shunning physical charm as the ultimate criterion, this selection stresses the predominant value of fear of the Lord. This is not a servile fear, whereby one cringes in the presence of the master. Rather, it is an attitude of profound respect that moves the person to pursue the good of the deity. In Israel, the good of Yahweh is always linked to the good of Yahweh's people.

The author offers a very concrete picture of this fear when he shows how the abilities of this beautiful woman redound to the good of her husband, her family, and her community. Thus she demonstrates all the domestic virtues. Her interests also extend beyond her household to include the poor and the needy. They are beneficiaries of her well-run home. It is only fitting, therefore, that her dedication and concern receive due recognition at the city gates.

Psalm 28 is a wisdom psalm. As such, it reflects the correct manner of living. It sees fear of the Lord as that all-encompassing value that impacts the whole of life. Thus to fear the Lord = to walk in God's ways = to be blessed. One should note, however, that the psalm does not understand prosperity and success as purely personal attainments. Rather, the psalm sees them as directly related to community.

Risk-taking

Matthew provides an insightful parable on the use of abilities and gifts. He recognizes that abilities and gifts presuppose action and even involve some risk. Paradoxically, he teaches that to use the gift for others is to improve the gift. The giver is perfected in the act of giving.

In the parable, a wealthy businessman, prior to embarking on a journey, entrusts his extra money to three servants. They are to invest the master's money and increase his wealth. While the first two double their sum by using the exorbitant interest rates, the third chooses to run no risk. He elects to bury the money, thereby precluding a profit, even a minimal amount of interest from the bankers. Hence, he refuses to use his talent for his master.

Today's Good News

When we speak of talents and gifts, we are prone to focus on college degrees and job performance. While these are certainly important, perhaps we would do well to consider other possibilities. How often do we use our ability to console by offering hope to a distraught person? How often do we use our ability to encourage by presenting a new world view to a despairing person? How often do we use our ability to lead by suggesting a new approach to an aimless person? How often do we use our ability to recognize talent by indicating a new form of life to a searching person? In all these instances, our positive actions reaffirm that personal gifts are common property.

Points for Reflection and Discussion

1. What special gifts and talents have you been blessed with? How are you using them for the good of others?

_____

_____

_____

_____

2. Read the entire passage from which the first reading has been taken (Prv 31:10-31). Does hearing the uncut proverb change its message in any way(s)? If so, how?

_____

_____

_____

_____

Themes
Ability, Talent
    M3, Your Special Gifts
Investment
    M6, Discernment
    M7, Holiness

Reading 1, Ezekiel 34:11-12,15-17

Thus says the Lord God: "I myself will search for my sheep, and will seek them out. As shepherds seek out their flocks when they are among their scattered sheep, so I will seek out my sheep. I will rescue them from all the places to which they have been scattered on a day of clouds and thick darkness.

"I myself will be the shepherd of my sheep, and I will make them lie down," says the Lord God. "I will seek the lost, and I will bring back the strayed, and I will bind up the injured, and I will strengthen the weak, but the fat and the strong I will destroy. I will feed them with justice.

"As for you, my flock," thus says the Lord God: "I shall judge between sheep and sheep, between rams and goats."

Psalm 23:1-2,2-3,5-6

Reading 2, 1 Corinthians 15:20-26,28

Christ has been raised from the dead, the first fruits of those who have died. For since death came through a human being, the resurrection of the dead has also come through a human being; for as all die in Adam, so all will be made alive in Christ. But each in his own order: Christ the first fruits, then at his coming those who belong to Christ. Then comes the end, when he hands over the kingdom to God the Father, after he has destroyed every ruler and every authority and power. For he must reign until he has put all his enemies under his feet. The last enemy to be destroyed is death.

When all things are subjected to him, then the Son himself will also be subjected to the one who put all things in subjection under him, so that God may be all in all.

Gospel, Matthew 25:31-46

[Jesus said to his disciples:] "When the Son of Man comes in his glory, and all the angels with him, then he will sit on the throne of his glory. All the nations will be gathered before him, and he will separate people one from another as a shepherd separates the sheep from the goats, and he will put the sheep at his right hand and the goats at the left. Then the king will say to those at his right hand, 'Come, you that are blessed by my Father, inherit the kingdom prepared for you from the foundation of the world; for I was hungry and you gave me food, I was thirsty and you gave me something to drink, I was a stranger and you welcomed me, I was naked and you gave me clothing, I was sick and you took care of me, I was in prison and you visited me.'

"Then the righteous will answer him, 'Lord, when was it that we saw you hungry and gave you food, or thirsty and gave you something to drink? And when was it that we saw you a stranger and welcomed you, or naked and gave you clothing? And when was it that we saw you sick or in prison and visited you?' And the king will answer them, 'Truly I tell you, just as you did it to one of the least of these who are members of my family, you did it to me.'

"Then he will say to those at his left hand, 'You that are accursed, depart from me into the eternal fire prepared for the devil and his angels; for I was hungry and you gave me no food, I was thirsty and you gave me nothing to drink, I was a stranger and you did not welcome me, naked and you did not give me clothing, sick and in prison and you did not visit me.'

"Then they also will answer, 'Lord, when was it that we saw you hungry or thirsty or a stranger or naked or sick or in prison, and did not take care of you?' Then he will answer them, 'Truly I tell you, just as you did not do it to one of the least of these, you did not do it to me.' And these will go away into eternal punishment, but the righteous into eternal life."

A Priestly People

John F. Craghan

Usually we reserve the title, "pastor," for the leader of a religious community. The pastor is to shepherd, that is, provide for the religious needs of the flock. But perhaps we fail to recognize that every believer is also commissioned, through baptism, to look to the needs of others. Even if we acknowledge this fact, we may find it exceedingly difficult to open ourselves to the world of the hurting. But we are all a priestly people—and priestly people "pastor."

The Shepherd-King

Ezekiel responded to the needs of his despondent exilic community in the early sixth century BC. To encourage them, he presented God as a shepherd. This was hardly a strange image, since kings in the ancient Near East often received the title of "shepherd," which implied, at least ideally, their concern for the people. This concern especially envisioned the legally helpless, for example, the widow and the orphan. "Shepherd" connoted interest in the welfare of the people.

Ezekiel described Yahweh as looking to the needs of the scattered sheep. Yahweh would rescue them from the land of their exile and lead them home. Specifically, he would give them rest, but, more importantly, Yahweh would focus attention on the lost, the strayed, the injured, and the sick. In addition, the Shepherd would assume a judicial role, passing judgment on all those, especially the upper classes, who mishandled the sheep.

The Shepherd-Host

Psalm 23, a psalm of trust or confidence, applied the shepherd image to Israel's prayer life. The author skillfully combined the image with that of host. Thus the one who guarded the desert traveler also provided hospitality in his tent and protection from all the enemies of the desert. The shepherd-host personified security.

The psalmist captured this pastoral concern by using a few concrete verbs, like "leads" and "restores." Pastures and water symbolized the complete involvement of the shepherd in the life of the sheep. The psalmist also depicted the social graces of the shepherd: "prepare a table" and "anoint my head with oil." The expression, "in the presence of my enemies," may suggest that the psalmist's former enemies now witness the great reversal that had occurred. Instead of harassment, Yahweh's guest now experienced all the pleasures of desert hospitality.

The Shepherd-Judge

In the gospel scene of the Final Judgment, Matthew presents Jesus as a king who will sit upon his royal throne and pass judgment on all the nations. Significantly, he exercises his royal duty by functioning as a shepherd. Just as the shepherd separates sheep from goats, so the Son of Man separates the blessed from the condemned. Fittingly, he places the sheep on the right and the goats on the left.

In the dialogue with the two groups, the Shepherd identifies with all who suffer. In passing judgment, he recognizes only one criterion: "Truly I tell you, just as you did it to one of the least of these brothers and sisters of mine, you did it to me." In recognizing Jesus in the needs of their sisters and brothers, the blessed affirm: We are a priestly people—and priestly people "pastor."

Today's Good News

Today's hurting ones can be found in our home, our work place, our places of amusement, even our Church. Instead of leaving these hurting people entirely to the care of social agencies or government subsidies, we are asked to pastor them with our own gifts and blessings. To offer food and drink to the destitute is to imitate the psalmist's God. To recognize the face of Jesus in the faces of the drug and alcohol dependent is to imitate Matthew's God. We are a priestly people—and priestly people "pastor."

Points for Reflection and Discussion

1. In responding to the needy, how do you reconcile a prudent need for caution with your baptismal mandate to pastor?

_____

_____

_____

_____

2. Read today's second reading, and compare its images to those of Shepherd that are found in the other readings of the day. When you think about Christ as King, what image most readily comes to your mind?

_____

_____

_____

_____

_____

Themes

Judgment
    Q2, What Do Catholics Believe?
Leadership
    Q9, Who's Who in the Church
    M2, The Laity: Called to Build God's Kingdom
    M3, Your Special Gifts
Parousia
    Q1, Journey of Faith
    M1, Conversion: A Lifelong Process

THEMATIC INDEX

Boldface numbers refer to pages in this book.
Numbers preceded by a letter refer to Handouts:
Q = Inquiry; C = Catechumenate; L = Lent; M = Mystagogy.
Example: Advent...**10-17**, Q11. Information on Advent may be found in this book on pages 10-17. Further information may be found in the Inquiry Handout number 11.

Abortion...C14, C15
Abraham...**40-41, 74-75**
Absolution...C5
Abstinence...Q11, L1
Acolyte...Q9
Acts of the Apostles (the Book of)...**22-23, 52-67**
Adam (and Eve)...**38-39**
Advent...**10-17**, Q11
All Saints Day...Q11
Altar...Q8
American Church...C12, C15, C16
Angel...**88-89**, L7
Angelus...Q11
Annulment...C7
Annunciation...**16-17**, Q7, Q10
Anointing...C2, C3, C6
Apostles' Creed...Q10
Apostolic...**26-27, 40-41, 54-55, 60-61, 74-75, 78-79, 116-117**, Q9, Q12, C11
Archbishop...Q9
Arms Control...C14
Ascension...Q10, Q11, C11
Ashes (Ash Wednesday)...L1
Assumption...Q7, Q10
Authority...**12-13, 96-97**
Awe (Wonder)...**54-55**, L8, M4, M7
Baptism...**12-13, 22-25, 54-55, 62-63, 66-67, 80-81, 94-95, 108-109**, C2, L7, L8, M1
Baptismal Font...Q8
Beatitudes...**28-29**
Belief...Q2, M1
Benediction...Q11
Bible...**56-57**, Q3, Q4, Q5, Q12, C13, M3, M5, M6
Bishop...Q9, C3, C8, C15, C16
Blessing...**40-41, 68-73**, Q11, C1, C6, M3
Body of Christ (Corpus Christi)...**66-67, 70-71**, Q9, Q12, C2, C9, C11, C12, C14, L6, M5
Bread...**52-57, 70-71**, Q3, Q6, Q9, Q10, C4, C11, L6, M3, M5, M6
Breviary...Q11
Call...**22-27, 74-75, 110-111**, Q1, Q12, C1, C13, L2, M1
Candles...Q8, C2, L7
Capital Punishment...C14, C15
Cardinal...Q9
Catechumenate...**52-53**, C2, L1, L8
Cathedral...Q8
Catholic...Q1, C1, C10, C12
Celebration...**70-71, 110-111**, C1, C4
Celibacy...C8
Chancery...Q8
Charismatic...Q11, C6
Charity...Q6, C16, M2, M3
Children...**16-17, 62-63**
Chosen...**44-45, 60-61, 108-109**, L2, M2
Chrism...C3, L7
Christmas...**16-21**, Q11
Church...**54-55, 64-65, 94-95, 100-101, 112-113**, Q7, Q8, Q9, Q12, C1, C2, C4, C8, C9, C11, C12, C13, L2, L4, M2
Civil Rights...C14

Code of Canon Law...Q11, C13
Colossians (the Letter to)...**18-19, 52-53**
Commandments...**32-33, 62-63, 100-101, 114-115**, C10, C13
Community...**30-31, 54-55, 100-101, 110-111, 114-115**, Q3, Q12, C2, C4, C11, L2, L4, M2, M5
Compassion...**48-51, 76-77, 82-83, 104-105, 114-115**, Q12, C15, L5, M4, M8
Confirmation...**24-25, 66-67**, C3
Conscience...**34-35**, C13, L3, M6
Contemplation...Q11, M6
Convent...Q8
Conversion...**26-27, 44-45, 54-59, 64-65, 80-83, 92-93**, Q1, C2, C3, C5, C11, C13, C15, L8, M1
Corinthians (the Letters to)...**24-37, 52-53, 66-71, 122-123**
Covenant...**22-23, 68-69, 72-73, 76-77, 114-117**, Q4, C9, C12, M2, M4
Creation...**38-39, 84-85**, C16, L8
Creed...Q2, Q10, L4
Cross...Q8, Q10, Q12, L1, L5, L7, M2
Crucifixion...**48-51**, Q10, L5, L7, M7
Crusades...C12
Deacon...**60-61**, Q9, C8
Death...**38-39, 46-47, 78-83, 118-123**, Q1, C2, L1, L5, L7, L8, M1
Decision-Making...**44-45, 90-91, 112-113**, M4, M6
Desert...**14-15, 38-39, 70-71**, L1
Deuteronomy (the Book of)...**70-73**
Devil...**38-39, 98-99**
Diocese...Q8
Discernment...**60-63, 66-67, 82-83, 90-91, 98-99, 112-113, 120-121**, M3, M4, M6
Discipleship...**60-61, 64-65, 76-81, 94-95, 108-109**, Q6, C9, C11, C13, L2, L5, M2, M3, M7, M8
Discipline...Q2, M2
Discrimination...**60-61, 80-81, 94-95, 106-107**
Dissent...C13
Divorce...C7
Doubt...Q1, Q5, L3, M1
Doxology...Q10
Early Church...**10-15, 20-21, 30-31**, Q6, Q7, Q12, C11
Easter...**52-67**, Q11, L7
Easter Vigil...L7, L8
Economy...C14, C16
Ecumenism...**12-13**, C13, C14, M8
Election, Rite of...L2
Elijah...**40-41, 92-93**
Elisha...**80-81**
Emmaus...**56-57**
Encyclical...C14
End Times (Parousia, Second Coming)...**14-15, 80-81, 118-123**, C10, M1, M7
Ephesians (the Letter to)...**20-21, 44-45**
Epiphany...**20-21**, C1
Equality...Q12, M2
Ethics (Morals)...**12-13, 18-21, 28-29, 32-37, 108-109**, C15
Eucharist...**30-31, 48-51, 70-71**, Q3, Q6, Q9, C4, C11, L6, L7, M2, M3, M5, M6, M7
Euthanasia...C15
Evangelization...**56-59, 66-67, 78-79, 106-107**, Q12, M8
Evil...**38-39**, Q10, C16, L6
Exodus (the Book of)...**42-43, 68-69, 76-77, 114-115**
Ezekiel (the Book of)...**46-47, 100-101, 106-107, 122-123**
Faith...**54-55, 64-65, 72-77, 92-93, 116-117**, Q1, C2, C3, L4, M1, M3, M6, M7

Faithfulness...**68-69, 74-75, 84-85**, Q6, Q7, Q12, C7, L5, M1, M6, M7
Family...**18-19, 58-59, 120-121**, C7, C13, C14, L2, M2, M4
Family Planning...C13, C15
Fast...**38-39**, Q11, L1
Food...**70-71, 90-91**, Q10, M5
Forgiveness...**34-35, 54-55, 102-103**, Q1, Q2, Q3, Q6, Q11, C5, C7, C10, C15, L1, L2, L3, L5, L6, L7, M1, M2, M5, M6
Freedom...**104-105**, C9, M1
Fulfillment...Q1, M6
Genesis (the Book of)...**38-41**
Genre (Literary)...Q5
Genuflect...Q11
Gifts...**54-55, 58-63, 66-67, 78-79, 120-121**, M3, M4
Glory...**64-65**, M7
God (the Father)...**56-57, 62-63, 68-69, 72-73, 82-83**, L4, L6
Godparent...C2
Good Friday...**56-57**, L7
Grace...**78-79**, C1, L3
Greed...Q1, M1
Hail Mary...Q10
Healing...**44-45, 76-77, 94-95**, Q10, C6, C15, L4, M3, M4, M5
Heresy...C12
Hierarchy...Q9
History...**14-17, 20-21, 32-33**, Q5, Q12, C10, C11, C12
Holiness...**24-25, 34-35, 56-57, 66-67, 76-77**, Q6, C13, C15, M7
Holy Days...Q11
Holy Family...**18-19**, C7
Holy Orders...**12-13, 22-23, 26-27, 32-33**, C8, L7
Holy See...Q9
Holy Spirit...**22-25, 38-39, 46-47, 54-55, 58-63, 66-67, 82-85, 92-93, 114-115**, Q5, Q12, C2, C3, C6, C8, C10, L3, L4, M3, M4, M6, M7, M8
Holy Thursday...L7
Holy Water...Q8
Holy Week...**40-41, 46-47, 52-53**, L7
Hope...**42-43, 116-117**, C5, C6, M1, M6, M7
Hosea (the Book of)...**74-75**
Hospitality...Q12, M2
Humility...**106-107, 116-117**, Q6, Q7, M6, M7
Hunger...**90-91, 122-123**, Q3, C4, M8
Idolatry...Q6, L4, L7
Immaculate Conception...Q7, Q11
Infallibility...Q9
Intercession...Q6, Q7
Isaiah (the Book of)...**10-17, 20-27, 30-31, 36-37, 48-51, 84-85, 90-91, 94-97, 104-105, 108-113**
James (the Letter of)...**14-15**
Jeremiah (the Book of)...**78-79, 98-99**
Jesus Christ...**10-11, 14-17, 30-31, 36-37, 44-45, 82-83, 96-97, 106-107**, Q9, C1, C3, C8, C10, L2, L4, L5, L7, M5
Jesus Prayer...Q11, M5
John (the Gospel of)...**24-25, 42-47, 52-55, 58-69**
John the Baptist...**12-15, 22-27, 90-91**
Joseph...**16-19**, C9
Journey...Q1, Q12, C9, M1
Judas Iscariot...**48-51**
Judgment...**122-123**, C13, M6
Justice...**18-19, 22-23, 30-31, 94-95, 104-109, 114-115**, Q9, Q12, C13, C14, C16, M2, M8
King (Queen)...**88-91, 112-113, 116-117, 122-123**, C3, C9, M2

Kingdom...**10-11, 66-67, 72-73, 76-77, 86-91, 94-95, 104-105, 118-119,** Q10, C2, C10, L6, M2, M6, M7, M8

Kings (the Books of)...**80-81, 88-89, 92-93**

Laity...**54-57, 60-61, 66-67,** Q6, Q9, Q12, C12, M2

Last Rites...C6

Law...**12-13, 18-19, 32-33, 72-73, 100-101,** C13, L4, M6

Lazarus...**46-47**

Lectern...Q8

Lector...Q4, Q9, M2, M3

Lent...**38-51,** Q11, L1, L2, L3, L4, L5, L6

Leviticus (the Book of)...**34-35**

Life...**10-11, 18-19, 28-31, 36-39, 46-47, 52-53, 70-71, 74-75, 80-83, 122-123,** Q1, Q2, Q6, Q9, C2, C10, C15, C16, L1, L7, L8, M1, M3, M4, M7

Light...**44-45, 78-79**

Litany...Q11

Liturgy...Q3, Q9, Q11, C9, C12, L7, M5

Lord's Prayer...**38-39, 48-51,** Q10, L6

Love...**12-13, 18-19, 34-35, 42-43, 52-53, 62-63, 68-69, 100-101, 114-115,** Q2, Q3, Q7, Q11, C1, C7, C15, L5, L6, L8, M1, M7, M8

Luke (the Gospel of)...**56-57**

Magi...**18-21**

Magisterium...**32-33,** Q9, C15

Malachi (the Book of)...**116-117**

Marriage...**16-19, 22-23, 26-27, 120-121,** C7, M2, M4

Martyr...Q1, Q6, C11, C12, M7

Mary...**16-17, 64-65,** Q7, Q10, Q11, C9

Mass...**70-71, 92-93,** Q3

Matthew (the Gospel of)...**10-23, 26-41, 48-53, 72-123**

Meal...C4, L7

Medals...Q11

Mercy...**86-87, 94-95, 104-105,** Q3, Q7, C14, C15, M7

Messiah...**14-17, 96-97,** C3, C10, C11

Ministry...**66-67, 78-79, 90-91,** Q1, Q9, C6, C8, C9, C13, M2, M3, M6

Mission (or Missionary)...**20-21, 62-63, 94-95,** Q8, Q12, C12, M3, M8

Monastery...Q8, C12

Monsignor...Q9

Moses...**34-35, 40-43, 68-69, 72-73, 76-77, 116-117**

Music...Q9

Mystagogy...M1, M2, M3

Name...**52-53, 58-59, 62-63, 100-101, 106-107,** Q10, C3, M3

Nativity...**16-21,** Q10, Q11

Neophyte...M1

Nicene Creed...Q2, L4

Novena...Q11

Nun...Q9

Obedience...L2

Ordinary Time...**22-37, 72-125,** Q11

Ordination...C8, L7

Original Sin...**38-39,** L3

Palms (Palm Sunday)...**48-51,** L1, L7

Parables...**84-87**

Parish...M2

Parish Center...Q8

Parousia (End Times, Second Coming)...**14-15, 80-81, 118-123,** C10, M1, M7

Passion...**48-51,** C9, C16, L7

Passover...**48-53,** C1

Pastor...Q9

Patience...**14-15, 118-119,** Q10, M6

Peace...**54-55, 66-67,** C15, C16, L3, L6, L8, M8

Penance...**10-13, 20-21, 26-27, 34-35,** C5, L1, L3

Pentecost...**56-59, 66-67,** C3, C10, C11, M3, M4

Persecution...**62-65, 78-79, 114-115,** C9, C11, C16

Perseverance...**84-85, 118-119,** Q1, Q10, Q11, Q12, L5, M1, M5, M6

Peter...**22-23, 26-27, 40-41, 48-51, 56-59, 92-93, 96-99, 102-103**

Peter (the Letters of)...**54-65**

Philippians (the Letter to)...**48-51, 104-111**

Poor (Poverty)...**28-29,** Q5, Q6, Q11, C12, C15, C16, M3, M6, M7

Pope...Q9, C12, C16

Power...**86-89, 96-97,** C3, C14, C15, M2

Praise...Q3, Q10, Q11, M3, M5, M6

Prayer...**38-39, 58-59, 64-65, 76-77, 100-101, 126-129,** Q6, Q7, Q10, Q11, C3, C5, L1, L3, L4, L5, L6, L8, M5, M6

Preparedness...**10-11, 118-119,** Q2, M7

Presence (Divine)...**92-93**

Priest...Q9, C8, L7, M2

Promise...**16-17, 36-37,** Q1, M7

Prophecy...L7, M3, M4, M7

Prophet...**78-81, 100-101,** Q6, C9, C14, L8, M2, M4

Protestant...C12

Proverbs (the Book of)...**120-121**

Providence (Divine)...**56-57**

Psalms...**52-53, 64-65, 82-87, 90-91, 96-97, 104-105, 112-113, 118-121**

Purification...L1

Racism...C16

Reconciliation...**18-21, 26-27, 94-95, 102-103,** Q2, Q3, Q8. Q10, Q11, C5, C6, L1, L3, M1, M5

Rectory...Q8

Reformation...C12

Relationship...**10-11, 18-19, 30-31, 58-59,** C5, C7, C9, C11, L8, M4, M8

Remembrance...**48-51, 70-71,** Q3, C1, C4, C11, L7, M6

Repentance...**12-13, 58-59,** Q2, Q10, Q11, C5, L1, L3, M1, M6, M7

Resurrection...**52-55, 66-67, 82-83, 118-119, 122-123,** Q2, L1, L5, L7, L8, M7

Retreat...**52-53,** Q11, L8

Revelation...M6

Revenge...**48-51**

Reward...Q1, M1

Romans (the Letter to)...**10-13, 16-17, 38-39, 42-43, 46-47, 72-103**

Rosary...Q10

Sabbath...M7

Sacrament...**10-13, 16-17, 30-31,** C1, C2, C3, C4, C5, C6, C7, C8, L3, M5

Sacramental...Q11

Sacramentary...Q8

Sacrifice...**74-75,** C4, C8, L5, L7, L8

Sacristy...Q8

Saint...Q6, Q11, C11, C12, C15, L4

Salvation...**56-57, 72-77, 106-107,** Q2, C6, C10, M7

Samuel (the Books of)...**44-45**

Sanctuary, Sanctuary Lamp...Q8

Scrutinies...L3

Second Coming (End Times, Parousia)...**14-15, 80-81, 118-123,** C10, M1, M7

Secular...Q11

Servant...**22-23, 40-41, 48-51, 58-59, 116-117,** C8, L2, M2

Server...Q9

Service...**60-61,** Q9, C8, C12, C14, C15, L7, M2, M3, M8

Sexism...Q9, C16, M3

Shepherd...**58-59, 76-77, 122-123,** C8

Shrine...Q8

Sign of the Cross...Q10, C2, C3, C6

Sin...**38-39, 72-73, 76-79, 106-107,** Q1, Q2, Q3, Q10, Q11, C2, C5, C16, L3, L6, M1, M6, M7

Single (Unmarried, Widowed)...M2, M4

Sirach (the Book of)...**18-19, 32-33, 102-103**

Sister...Q9

Slavery...C9

Social Justice...**18-21, 28-29, 32-35,** C14, C16

Solomon...**88-89**

Sponsor...C3

Stations of the Cross...**48-51,** Q8, L5

Stewardship...**36-37, 108-109,** Q1, Q3, C16, M2, M8

Stipend...Q11

Suffering...**40-41, 48-51, 58-59**

Symbol (Sign)...Q11,C1, L1, M6

Tabernacle...Q8, L8

Temple...**34-35,** C9, C11

Temptation...**38-39,** Q10, L1, L3, L6

Thanksgiving...Q10, M5, M6, M7

Theology...C13

Thessalonians (the Letters to)...**112-121**

Thomas...**54-55**

Timothy (the Letters to)...**40-41**

Tongues (Speaking in)...**66-67,** M3

Tradition...**116-117,** Q12

Transfiguration...**40-41,** C10, M1

Triduum...Q11, L7

Trinity...**68-69, 82-83,** Q2, C1, L4, M4, M7

Trust...**36-37, 64-65, 78-79,** L2

Truth...Q12, C10, M1

Unity...**20-21,** C7, M7, M8

Universality...**62-63, 72-73, 76-77, 110-111,** Q12, C11, L4, M8

Values...C15, C16, M6, M8

Vanity...Q6, Q7, M3

Vatican...Q8, Q9

Vatican Council II...Q12, C6, C7, C12, C14, C16

Vestments...Q8, Q11,L1

Violence...**48-51**

Virgin...Q7

Vocation...**26-27,** C1, C7, C8, C9, M2, M3

Waiting...**14-15, 118-119,** Q11, C11

Wake Service...Q11

War...C14, C15

Water...**42-43, 90-91,** Q8, C2, L7, M1

Way (The)...**76-77,** C10, C11, L8

Way of the Cross...**40-41,** L5, L7

Will...**74-75, 88-89, 98-99,** Q10, C13, L6

Wisdom...**32-33, 82-83, 88-89, 118-121,** Q6, L8, M3, M6, M7

Wisdom (the Book of)...**86-87, 118-119**

Witness...**76-77,** C3, M3, M8

Word...**72-73, 76-77, 84-85, 92-93, 98-99,** Q3, Q4, Q5, L7, L8

Workers' Rights...C14, C16, M2

Works of Mercy...**30-31, 54-55, 60-61, 76-77, 106-107,** Q11, M3

Zechariah (the Book of)...**82-83**

Zephaniah (the Book of)...**28-29**

SUPPLEMENTAL MATERIALS FOR EASTER TRIDUUM AND OCCASIONAL SUNDAYS

These supplemental materials "complete" the total **JOURNEY OF FAITH** program.

Here you will find:

- The *readings* for the *Easter Triduum*
- The *cycle A readings* for the *third, fourth, and fifth Sundays of Lent*
- The *readings* for those occasional *Sundays that supersede ordinary time* readings
- *Scripture commentary* for every set of readings
- *Discussion and/or reflection questions* for every set of readings
- Every set of readings is *cross-referenced to the catechetical handouts*

TABLE OF CONTENTS

Immaculate Conception of Mary
      December 8 128

The Birth of the Lord (Christmas)
      December 25 130

Mary, Mother of God
      January 1 132

❀ ❀ ❀

Presentation of the Lord
      February 2 134

Saint Joseph, Husband of Mary
      March 19 136

Annunciation of the Lord
      March 25 138

❀ ❀ ❀

Third Sunday of Lent
      Cycle A 140

Fourth Sunday of Lent
      Cycle A 142

Fifth Sunday of Lent
      Cycle A 144

❀ ❀ ❀

Easter Triduum
      Holy Thursday 146

Easter Triduum
      Good Friday 148

Easter Triduum
      Holy Saturday 152

❀ ❀ ❀

Ascension of the Lord 156

❀ ❀ ❀

Birth of Saint John the Baptist
      June 24 158

Saints Peter and Paul
      June 29 160

Transfiguration of the Lord
      August 6 162

Assumption of Mary
      August 15 164

❀ ❀ ❀

Triumph of the Cross
      September 14 166

All Saints
      November 1 168

All Souls
      November 2 170

Dedication of Saint John Lateran
      November 9 172

❀ ❀ ❀

Gathering Prayers 174
Dismissal Prayers 176

Reading 1 (ABC), Gensis 3:9-15,20

The Lord God called to the man, and said to him, "Where are you?" He said, "I heard the sound of you in the garden, and I was afraid, because I was naked; and I hid myself." He said, "Who told you that you were naked? Have you eaten from the tree of which I commanded you not to eat?" The man said, "The woman whom you gave to be with me, she gave me fruit from the tree, and I ate."

Then the Lord God said to the woman, "What is this that you have done?" The woman said, "The serpent tricked me, and I ate." The Lord God said to the serpent, "Because you have done this, cursed are you among all animals and among all wild creatures; upon your belly you shall go, and dust you shall eat all the days of your life. I will put enmity between you and the woman, and between your offspring and hers; he will strike your head, and you will strike his heel."

The man named his wife Eve, because she was the mother of all living.

Psalm 98:1,2-3,3-4 (R verse 2)

Reading 2 (ABC), Ephesians 1:3-6,11-12

Blessed be the God and Father of our Lord Jesus Christ, who has blessed us in Christ with every spiritual blessing in the heavenly places, just as he chose us in Christ before the foundation of the world to be holy and blameless before him in love. He destined us for adoption as his children through Jesus Christ, according to the good pleasure of his will, to the praise of his glorious grace that he freely bestowed on us in the Beloved.

In Christ we have also obtained an inheritance, having been destined according to the purpose of him who accomplishes all things according to his counsel and will, so that we, who were the first to set our hope on Christ, might live for the praise of his glory.

Gospel (ABC), Luke 1:26-38

In the sixth month the angel Gabriel was sent by God to a town in Galilee called Nazareth, to a virgin engaged to a man whose name was Joseph, of the house of David. The virgin's name was Mary. And he came to her and said, "Greetings, favored one! The Lord is with you." But she was much perplexed by his words and pondered what sort of greeting this might be. The angel said to her, "Do not be afraid, Mary, for you have found favor with God. And now, you will conceive in your womb and bear a son, and you will name him Jesus. He will be great, and will be called the Son of the Most High, and the Lord God will give to him the throne of his ancestor David. He will reign over the house of Jacob forever, and of his kingdom there will be no end." Mary said to the angel, "How can this be, since I am a virgin?" The angel said to her, "The Holy Spirit will come upon you, and the power of the Most High will overshadow you; therefore the child to be born will be holy; he will be called Son of God. And now, your relative Elizabeth in her old age has also conceived a son; and this is the sixth month for her who was said to be barren. For nothing will be impossible with God."

Then Mary said, "Here am I, the servant of the Lord; let it be with me according to your word." Then the angel departed from her.

The Mother of All the Living

ELSIE HAINZ MCGRATH

Remember that when "God created humankind in his image…male and female he created them"; God gave them, the male and the female, the richness of the earth and its yield and dominion over all the other living creatures (see Gn 1:27-31). Today the story of the "fall" is presented as the reason why our world is filled with sin and toil and pain and shame. It explains why the good earth does not always yield good food, why folks generally are not fond of reptiles, and even why women are not equal to men. (This strongly suggests that the subordination of women in Israelite society was not intended by God. Note that the serpent and the woman are punished for their sins while the man is simply chastised; the *earth* is punished for the sin of the man!) The conclusion to be reached from this story, of course, is that all the world's imperfections are due to us—human beings—aspiring to be our own god.

Significantly, the man now gives the woman *another* name, Eve, meaning *life*, "but God said, 'You shall not eat of the fruit of the tree that is in the middle of the garden, nor shall you touch it, or you shall *die*'" (3:3). To *live*, as regards eating from the forbidden tree, meant to live *forever*, like God. To *live* as the child of Eve meant merely to live *until you die*, like an earth creature fashioned from dust by the only eternal God. That is the primary theology behind original sin and redemption. If we had not sinned we would not have known death; because we did, we could not live forever until we were saved by a Redeemer.

Children of God

The author of Ephesians reminds us today that we are no longer children of Eve: We are children of God, who has adopted us because of Christ, our Redeemer. Now we are assured of real and eternal *life;* life that we have not earned but that has been earned for us by the sacrifice of Jesus. This is why we bless God, "so that we, who were the first to set our hope on Christ, might live for the praise of his glory."

The gospel gives us the story of the Annunciation: the angel Gabriel announces the impending birth of the Redeemer to his mother, Mary, and she humbly accepts the awesome challenge. This is why Mary is sometimes called "the new Eve." By giving birth to the One who will redeem humankind from death, *she* assumes the role of "mother of all the living." In the same way, Jesus is often referred to as "the new Adam." Through Adam sin and death entered the world, through Jesus salvation and life are restored (see Rom 5:12-16, for example).

The feast we celebrate today is not about sin and death. It is about birth and life: the birth and life of Mary. Specifically, it is about the conception of Mary, believed to be free from the stain of that "original" sin we all inherited in the Garden of Eden because she was predestined to become the Mother of God. As all great truths, this truth is a Mystery, something that cannot be logically and rationally explained but only believed in faith. Also as all great truths, this truth came to be defined as dogma precisely because the Tradition of the Church has believed it for centuries.

Today's gospel tells us that Gabriel addressed Mary not as "Mary" but as "favored one." This name indicates the divine gifts bestowed upon one who has been elected for bearing the Light of the world. "If this election is fundamental for the accomplishment of God's salvific designs for humanity, and if the eternal choice in Christ and the vocation to the dignity of adopted children is the destiny of everyone, then the election of Mary is wholly exceptional and unique. Hence also the singularity and uniqueness of her place in the mystery of Christ." (*Mother of the Redeemer,* Pope John Paul II.)

Today's Good News

Mary's immaculate conception was not what kept her from making bad decisions, any more than our baptisms keep us from sin. We *all* know that baptism, while opening us up to the possibility of salvation, does *not,* in-and-of-itself, keep us free from sin! Thus was it Mary's responsibility to choose to be holy and it was wholly *her* choice to take on the responsibility of divine maternity.

Those of us who wish to "be perfect" (Mt 5:48) would do well to emulate Mary. She truly is "one of us" who is yet without sin. She is not so far removed from our world as to be just a plaster statue. Mary lived and loved. She knew pain and fear and heartbreak. She risked divorce from the man she loved, even death from those who thought her guilty of the sin of adultery, when she said those poignant words to Gabriel: "Here am I, the servant of the Lord; let it be with me according to your word." Mary can be our beacon in this world of selfishness and violence and death; she shows us the way to love and service and life.

Points for Reflection and Discussion

1. Say these words to yourself: "Let it be with me according to your Word." As you say them, think about those things you must immediately change in your life in order to really mean them.

_____

_____

_____

_____

2. How does the society in which we live look at life? How does the contemporary view differ from the view of life we are offered in today's readings?

_____

_____

_____

_____

Themes

Immaculate Conception, Mary
    C9, The People of God
    C10, Who is Jesus Christ?
Life
    C2, The Sacrament of Baptism
    C6, The Sacrament of the Anointing of the Sick
    C15, The Consistent Life Ethic
    C16, The Dignity of Life
Sin
    C5, The Sacrament of Penance

Reading 1 (ABC), Isaiah 9:2-4,6-7

The people who walked in darkness have seen a great light; those who lived in a land of deep darkness—on them light has shined. You have multiplied the nation, you have increased its joy; they rejoice before you as with joy at the harvest, as people exult when dividing plunder. For the yoke of their burden, and the bar across their shoulders, the rod of their oppressor, you have broken as on the day of Midian.

For a child has been born for us, a son given to us; authority rests upon his shoulders; and he is named Wonderful Counselor, Mighty God, Everlasting Father, Prince of Peace. His authority shall grow continually, and there shall be endless peace for the throne of David and his kingdom. He will establish and uphold it with justice and with righteousness from this time onward and forevermore. The zeal of the Lord of hosts will do this.

Psalm 96:1-2,3-4,11-12,13 (*R* Lk 2:11)

Reading 2 (ABC), Titus 2:11-14

The grace of God has appeared, bringing salvation to all, training us to renounce impiety and worldly passions, and in the present age to live lives that are self-controlled, upright, and godly, while we wait for the blessed hope and the manifestation of the glory of our great God and Savior, Jesus Christ. He it is who gave himself for us that he might redeem us from all iniquity and purify for himself a people of his own who are zealous for good deeds.

Gospel (ABC), Luke 2:1-14

In those days a decree went out from Emperor Augustus that all the world should be registered. This was the first registration and was taken while Quirinius was governor of Syria. All went to their own towns to be registered. Joseph also went from the town of Nazareth in Galilee to Judea, to the city of David called Bethlehem, because he was descended from the house and family of David. He went to be registered with Mary, to whom he was engaged and who was expecting a child.

While they were there, the time came for her to deliver her child. And she gave birth to her firstborn son and wrapped him in bands of cloth, and laid him in a manger, because there was no place for them in the inn.

In that region there were shepherds living in the fields, keeping watch over their flock by night. Then an angel of the Lord stood before them, and the glory of the Lord shone around them, and they were terrified. But the angel said to them, "Do not be afraid; for see—I am bringing you good news of great joy for all the people: to you is born this day in the city of David a Savior, who is the Messiah, the Lord. This will be a sign for you: you will find a child wrapped in bands of cloth and lying in a manger." And suddenly there was with the angel a multitude of the heavenly host, praising God and saying, "Glory to God in the highest heaven, and on earth peace among those whom he favors!"

Royal Titles

JOHN F. CRAGHAN

Titled people are committed people. This may strike us as a little odd. In our world we simply assume that people with titles are people with power and prestige. As such, these people expect others to serve them and provide for them. Those serving and providing must be committed to the titled people. To reverse the process is to promote chaos.

The readings we hear tonight fly in the face of our basic assumption. They speak of titled people, i.e., the Davidic king and Jesus, but they also speak of them as committed people. Title-bearers are thus people who take on obligations for others. They are true to their titles only insofar as they are committed to their people.

Wonderful Counselor and Mighty God

Before tonight's reading, Isaiah of Jerusalem spoke of the downfall of the northern kingdom of Israel (see Is 8:22). Only after the gloom and despair of that experience will the Lord raise up an ideal Davidic king who will reunite the tribes of Israel. For the people who walked in darkness, it will indeed be a day of great light and joy comparable to harvest time and the division of spoils after a battle. The yoke symbolizes allegiance to a foreign power, here the neo-Assyrians. The Lord, however, will smash and utterly destroy that yoke after the manner of Gideon's defeat of the Midianites (see Jgs 7:16-25).

Isaiah next describes the ideal Davidic king and his commitment to the people through the use of titles. The king is God's adopted son/child on the day of his coronation (see Ps 2:7). His relationship to the people is captured in throne names or titles like "Everlasting Father" and "Prince of Peace." According to the former, the Davidic king is to lavish paternal love and care on his people. According to the latter, he is to effect peace and prosperity for them. It is, however, only the practice of justice and righteousness that will ensure the well-being of the king's subjects. For Isaiah, titled people are committed people.

God and Savior

In 2:2-10, the author of Titus enumerates the rules for the household, including old men, old and young women, young men, and slaves. In 2:11-14, the author offers a theological basis for the previously-listed duties. This basis is the fact that God has manifested his goodness to all people and calls for a response in the form of a truly Christian life now.

The author uses the title "Savior" for Jesus. While this title was applied to gods, kings, emperors, and so forth in the Greco-Roman world, it takes on very special significance in this letter. Jesus is Savior insofar as he "gave himself for us that he might redeem us...". Jesus' self-giving is epitomized in his suffering and death on behalf of humanity. For the author of Titus, titled people are committed people.

Messiah and Lord

Playing on some Hebrew Testament texts, Luke interprets the significance of Jesus' birth. The manger may refer to Isaiah 1:13. Now, however, Israel recognizes the presence of its Lord who provides for his people. The inn may suggest Jeremiah 14:8, where only the passing traveler spends the night. Now, however, God in Jesus is permanently present to Israel by not lodging in an inn. The bands of cloth may allude to Wisdom 7:4-5, where King Solomon is said to be swaddled. Jesus indeed possesses royal dignity.

While relying upon the titles of the Davidic king in Isaiah 9:6, Luke substitutes his own, which comes from the Christian proclamation of Jesus. Jesus is a "Savior." In the Hebrew Scriptures this title refers to those who deliver God's people, e.g., the judges (see Jgs 3:9,15) and God himself (see Is 45:15,21). Caesar Augustus was known as savior of the whole world, especially in view of the peace he brought to the empire. By linking "Savior" and peace, Luke is suggesting that real peace comes only from Jesus.

Jesus is also "Messiah." From its Jewish roots this title designates Jesus as God's anointed agent who is the bearer of a new form of salvation. Luke, however, is careful to connect Jesus' messiahship with his suffering and death. "Was it not necessary that the Messiah should suffer these things and then enter into his glory?" (Lk 24:26). For Luke, titled people are committed people.

Today's Good News

These authors present us with a formidable challenge. Essentially, they urge us to discover the meaning of titles within the context of community. They impel us to look beyond the status implied by titles and bring to light those people who are to benefit from the title-bearers.

For example, the title "Mr. and Mrs." bespeaks mutual support and concern; the title of the married couple is a call to unflagging service. The title "father and mother" implies dedication to the members of the family; to acknowledge this title is to devote all their energies and talents to the common good. The title "teacher" expresses the giving of oneself to the total formation of those taught; it is the awareness that the success of one's pupils is the goal of the classroom enterprise. The title "employer" articulates the association of oneself with the needs as well as with the talents of others; the title suggests more than the overseer of the means of production—ideally it is a bond uniting owners and workers in a truly human experience of growth. For all such persons, titled people are committed people.

Points for Reflection and Discussion

1. What "titles" do you hold? To what and/or whom do your titles hold you accountable?

_____

_____

_____

_____

2. Imagine a newborn baby, wrest from his mother's womb into the midst of a cold and prickly stable/cave and hearing the sounds of animals competing with the sounds of angels. Listen to this baby's titles resound in your heart while your mind's eye sets the scene. Pray over the wonder of this moment.

_____

_____

_____

_____

Themes

Christmas, Savior
    C4, The Eucharist
    C10, Who is Jesus Christ?
    C16, The Dignity of Life
Commitment
    C3, The Sacrament of Confirmation
    C7, The Sacrament of Marriage
    C8, The Sacrament of Holy Orders
    C9, The People of God
    C13, Christian Moral Living
    C14, Social Justice

Reading 1 (ABC), Numbers 6:22-27

The Lord spoke to Moses, saying: Speak to Aaron and his sons, saying, Thus you shall bless the Israelites: You shall say to them, The Lord bless you and keep you; the Lord make his face to shine upon you, and be gracious to you; the Lord lift up his countenance upon you, and give you peace. So they shall put my name on the Israelites, and I will bless them.

Psalm 67:1-2,4-5,6-7 (*R verse 1*)

Reading 2, Galatians 4:4-7

When the fullness of time had come, God sent his Son, born of a woman, born under the law, in order to redeem those who were under the law, so that we might receive adoption as children. And because you are children, God has sent the Spirit of his Son into our hearts, crying, "Abba! Father!" So you are no longer a slave but a child, and if a child then also an heir, through God.

Gospel, Luke 2:16-21

[The shepherds] went with haste and found Mary and Joseph, and the child lying in the manger. When they saw this, they made known what had been told them about this child; and all who heard it were amazed at what the shepherds told them. But Mary treasured all these words and pondered them in her heart. The shepherds returned, glorifying and praising God for all they had heard and seen, as it had been told them.

After eight days had passed, it was time to circumcise the child; and he was called Jesus, the name given by the angel before he was conceived in the womb.

Theotokos

ELSIE HAINZ MCGRATH

Mary's oldest and most consistent "title" has been that of *Theotokos* (Mother of God). This is dogma, first defined at the Council of Ephesus in A.D. 431. It helps us to define Jesus as "true God and true man." Mary is called Mother of God not in the sense of having existed *before* God, but as affirmation of the Incarnation. Saint Cyril of Alexandria put it this way: "If we are to confess that Emmanuel is truly God, we must also confess that the Holy Virgin is *Theotokos;* for she bore according to the flesh the Word of God made flesh."

The letter Saint Paul wrote to Galatia (c 48-55) gives an earlier definition of Mary's maternity. That Jesus was "born of a woman" emphasizes the human condition of the baby; it was necessary that Jesus be fully human in order to accomplish the divine mission. That the Son was sent by God so we would be "no longer slaves" emphasizes the divinity of the baby; we could not be freed of the law through merely human intervention.

Proclaimed by Shepherds

Today's gospel celebrates Mary's maternity in still another way. An angel has visited the shepherds who are watching their flocks from the Tower of David that overlooked Bethlehem, and has announced the birth of the Messiah. We pick up the story at the point where the shepherds make their way down the hillside and see the Christ-child for themselves, whereupon they recount the angel's message to Mary and Joseph, praise God, and set about proclaiming his birth to all who would hear them.

Thus it is that the first ones to know about Jesus' birth are the very persons who are most despised of all by "good" Jews. Ordinary shepherds were *anathema* (excommunicated) for their lowly profession. Paradoxically, the shepherds in Bethlehem were of the highly esteemed caste of temple slaves. In fact, Jewish tradition held that the first announcement of the Messiah's coming would be made to shepherds in the Tower of David. These were *special* shepherds. They were in charge of the sheep that *would be sacrificed* in the Temple.

"But Mary treasured all these words and pondered them in her heart." We may or may not presume that she knew of the tradition about the Tower of David, as we wish, but shepherds appearing in her birthing chamber and announcing angels and heavenly hosts had to be unnerving! In her pondering, did she connect the fact that these men were in charge of the sheep that would be sacrificed? Did she wonder why the birth of her God-son was made known to temple slaves instead of temple priests? Did she realize, as she tried to comfort herself and her newborn babe in the cold, dark, smelly confines of a stable-cave, that this miraculous Nativity was destined for life and death among the *anawim* (the lowly ones of God)?

Today's Good News

It is fitting that the solemnity of the Mother of God is celebrated on the same day as the "World Day of Peace" because it has always been Mary who has inspired people to work for peace in the world. Witness the well-established devotions to Mary, and the numerous Marian apparitions calling for prayers for peace. Pope Paul VI first instituted the "World Day of Peace" on this day because the "Solemnity of Mary...is meant to commemorate the part played by Mary in this mystery of salvation...to exalt the singular dignity which this mystery brings to the holy Mother...for imploring to God, through the Queen of Peace, the supreme gift of peace." (*Devotion to the Blessed Virgin Mary,* Pope Paul VI.)

The Second Vatican Council further explicated the place of Mary in our world by stressing the "title" of Mother of the Church. Here the emphasis is on Mary's spiritual motherhood, scripturally established at Calvary when Jesus symbolically "gave" Mary over to all of us by telling the beloved disciple, "Here is your mother" (Jn 19:26-27). Because Mary is believed to be pure and holy, the perfect disciple who was assumed into heaven to be with God and watch over us, she is the fulfillment of the Church (the body of Christ...the people of God...you and me). She is the person we need to emulate. Hers are the virtues we need to acquire. When we have accomplished her perfection, we too will have reached our fulfillment.

Points for Reflection and Discussion

1. Today's first reading gives us an ancient priestly blessing. Read it now, and reflect on it reverently. What is it saying to you?

_____

_____

_____

_____

2. Mary is believed to have been twelve or fourteen years old when Jesus was born. Imagine yourself in her situation (or in Joseph's)—giving birth to a baby in the middle of an alien land without even the comfort of a warm room and a bed, much less a physician or midwife. Talk about the experience.

_____

_____

_____

_____

Themes

Mary
 C9, The People of God
 C10, Who is Jesus Christ?
Parenthood
 C7, The Sacrament of Marriage
 C16, The Dignity of Life
Shepherd
 C8, The Sacrament of Holy Orders
 C14, Social Justice

Reading 1 (ABC), Malachi 3:1-4

The Lord God said: See, I am sending my messenger to prepare the way before me, and the Lord whom you seek will suddenly come to his temple. The messenger of the covenant in whom you delight—indeed, he is coming, says the Lord of hosts. But who can endure the day of his coming, and who can stand when he appears? For he is like a refiner's fire and like fullers' soap; he will sit as a refiner and purifier of silver, and he will purify the descendants of Levi and refine them like gold and silver, until they present offerings to the Lord in righteousness. Then the offering of Judah and Jerusalem will be pleasing to the Lord as in the days of old and as in former years.

Psalm 24:7,8,9,10 (*R* verse 10)

Reading 2 (ABC), Hebrews 2:14-18

Since…the children [of God] share flesh and blood, [Jesus] likewise shared the same things, so that through death he might destroy the one who has the power of death, that is, the devil, and free those who all their lives were held in slavery by the fear of death. For it is clear that he did not come to help angels, but the descendants of Abraham. Therefore he had to become like his brothers and sisters in every respect, so that he might be a merciful and faithful high priest in the service of God, to make a sacrifice of atonement for the sins of the people. Because he himself was tested by what he suffered, he is able to help those who are being tested.

Gospel (ABC), Luke 2:22-40

When the time came for their purification according to the law of Moses, [Mary and Joseph] brought [Jesus] up to Jerusalem to present him to the Lord (as it is written in the law of the Lord, "Every firstborn male shall be designated as holy to the Lord"), and they offered a sacrifice according to what is stated in the law of the Lord, "a pair of turtledoves or two young pigeons."

Now there was a man in Jerusalem whose name was Simeon; this man was righteous and devout, looking forward to the consolation of Israel, and the Holy Spirit rested on him. It had been revealed to him by the Holy Spirit that he would not see death before he had seen the Lord's Messiah. Guided by the Spirit, Simeon came into the temple; and when the parents brought in the child Jesus, to do for him what was customary under the law, Simeon took him in his arms and praised God, saying, "Master, now you are dismissing your servant in peace, according to your word; for my eyes have seen your salvation, which you have prepared in the presence of all peoples, a light for revelation to the Gentiles and for glory to your people Israel."

And the child's father and mother were amazed at what was being said about him. Then Simeon blessed them and said to his mother Mary, "This child is destined for the falling and the rising of many in Israel, and to be a sign that will be opposed so that the inner thoughts of many will be revealed—and a sword will pierce your own soul too."

There was also a prophet, Anna the daughter of Phanuel, of the tribe of Asher. She was of a great age, having lived with her husband seven years after her marriage, then as a widow to the age of eighty-four. She never left the temple but worshiped there with fasting and prayer night and day. At that moment she came, and began to praise God and to speak about the child to all who were looking for the redemption of Jerusalem.

When they had finished everything required by the law of the Lord, they returned to Galilee, to their own town of Nazareth. The child grew and became strong, filled with wisdom; and the favor of God was upon him.

Being Purified, Being Presented

ELSIE HAINZ MCGRATH

Today's gospel combines two rituals into one story. The first is the purification. "When the time came for *their* purification" is not a fully accurate statement. The law of Moses held that the *woman* who had delivered a child be "purified" in a Temple rite after the birth. This rite required a sacrifice. If the family was rich, the sacrifice was a lamb; if poor, two turtledoves were accepted (see Lv 12:1-8).

The presentation is another ritual, *bekor* in Hebrew. Only the firstborn son of a mother whose husband was not a priest (of the tribe of Levi) was presented. This presentation of the firstborn son was originally a human sacrifice (see Ex 13:1-2). Human sacrifice was not wholly discontinued until after the time of King David.

In today's account, Anna is the female counterpart to Simeon. Luke consistently gives us stories that illustrate men and women are equal and treated equally by Jesus. A "prophet," Anna was an equivalent of today's Sisters. She took vows of poverty and chastity, participated in daily prayer, and was committed to apostolic action.

A Sword to the Soul

Pope John Paul II says this about Simeon's words to Mary: They "seem like a second Annunciation, for they tell her of the actual historical situation in which the Son is to accomplish his mission, namely, in misunderstanding and sorrow. While this announcement on the one hand confirms her faith in the accomplishment of the divine promises of salvation, on the other hand it also reveals to her that she will have to live her obedience of faith in suffering, at the side of the suffering Savior, and that her motherhood will be mysterious and sorrowful" (*Mother of the Redeemer*).

The conclusion of Luke's account of these happenings is mysterious indeed. "When they had finished everything required by the law of the Lord, they returned to Galilee, to their own town of Nazareth. The child grew and became strong, filled with wisdom; and the favor of God was upon him." In short, there isn't much more to tell until Jesus begins his public ministry. There is the incident in the Temple when he is twelve, but for the most part his formative years are "hidden." These years of Mary's life are "hidden" too. Surely we may safely conjecture that as Jesus "grew and became strong," so did his mother.

The Messenger of the Covenant

"The Lord whom you seek will suddenly come into his temple," says Malachi in today's first reading. It is as if he is speaking directly to Simeon, who is "looking forward to the consolation of Israel." This "consolation" would be the comforter, the Messiah. Simeon was a minor judge who wanted to be freed from the disgrace and drudgery of his state in life. Considered a failure by his father, Simeon could not even use his full identifying name. Disconnected from his family heritage, he was in a very real sense under the yoke of the slavery of death and sin ("dismiss your servant in peace"). And suddenly the Lord was there, in the Temple, just as Malachi had promised.

Malachi means *messenger,* and his message today does appear to announce the coming of the Messiah in much the same way as John the Baptist announces him as an adult (see Jn 1:6-9). Very little is known about Malachi, not even when the book was written. It is a prophetic book and as such it gives its readers hope, but the hope offered seems to be more elusive and distant—maybe as distant as the birth of the Messiah.

Today's Good News

The Letter to the Hebrews reminds those of us who tend to get mired down in day-to-day problems and the catastrophic events of contemporary society that there is Light at the end of the tunnel. We need no longer be slaves to fear because our High Priest is both faithful and merciful. Our temptations to turn away from God are not abhorrent to our Lord because he was tempted in every way we are (see Lk 4:1-13; Mt 4:1-11; Mk 1:12-13); he was *one of us.* Death, whether death of body or soul or spirit, has been defeated by the One who humbled himself to be born into the degradation of human nature.

Mary's example for us, displayed once again in today's readings, is one of faithfulness and steadfastness. She kept all the laws of her Jewish faith, fulfilling the rituals demanded of herself and her son. She wondered at the prophecies she heard from Simeon and Anna, and went home to reverently ponder the meaning of it all. And she quietly and faithfully assumed the roles of wife and mother that she had committed herself to.

Points for Reflection and Discussion

1. Mary's example is one of fidelity to her commitments, no matter how difficult keeping them might be. Think about a commitment you have been faithful to despite temptations to break it. Has keeping that commitment strengthened you in any way(s)? If you're comfortable doing so, talk about that commitment and its effect on your life.

_____

_____

_____

_____

2. How much do you think Mary understood about who Jesus was when she and Joseph presented him at the Temple?

_____

_____

_____

_____

Themes
Incarnation
    C1, The Sacraments: An Introduction
    C2, The Sacrament of Baptism
    C4, The Eucharist
    C10, Who is Jesus Christ?
Mary
    C7, The Sacrament of Marriage
Prophecy
    C3, The Sacrament of Confirmation

Reading 1 (ABC), 2 Samuel 7:4-5,12-14,16

The word of the Lord came to Nathan: Go and tell my servant David: "When your days are fulfilled and you lie down with your ancestors, I will raise up your offspring after you, who shall come forth from your body, and I will establish his kingdom. He shall build a house for my name, and I will establish the throne of his kingdom forever. I will be a father to him, and he shall be a son to me. Your house and your kingdom shall be made sure forever before me; your throne shall be established forever."

Psalm 89:1-2,3-4,26,28 (R verse 36)

Reading 2 (ABC), Romans 4:13,16-18,22

The promise that he would inherit the world did not come to Abraham or to his descendants through the law but through the righteousness of faith. For this reason it depends on faith, in order that the promise may rest on grace and be guaranteed to all his descendants, not only to the adherents of the law but also to those who share the faith of Abraham (for he is the father of all of us, as it is written, "I have made you the father of many nations")— in the presence of the God in whom he believed, who gives life to the dead and calls into existence the things that do not exist. Hoping against hope, he believed that he would become "the father of many nations," according to what was said, "So numerous shall your descendants be." Therefore his faith "was reckoned to him as righteousness."

Gospel (ABC), Matthew 1:16,18-21,24*

Jacob [was] the father of Joseph the husband of Mary, of whom Jesus was born, who is called the Messiah. Now the birth of Jesus the Messiah took place in this way. When his mother Mary had been engaged to Joseph, but before they lived together, she was found to be with child from the Holy Spirit. Her husband Joseph, being a righteous man and unwilling to expose her to public disgrace, planned to dismiss her quietly. But just when he had resolved to do this, an angel of the Lord appeared to him in a dream and said, "Joseph, son of David, do not be afraid to take Mary as your wife, for the child conceived in her is from the Holy Spirit. She will bear a son, and you are to name him Jesus, for he will save his people from their sins." When Joseph awoke from sleep, he did as the angel of the Lord commanded him; he took [Mary] as his wife.

*(or) Luke 2:41-51

Every year [Jesus'] parents went to Jerusalem for the festival of the Passover. And when he was twelve years old, they went up as usual for the festival. When the festival was ended and they started to return, the boy Jesus stayed behind in Jerusalem, but his parents did not know it. Assuming that he was in the group of travelers, they went a day's journey. Then they started to look for him among their relatives and friends.

When they did not find him, they returned to Jerusalem to search for him. After three days they found him in the temple, sitting among the teachers, listening to them and asking them questions. And all who heard him were amazed at his understanding and his answers.

When his parents saw him they were astonished; and his mother said to him, "Child, why have you treated us like this? Look, your father and I have been searching for you in great anxiety." He said to them, "Why were you searching for me? Did you not know that I must be in my Father's house?" But they did not understand what he said to them.

Then he went down with them and came to Nazareth, and was obedient to them.

Investing in the Future

JOHN F. CRAGHAN

Faith means the family's future. In the act of believing, we root ourselves in God but often hesitate to root ourselves in the lives of others. In the act of believing, we open ourselves up to God's person but are often reluctant to open ourselves up to other persons and their concerns. In the act of believing, we strengthen ourselves by leaning upon God but are often loath to strengthen ourselves by having others lean upon us. Faith directs us beyond the person of our God. By involving us in our God, faith also involves us in our God's world of problems.

Today's readings touch upon the faith of the Davidic king, of Abraham, and of Joseph. Their faith, however, is not limited to the world of purely personal concerns; rather, it is necessarily bound up with the good of their community. Faith means the family's future.

Faith and Family

Psalm 89 is probably a lament of the community (verses 38-51) that includes praise of Israel's God (verses 1-18) and the oracle to the Davidic dynasty assuring its kings of God's perpetual care and protection (verses 19-37). The psalm opens with the accent on God's favors in the past. In verses 3-4 there is the clear statement of God's unconditional promise to David and his line. As a father to the Davidic king (see Ps 2:7), this God is indeed "the Rock of my salvation!" (verse 26).

Beginning in verse 38, the psalm seems to question God's promise, e.g., "Lord, where is your steadfast love of old...?" (verse 49). Faced with some political crisis, the king and the community challenge their God to act on their behalf and resolve the problem. It is the faith of both the king and the community that makes such a demand possible. In this impasse, faith in the God of Israel means the family's future.

Father of Nations

In the passage from Romans, Paul illustrates the meaning of righteousness by discussing the faith of Abraham. Paul points out that the promise of inheritance depends on the righteousness of faith, not the Mosaic law. For Paul, to live by faith is to live by grace. Abraham's faith is not a purely private enterprise, however—it has impact on all, both Jews and Gentiles.

For Paul, Abraham's life means total dedication to God that, in turn, has impact on the community. Hence others will be the beneficiaries: "I have made you the father of many nations." Although his wife was barren and advanced in years, Abraham continued to believe on behalf of others: "'Look toward heaven and count the stars, if you are able to count them.' Then he said to him, 'So shall your descendants be'" (Gn 15:5). Clearly, Abraham's faith means the family's future.

Husband of Mary

Matthew concludes his genealogy (1:16) by registering Joseph as the son of Jacob. In this very same verse, however, he also observes that Jesus, the Messiah, is born of Mary, not Joseph. What follows in verses 18-25 is an expanded footnote that is intended to explain the irregularity of the genealogy. If Jesus does not have a human father, then how is it possible to call him "son of David" (1:1)? Matthew responds to the difficulty by noting that Joseph, although perplexed, was willing to accept legal paternity of Jesus because of the angel's revelation. Fittingly, Joseph is addressed in verse 20 as "son of David."

For Matthew, Joseph is a great example of faith ("righteous man"). He believes the angel's message that explains Mary's conception, namely, through the Holy Spirit. He also accepts the mission to act on behalf of Mary and the child. Matthew summarizes Joseph's faith by remarking: "He did as the angel of the Lord commanded him...". For Matthew, Joseph's faith means the family's future.

Today's Good News

These readings ought to challenge us to rethink our notion of faith. They urge us to move away from a purely one-on-one relationship with our God to a community-oriented relationship. In saying "we believe in God," we implicitly include the world of our community. Faith in this God is necessarily linked to this God's community—everyone.

For example, parents who devote themselves to the total education of their family demonstrate their faith. Educators who seek to form the whole person in view of society's needs prove their faith. The sick and the dying who see their condition as the opportunity to encourage others show their faith. Leaders in both civil and church society who view their position as the chance to improve the condition of others indicate their faith. All such people link their faith in God to the needs of others. For them faith clearly means the family's future.

Points for Reflection and Discussion

1. Today's readings emphasize the part faith has consistently played in the preservation of the family of God. What part has faith played in the preservation of your biological family?

——————————————————————

——————————————————————

——————————————————————

——————————————————————

2. Society claims that faith is a private matter, something strictly between an individual and God. Scripture disputes that claim. Imagine what the world would be like if everyone followed the dictates of society. Imagine what the world would be like if everyone followed the dictates of Scripture. Discuss the differences.

——————————————————————

——————————————————————

——————————————————————

——————————————————————

Themes
Faith
 L2, Saying Yes to Jesus
 L4, The Nicene Creed
Family
 L7, The Meaning of Holy Week
 L8, Catechumenate Retreat Day
Future
 L3, Take a Look
 L5, The Way of the Cross

Reading 1 (ABC), Isaiah 7:10-14

The Lord spoke to Ahaz, saying, "Ask a sign of the Lord your God; let it be deep as Sheol or high as heaven." But Ahaz said, "I will not ask, and I will not put the Lord to the test."

Then Isaiah said: "Hear then, O house of David! Is it too little for you to weary mortals, that you weary my God also? Therefore the Lord himself will give you a sign. Look, the young woman is with child and shall bear a son, and shall name him Immanuel."

Psalm 40:6,7-8,9,10 (R verses 7-8)

Reading 2 (ABC), Hebrews 10:4-10

It is impossible for the blood of bulls and goats to take away sins. Consequently, when Christ came into the world, he said, "Sacrifices and offerings you have not desired, but a body you have prepared for me; in burnt offerings and sin offerings you have taken no pleasure. Then I said, 'See, God, I have come to do your will, O God' (in the scroll of the book it is written of me)."

When he said above, "You have neither desired nor taken pleasure in sacrifices and offerings and burnt offerings and sin offerings" (these are offered according to the law), then he added, "See, I have come to do your will." He abolishes the first in order to establish the second.

And it is by God's will that we have been sanctified through the offering of the body of Jesus Christ once for all.

Gospel (ABC), Luke 1:26-38

In the sixth month the angel Gabriel was sent by God to a town in Galilee called Nazareth, to a virgin engaged to a man whose name was Joseph, of the house of David. The virgin's name was Mary. And he came to her and said, "Greetings, favored one! The Lord is with you." But she was much perplexed by his words and pondered what sort of greeting this might be. The angel said to her, "Do not be afraid, Mary, for you have found favor with God. And now, you will conceive in your womb and bear a son, and you will name him Jesus. He will be great, and will be called the Son of the Most High, and the Lord God will give to him the throne of his ancestor David. He will reign over the house of Jacob forever, and of his kingdom there will be no end."

Mary said to the angel, "How can this be, since I am a virgin?" The angel said to her, "The Holy Spirit will come upon you, and the power of the Most High will overshadow you; therefore the child to be born will be holy; he will be called Son of God. And now, your relative Elizabeth in her old age has also conceived a son; and this is the sixth month for her who was said to be barren. For nothing will be impossible with God."

Then Mary said, "Here am I, the servant of the Lord; let it be with me according to your word." Then the angel departed from her.

God's Signposts

ELSIE HAINZ MCGRATH

Today's first reading has the prophet Isaiah wanting King Ahaz to ask God for a "sign" that the kingdom will be saved, but Ahaz refuses. He has already decided to allow Judah to become a vassal to Assyria, a means of saving himself from being deposed by the nations of Syria and Israel; his refusal to "test" the Lord is probably more a refusal to change his own mind.

The sign is given despite Ahaz's stubbornness: A woman is to bear a son named Immanuel, "for God is with us." The "young woman," often incorrectly translated as "virgin," is probably the wife of Ahaz. The child will consequently preserve the house of David from being overthrown.

Centuries later, the angel Gabriel greets Mary with the words, "The Lord is with you." Mary, a virgin, is to bear a son, "the Son of the Most High…[who]…will reign over the house of Jacob forever." Gabriel *volunteers* a sign, so that Mary may believe "nothing will be impossible with God"; her sign is to find her cousin to be also with child, even though beyond childbearing years.

Preserving the House of David

God is with the house of David, and the kingdom is preserved through new life. The annunciation to Mary differed from the annunciations to Ahaz (father of Hezekiah) and to Zechariah (father of John the Baptist) in significant ways, however. First, it was Mary herself—the mother, *not* the father—who received both the prophecy and the sign. And it was Mary's openness to God's promise of intimacy that made her pregnancy possible. The Annunciation, in fact, has little to do with motherhood and much to do with discipleship: Mary is the one who listens attentively, hears God's Word, and acts on it—precisely the means by which one comes to be called a disciple according to Jesus himself (see, for example, Lk 8:15,21;11:27-28; Acts 1:14).

The pivotal moment of Christian history was Mary's *fiat* to the angelic announcement. Her YES is our paradigm for all ages, which is why "all ages shall call me blessed." It was not *just* important to God that Mary say YES; it was *absolutely necessary* because redemption establishes a relationship between God and humanity that must be sealed at both ends by a free and personal decision. So it is that the celebration of the Annunciation is a "joint" celebration; we honor not only Mary's YES but God's initiative.

Today's Good News

Signs are given to us too, so we can recognize God's initiative in *our* lives, especially signs of new life. Remember when you or someone close to you was first discovered to be with a wanted child? Recall the joy, the wonder of the moment, of knowing that new life was beginning. With the joy and the wonder, though, there is usually a touch of fear, especially with the first child; even a questioning of how this can be happening. (Imagine how Mary must have felt!) And then the interminable waiting begins, always with at least a little discomfort and anxiety. The body grows heavy and awkward and tires too quickly. The joy of the announcement is forgotten and the experience of carrying this new life takes on an aura of death. But finally the baby emerges and fulfills the promise of that long-ago announcement. (Again, imagine how Mary must have felt!)

Signs of new life do not only come with announcements of pregnancy and births of babies, of course. How often do we reflect on the human cycle of death and life, for example. A grandparent dies, a baby is born. Is the *visible* new life (the baby) the *only* new life? Isn't the grandparent also experiencing new life—with God? Don't we often *feel* the presence of that grandparent, talk to him or her, experience consolation? Are not these experiences "signs" of life?

New life is most apparent through the change of the seasons. We *know* that the dead of winter is going to give way to the resurrection of spring—from gray and white to shades of pastel. We *know* that the resurrection of spring is going to give way to the fullness of lush green summer life. We *know* that the fullness of life is going to give way to the autumn of life—displayed in the glorious and multi-colored hues that richly epitomize the dignity and diversity of the wholly-mature. And we *know* that the autumn of life is going to give way to the dead of winter. The cycle repeats itself, year after year, generation after generation. Death continually gives way to life because death has no hold on us who believe in the Resurrection.

Points for Reflection and Discussion

1. Saint Paul tells us today that redemption can only come through a person. The burnt offerings of the past do not please God. A living person, one who listens to the Word and does the will of God, pleases God. That is why Mary is often referred to as co-redeemer. Without her humble cooperation there could not have been an Incarnation; without the Incarnation there could not have been the perfect sacrifice on Calvary; without Calvary there would be no Resurrection and no redemption. Reflect on this magnificent Mystery during the coming week.

_____

_____

_____

_____

_____

2. Write a letter to Mary and share it with the community.

_____

_____

_____

_____

_____

Themes

Annunciation, Discipleship, Mary
   L2, Saying Yes to Jesus
Redemption
   L1, What Is Lent?
   L3, Take a Look
   L5, The Way of the Cross
   L7, The Meaning of Holy Week

Reading 1, Exodus 17:3-7

The people thirsted [in the wilderness] for water; and the people complained against Moses and said, "Why did you bring us out of Egypt, to kill us and our children and livestock with thirst?" So Moses cried out to the Lord, "What shall I do with this people? They are almost ready to stone me."

The Lord said to Moses, "Go on ahead of the people, and take some of the elders of Israel with you; take in your hand the staff with which you struck the Nile, and go. I will be standing there in front of you on the rock at Horeb. Strike the rock, and water will come out of it, so that the people may drink." Moses did so, in the sight of the elders of Israel.

He called the place Massah and Meribah, because the Israelites quarreled and tested the Lord, saying, "Is the Lord among us or not?"

Psalm 95:1-2,6-7,7-9 (R verses 7c, 8a)

Reading 2, Romans 5:1-2,5-8

Since we are justified by faith, we have peace with God through our Lord Jesus Christ, through whom we have obtained access to this grace in which we stand; and we boast in our hope of sharing the glory of God.

And hope does not disappoint us, because God's love has been poured into our hearts through the Holy Spirit that has been given to us. For while we were still weak, at the right time Christ died for the ungodly. Indeed, rarely will anyone die for a righteous person—though perhaps for a good person someone might actually dare to die. But God proves his love for us in that while we still were sinners Christ died for us.

Gospel, John 4:5-42

[Jesus] came to a Samaritan city called Sychar, near the plot of ground that Jacob had given to his son Joseph. Jacob's well was there, and Jesus, tired out by his journey, was sitting by the well. It was about noon.

A Samaritan woman came to draw water, and Jesus said to her, "Give me a drink." (His disciples had gone to the city to buy food.) The Samaritan woman said to him, "How is it that you, a Jew, ask a drink of me, a woman of Samaria?" (Jews do not share things in common with Samaritans.) Jesus answered her, "If you knew the gift of God, and who it is that is saying to you, 'Give me a drink,' you would have asked him, and he would have given you living water." The woman said to him, "Sir, you have no bucket, and the well is deep. Where do you get that living water? Are you greater than our ancestor Jacob, who gave us the well, and with his sons and his flocks drank from it?" Jesus said to her, "Everyone who drinks of this water will be thirsty again, but those who drink of the water that I will give them will never be thirsty. The water that I will give will become in them a spring of water gushing up to eternal life." The woman said to him, "Sir, give me this water, so that I may never be thirsty or have to keep coming here to draw water."

Jesus said to her, "Go, call your husband, and come back." The woman answered him, "I have no husband." Jesus said to her, "You are right in saying, 'I have no husband'; for you have had five husbands, and the one you have now is not your husband. What you have said is true!"

The woman said to him, "Sir, I see that you are a prophet. Our ancestors worshiped on this mountain, but you say that the place where people must worship is in Jerusalem." Jesus said to her, "Woman, believe me, the hour is coming when you will worship the Father neither on this mountain nor in Jerusalem. You worship what you do not know; we worship what we know, for salvation is from the Jews. But the hour is coming, and is now here, when the true worshipers will worship the Father in spirit and truth, for the Father seeks such as these to worship him. God is spirit, and those who worship him must worship in spirit and truth."

The woman said to him, "I know that Messiah is coming" (who is called Christ). "When he comes, he will proclaim all things to us." Jesus said to her, "I am he, the one who is speaking to you."

Just then his disciples came. They were astonished that he was speaking with a woman, but no one said, "What do you want?" or, "Why are you speaking with her?" Then the woman left her water jar and went back to the city. She said to the people, "Come and see a man who told me everything I have ever done! He cannot be the Messiah, can he?" They left the city and were on their way to him.

Meanwhile the disciples were urging him, "Rabbi, eat something." But he said to them, "I have food to eat that you do not know about." So the disciples said to one another, "Surely no one has brought him something to eat?" Jesus said to them, "My food is to do the will of him who sent me and to complete his work. Do you not say, 'Four months more, then comes the harvest'? But I tell you, look around you, and see how the fields are ripe for harvesting. The reaper is already receiving wages and is gathering fruit for eternal life, so that sower and reaper may rejoice together. For here the saying holds true, 'One sows and another reaps.' I sent you to reap that for which you did not labor. Others have labored, and you have entered into their labor."

Many Samaritans from that city believed in him because of the woman's testimony, "He told me everything I have ever done." So when the Samaritans came to him, they asked him to stay with them; and he stayed there two days. And many more believed because of his word. They said to the woman, "It is no longer because of what you said that we believe, for we have heard for ourselves, and we know that this is truly the Savior of the world."

Wellsprings

JOHN F. CRAGHAN

Love is its own reward. We live in a world of progress reports, work evaluations, and periodic reassessments. We hope to get a higher wage and/or a better position because of our improved output or more efficient management. We thereby assume that better performance means a better reward. In our *quid pro quo* atmosphere it is hard to believe that love can be its own reward.

Today's readings treat the graciousness of our God, a graciousness not prompted by our work ethic or motivated by our compelling desire to succeed. It is a graciousness that is only explicable on the basis of our God's capacity to love for the sake of loving.

A second level in the narrative of Massah and Meribah is Israel's dispute with Yahweh over the question of the exodus from Egypt. On this level the people's thirst serves as the occasion for attacking the very purpose of the exodus: "Why did you bring us out of Egypt?" On this level, Israel rejects God's whole plan of salvation.

The primary tradition concentrates on Yahweh's graciousness for the people. In the primary tradition, the people merely quarrel with Moses and constrain him to meet their demands. Moses' cry to the Lord results in a positive and prompt reply. There is no threat of punishment for the people. God meets their needs because it is the nature of God to do so.

Love is Its Own Reward

In his Letter to the Romans, Paul observes that the state of being right with God brings about unshakable peace. Through Christ Jesus, the Christian has access to God's presence. Despite the ups and downs of life, the Christian has a hope rooted in God's Spirit. The gift of the Spirit is the assurance of God's love.

Paul insists that Christ freely chose to die for godless humans. The self-giving of Christ seems so incomprehensible, his death is the great proof of God's love.

John demonstrates in today's gospel the truth that the sending of the Son is grounded in God's love for the world (see Jn 3:16). It is only this love that can adequately explain the happenings in this episode.

Jesus brings living water, that is, God's revelation, to the Samaritans—renegade or at least second-class Jews. It is significant that Jesus chooses to talk not only with a Samaritan but with a Samaritan woman—this is indeed a reversal of acceptable practice in first-century Judaism in Palestine. The outcome is that the woman brings the message of Jesus to her people, who end up by accepting Jesus as the Savior of the world. John sees this as the fulfillment of Jesus' mission: "God did not send the Son into the world to condemn the world, but in order that the world might be saved through him" (Jn 3:17).

Today's Good News

We are directed to reach out to our family, to assist our friends, to love and work with all peoples not simply because we will be amply compensated but because it is the nature of our God to love with no strings attached. Hence to accept God is to accept God's worldview. Our family, our friends, and our business associates are worthy of gratuitous love because the essence of our God is to look to the welfare of others. In our pragmatic world, the upsetting message is that love is its own reward.

Points for Reflection and Discussion

1. Try to imagine loving some one as unconditionally as God loves every one. How would your life change?

_____

_____

_____

_____

2. The water of life is imaged throughout today's readings. Who has been a source of life-giving water for you?

_____

_____

_____

_____

Themes

Hope
    L1, What Is Lent?
Love
    L2, Saying Yes to Jesus
Water
    L3, Take a Look

Reading 1, 1 Samuel 16:1,6-7,10-13

The Lord said to Samuel, "Fill your horn with oil and set out; I will send you to Jesse the Bethlehemite, for I have provided for myself a king among his sons."

When [the sons of Jesse] came, [Samuel] looked on Eliab and thought, "Surely the Lord's anointed is now before the Lord." But the Lord said to Samuel, "Do not look on his appearance or on the height of his stature, because I have rejected him; for the Lord does not see as mortals see; they look on the outward appearance, but the Lord looks on the heart."

Jesse made seven of his sons pass before Samuel, and Samuel said to Jesse, "The Lord has not chosen any of these." Samuel said to Jesse, "Are all your sons here?" And he said, "There remains yet the youngest, but he is keeping the sheep." And Samuel said to Jesse, "Send and bring him; for we will not sit down until he comes here." He sent and brought him in. Now he was ruddy, and had beautiful eyes, and was handsome. The Lord said, "Rise and anoint him; for this is the one."

Then Samuel took the horn of oil, and anointed him in the presence of his brothers; and the spirit of the Lord came mightily upon David from that day forward.

Psalm 23:1-3,3-4,5,6 (R verse 1)

Reading 2, Ephesians 5:8-14

Once you were darkness, but now in the Lord you are light. Live as children of light—for the fruit of the light is found in all that is good and right and true.

Try to find out what is pleasing to the Lord. Take no part in the unfruitful works of darkness, but instead expose them. For it is shameful even to mention what such people do secretly; but everything exposed by the light becomes visible, for everything that becomes visible is light. Therefore it says, "Sleeper, awake! Rise from the dead, and Christ will shine on you."

Gospel, John 9:1-41

As [Jesus] walked along, he saw a man blind from birth. His disciples asked him, "Rabbi, who sinned, this man or his parents, that he was born blind?" Jesus answered, "Neither this man nor his parents sinned; he was born blind so that God's works might be revealed in him. We must work the works of him who sent me while it is day; night is coming when no one can work. As long as I am in the world, I am the light of the world." When he had said this, he spat on the ground and made mud with the saliva and spread the mud on the man's eyes, saying to him, "Go, wash in the pool of Siloam" (which means Sent). Then he went and washed and came back able to see.

The neighbors and those who had seen him before as a beggar began to ask, "Is this not the man who used to sit and beg?" Some were saying, "It is he." Others were saying, "No, but it is someone like him." He kept saying, "I am the man." But they kept asking him, "Then how were your eyes opened?" He answered, "The man called Jesus made mud, spread it on my eyes, and said to me, 'Go to Siloam and wash.' Then I went and washed and received my sight." They said to him, "Where is he?" He said, "I do not know."

They brought to the Pharisees the man who had formerly been blind. Now it was a sabbath day when Jesus made the mud and opened his eyes. Then the Pharisees also began to ask him how he had received his sight. He said to them, "He put mud on my eyes. Then I washed, and now I see." Some of the Pharisees said, "This man is not from God, for he does not observe the sabbath." But others said, "How can a man who is a sinner perform such signs?" And they were divided. So they said again to the blind man, "What do you say about him? It was your eyes he opened." He said, "He is a prophet."

The Jews did not believe that he had been blind and had received his sight until they called the parents of the man who had received his sight and asked them, "Is this your son, who you say was born blind? How then does he now see?" His parents answered, "We know that this is our son, and that he was born blind; but we do not know how it is that now he sees, nor do we know who opened his eyes. Ask him; he is of age. He will speak for himself." His parents said this because they were afraid of the Jews; for the Jews had already agreed that anyone who confessed Jesus to be the Messiah would be put out of the synagogue. Therefore his parents said, "He is of age; ask him."

So for the second time they called the man who had been blind, and they said to him, "Give glory to God! We know that this man is a sinner." He answered, "I do not know whether he is a sinner. One thing I do know, that though I was blind, now I see." They said to him, "What did he do to you? How did he open your eyes?" He answered them, "I have told you already, and you would not listen. Why do you want to hear it again? Do you also want to become his disciples?" Then they reviled him, saying, "You are his disciple, but we are disciples of Moses. We know that God has spoken to Moses, but as for this man, we do not know where he comes from."

The man answered, "Here is an astonishing thing! You do not know where he comes from, and yet he opened my eyes. We know that God does not listen to sinners, but he does listen to one who worships him and obeys his will. Never since the world began has it been heard that anyone opened the eyes of a person born blind. If this man were not from God, he could do nothing." They answered him,

"You were born entirely in sins, and are you trying to teach us?" And they drove him out.

Jesus heard that they had driven him out, and when he found him, he said, "Do you believe in the Son of Man?" He answered, "And who is he, sir? Tell me, so that I may believe in him." Jesus said to him, "You have seen him, and the one speaking with you is he." He said, "Lord, I believe." And he worshiped him. Jesus said, "I came into this world for judgment so that those who do not see may see, and those who do see may become blind."

Some of the Pharisees near him heard this and said to him, "Surely we are not blind, are we?" Jesus said to them, "If you were blind, you would not have sin. But now that you say, 'We see,' your sin remains."

Points of View

JOHN F. CRAGHAN

Day after day we are offered a great number of facts, situations, events—especially in the media. We learn of murders, revolutions, natural disasters, and are required to assess all this material. Our conclusions to this process form our point of view about the world.

Today's readings dwell on light and darkness, sight and blindness, seeing and not seeing. They are timely reminders to reexamine our priorities and retest our standards for making judgments. They urge us to look within and ask whether or not our decisions are really Christian.

The author of 1 Samuel 16:1—2 Samuel 5:5 begins his narrative by painting an enthusiastic portrait of David's rise from a nobody to a royal somebody. He captures the upward movement of Israel's youthful hero. At the same time, he endorses key values of the decision-making process.

The story warns against judging by mere appearances since the well-to-do tend to be the elite. Hence there is the process whereby Samuel reviews the available sons of Jesse. The story highlights the motif of the selection of the most unlikely candidate. The shepherd boy, a marginal person, enters into the process and is ultimately chosen. God's Spirit can also rush on the lowly. Although the author notes David's handsome appearance, this is not the decisive factor because "the Lord looks on the heart."

Let There Be Light

The author of Ephesians contrasts the previously pagan lives of his audience with their new Christian lives by using the images of light and darkness, and the account from the Gospel of John contrasts the perceptions of the blind man and the Pharisees/Jews. The blind man progresses from darkness to light. Initially he regards Jesus as a man, but finally confesses that he is the Son of Man. The blind man sees (faith) that Jesus is "the light of the world."

The Pharisees/Jews first appear to accept the healing, but then begin to doubt that the man was blind from birth. They next deny Jesus' heavenly origins, and go on to mock the blind man. They adamantly refuse to see and thus end up blind.

Today's Good News

Taking this message to heart, modern Christians are called to look beyond appearances. We must decide whether the helpless, the indigent, the derelict are worthy of respect; or whether they are merely objects of disdain. These people are also the sisters and brothers of Jesus. It all depends on our point of view.

Modern Christians must judge wayward members of the family. Are they merely a disgrace to the family name? Or do they possibly exhibit genuine human qualities that we choose to ignore in order to concentrate on their clear excesses? It all depends on our point of view.

Modern Christians must evaluate the policies and programs of both Church and state. Are they right merely because authority has endorsed them? Do they really benefit the community? Or do too many people get hurt in the process of protecting the administration's policy? It all depends on our point of view.

Points for Reflection and Discussion

1. Do you generally derive your criteria for judgment from the gospel, or from the standard business procedures of our environment?

_____

_____

2. Imagine yourself blind. Whom do you trust to lead you?

_____

_____

Themes
Blindness
    L2, Saying Yes to Jesus
Conversion
    L3, Take a Look
Light
    L1, What Is Lent?

Reading 1, Ezekiel 37:12-14

Thus says the Lord God: "I am going to open your graves, and bring you up from your graves, O my people; and I will bring you back to the land of Israel. And you shall know that I am the Lord, when I open your graves, and bring you up from your graves, O my people. I will put my spirit within you, and you shall live, and I will place you on your own soil; then you shall know that I, the Lord, have spoken and will act," says the Lord.

Psalm 130:1-2,3-4,5-6,7-8 (*R* verse 7b)

Reading 2, Romans 8:8-11

Those who are in the flesh cannot please God. But you are not in the flesh; you are in the Spirit, since the Spirit of God dwells in you. Anyone who does not have the Spirit of Christ does not belong to him. But if Christ is in you, though the body is dead because of sin, the Spirit is life because of righteousness. If the Spirit of him who raised Jesus from the dead dwells in you, he who raised Christ from the dead will give life to your mortal bodies also through his Spirit that dwells in you.

Gospel, John 11:1-45

Now a certain man was ill, Lazarus of Bethany, the village of Mary and her sister Martha. Mary was the one who anointed the Lord with perfume and wiped his feet with her hair; her brother Lazarus was ill.

So the sisters sent a message to Jesus, "Lord, he whom you love is ill." But when Jesus heard it, he said, "This illness does not lead to death; rather it is for God's glory, so that the Son of God may be glorified through it." Accordingly, though Jesus loved Martha and her sister and Lazarus, after having heard that Lazarus was ill, he stayed two days longer in the place where he was.

Then after this he said to the disciples, "Let us go to Judea again." The disciples said to him, "Rabbi, the Jews were just now trying to stone you, and are you going there again?" Jesus answered, "Are there not twelve hours of daylight? Those who walk during the day do not stumble, because they see the light of this world. But those who walk at night stumble, because the light is not in them."

After saying this, he told them, "Our friend Lazarus has fallen asleep, but I am going there to awaken him." The disciples said to him, "Lord, if he has fallen asleep, he will be all right." Jesus, however, had been speaking about his death, but they thought that he was referring merely to sleep. Then Jesus told them plainly, "Lazarus is dead. For your sake I am glad I was not there, so that you may believe. But let us go to him." Thomas, who was called the Twin, said to his fellow disciples, "Let us also go, that we may die with him."

When Jesus arrived, he found that Lazarus had already been in the tomb four days. Now Bethany was near Jerusalem, some two miles away, and many of the Jews had come to Martha and Mary to console them about their brother. When Martha heard that Jesus was coming, she went and met him, while Mary stayed at home. Martha said to Jesus, "Lord, if you had been here, my brother would not have died. But even now I know that God will give you whatever you ask of him." Jesus said to her, "Your brother will rise again." Martha said to him, "I know that he will rise again in the resurrection on the last day." Jesus said to her, "I am the resurrection and the life. Those who believe in me, even though they die, will live, and everyone who lives and believes in me will never die. Do you believe this?" She said to him, "Yes, Lord, I believe that you are the Messiah, the Son of God, the one coming into the world." When she had said this, she went back and called her sister Mary, and told her privately, "The Teacher is here and is calling for you." And when she heard it, she got up quickly and went to him. Now Jesus had not yet come to the village, but was still at the place where Martha had met him. The Jews who were with her in the house, consoling her, saw Mary get up quickly and go out. They followed her because they thought that she was going to the tomb to weep there.

When Mary came where Jesus was and saw him, she knelt at his feet and said to him, "Lord, if you had been here, my brother would not have died." When Jesus saw her weeping, and the Jews who came with her also weeping, he was greatly disturbed in spirit and deeply moved. He said, "Where have you laid him?" They said to him, "Lord, come and see." Jesus began to weep. So the Jews said, "See how he loved him!" But some of them said, "Could not he who opened the eyes of the blind man have kept this man from dying?"

Then Jesus, again greatly disturbed, came to the tomb. It was a cave, and a stone was lying against it. Jesus said, "Take away the stone." Martha, the sister of the dead man, said to him, "Lord, already there is a stench because he has been dead four days." Jesus said to her, "Did I not tell you that if you believed, you would see the glory of God?" So they took away the stone. And Jesus looked upward and said, "Father, I thank you for having heard me. I knew that you always hear me, but I have said this for the sake of the crowd standing here, so that they may believe that you sent me."

When he had said this, he cried with a loud voice, "Lazarus, come out!" The dead man came out, his hands and feet bound with strips of cloth, and his face wrapped in a cloth. Jesus said to them, "Unbind him, and let him go." Many of the Jews therefore, who had come with Mary and had seen what Jesus did, believed in him.

Dry Bones

JOHN F. CRAGHAN

We sometimes reach a point where despair takes over and depression reigns supreme. We feel overwhelmed by life's shocks and incapacitated by our own failure. Self-pity often becomes the expression of our profound misery. We feel we are old bones incapable of new life.

Today's readings deal with the very real problems of anxiety and hopelessness. Yet they clearly announce a God who becomes involved in human tragedy. This is the God of the living who chooses to become concerned because concern is a manifestation of life. This God unequivocally enables old bones to have new life.

Preaching to a depressed exilic audience in the aftermath of the destruction of Jerusalem, Ezekiel personally experiences their sense of frustration. He even quotes their expression of despair: "Our bones are dried up, and our hope is lost; we are cut off completely" (37:11). The prophet is transported by God's Spirit to a place littered with dry human bones. At the prophet's word, the bones are reconstituted into human bodies and the breath/spirit/wind brings the bodies to life. In Ezekiel's interpretation, the vision is applied to God's despondent people. The bones are the graves of that people who now come back to life and are promised resettlement in their own land. The message is that old bones can have new life.

In Romans 7:14-25, Paul paints a vivid picture of human agony. "I do not do the good I want, but the evil I do not want is what I do" (7:19). In chapter eight of Romans, however, Paul develops the theme of new hope because of the life-giving Spirit. Christians experience God's power whereby a genuine moral life is possible and the threat of condemnation is lifted.

In today's reading, Paul teaches that Christians who allow the Spirit to determine their moral values actually live out their profound association with Christ. Even though the Spirit does not remove physical death, the Spirit does bring to human life that transforming experience of being right with God (justice—a gratuitous gift) that leads to resurrection. For Paul, the message of God in Christ is that old bones can have new life.

The Glory of God

John recounts the raising of Lazarus as a sign that transforms tragedy into hope. Lazarus' illness and subsequent death are an occasion for the manifestation of God's glory. God's presence is made visible through deeds of power. The primary focus of this incident is the glory of the Father, not the assistance of a friend.

Faith goes hand in hand with glory. The miracle also glorifies Jesus, and the disciples' faith in Jesus will lead to the further display of God's glory (see also Jn 2:11). To accept Jesus is to make oneself open to that whole process of transformation. The disciple glorifies the Father just as the Son did by sharing in the passion/death/resurrection.

Today's Good News

Human despair takes many forms. Whatever form it takes, the process of overcoming despair is fundamentally the same. It is to be in the presence of God and to breathe the Spirit upon our world. Hope then becomes possible and life becomes livable.

To provide jobs for the unemployed is clearly in the tradition of Ezekiel: Graves open and the Spirit breathes new life. To care for the elderly and the shut-ins is certainly in the tradition of Paul: The Spirit influences our moral choices and outreach to others implies we belong to Christ. To alleviate the hunger of the world's stricken is obviously in the tradition of John. So too are the many acts of charity we all are called upon to perform. We thus manifest the glory of God and strengthen the faith of our sisters and brothers. We participate in God's great work of giving old bones new life.

Points for Reflection and Discussion

1. God is a God of the living. What area in your existence needs to be untied, as Lazarus was, in order to come back to life?

_____

_____

_____

_____

_____

2. Do you fear death? Talk about your experiences of death.

_____

_____

_____

_____

Themes
Death
    L1, What Is Lent?
Spirit
    L7, The Meaning of Holy Week

Reading 1 (ABC), Exodus 12:1-8,11-14

The Lord said to Moses and Aaron in the land of Egypt: This month shall mark for you the beginning of months; it shall be the first month of the year for you. Tell the whole congregation of Israel that on the tenth of this month they are to take a lamb for each family, a lamb for each household. If a household is too small for a whole lamb, it shall join its closest neighbor in obtaining one; the lamb shall be divided in proportion to the number of people who eat of it. Your lamb shall be without blemish, a year-old male; you may take it from the sheep or from the goats. You shall keep it until the fourteenth day of this month; then the whole assembled congregation of Israel shall slaughter it at twilight. They shall take some of the blood and put it on the two doorposts and the lintel of the houses in which they eat it. They shall eat the lamb that same night; they shall eat it roasted over the fire with unleavened bread and bitter herbs.

This is how you shall eat it: your loins girded, your sandals on your feet, and your staff in your hand; and you shall eat it hurriedly. It is the passover of the Lord. For I will pass through the land of Egypt that night, and I will strike down every firstborn in the land of Egypt, both human beings and animals; on all the gods of Egypt I will execute judgments: I am the Lord. The blood shall be a sign for you on the houses where you live: when I see the blood, I will pass over you, and no plague shall destroy you when I strike the land of Egypt. This day shall be a day of remembrance for you. You shall celebrate it as a festival to the Lord; throughout your generations you shall observe it as a perpetual ordinance.

Psalm 116:12-13,15-16,17-18 (*R* 1 Cor 10:16)

Reading 2 (ABC), 1 Corinthians 11:23-26

I received from the Lord what I also handed on to you, that the Lord Jesus on the night when he was betrayed took a loaf of bread, and when he had given thanks, he broke it and said, "This is my body that is for you. Do this in remembrance of me." In the same way he took the cup also, after supper, saying, "This cup is the new covenant in my blood. Do this, as often as you drink it, in remembrance of me." For as often as you eat this bread and drink the cup, you proclaim the Lord's death until he comes.

Gospel (ABC), John 13:1-15

Before the festival of the Passover, Jesus knew that his hour had come to depart from this world and go to the Father. Having loved his own who were in the world, he loved them to the end. The devil had already put it into the heart of Judas son of Simon Iscariot to betray him. And during supper Jesus, knowing that the Father had given all things into his hands, and that he had come from God and was going to God, got up from the table, took off his outer robe, and tied a towel around himself. Then he poured water into a basin and began to wash the disciples' feet and to wipe them with the towel that was tied around him. He came to Simon Peter, who said to him, "Lord, are you going to wash my feet?" Jesus answered, "You do not know now what I am doing, but later you will understand." Peter said to him, "You will never wash my feet." Jesus answered, "Unless I wash you, you have no share with me." Simon Peter said to him, "Lord, not my feet only but also my hands and my head!" Jesus said to him, "One who has bathed does not need to wash, except for the feet, but is entirely clean. And you are clean, though not all of you." For he knew who was to betray him; for this reason he said, "Not all of you are clean."

After he had washed their feet, had put on his robe, and had returned to the table, he said to them, "Do you know what I have done to you? You call me Teacher and Lord— and you are right, for that is what I am. So if I, your Lord and Teacher, have washed your feet, you also ought to wash one another's feet. For I have set you an example, that you also should do as I have done to you."

Service

JOHN F. CRAGHAN

Self-service is no service. Somehow we seem programmed to look only to our own concerns; we find it hard to include the concerns of others. We believe that we are to be served and waited upon; we find it difficult to serve and wait upon others. We are driven to pursue our personal advantage; we find it distasteful to pursue the advantage of others. Nonetheless the whole thrust of Holy Thursday is that to be Christian means to serve others. Hence self-service is no service.

An Unblemished Lamb

Originally the Passover was the feast of shepherds for the welfare of their flocks when they set out for new pasture grounds. It was a critical time in the spring when the young of the sheep and goats would be born. In this feast, the blood is smeared on the tent poles to ward off any danger to humans and animals.

In its Israelite context the Passover is the celebration of the new pasture grounds that follows the exodus, i.e., the Promised Land. It is the celebration of the Lord's liberating action. The blood rite is now the link between the tenth plague and the Passover. The Lord will strike down the Egyptian firstborn but will pass over or spare the inhabitants of the blood-smeared houses.

In Christian use, and especially on Holy Thursday, Jesus is the Passover lamb who delivers the world from sin. There is a link, therefore, with the Passover lamb of Exodus whose blood delivered the Israelites from the "destroyer" (see Ex 12:23). In its Christian context, Jesus' self-giving in death is the supreme act whereby sin may be overcome. Hence it is that self-giving that looks to the needs of others. To that degree self-service is no service.

Remembering the Lord

The celebration of the Lord's Supper in Corinth involved two elements: a common meal in which one would share one's food and drink with other members of the community, and the Eucharist itself. It is clear from 1 Cor 11:17-22, however, that the Corinthian community was not really a community but an amalgam of various factions. The wealthier members arrived first and consumed the food and drink to the extent that some became intoxicated. The poorer members arrived later only to find that the meal was virtually ended, to such a degree that some of them went hungry.

At this point Paul upbraids his community, pointing out that the Corinthians are really unable to eat the Lord's Supper. Clearly their lack of charity does not dispose them to take part in the self-giving of Jesus. Paul quotes the tradition he received about the words of institution for the Eucharist. He insists that proclaiming the death of the Lord and remembrance imply a sharing now in the Lord's body and blood. But such sharing presupposes a bonded community, not a multiplication of factions. For Paul, Eucharist without community is no Eucharist. For Paul, self-service is no service.

Setting Examples

The opening verse of the gospel understands Jesus' death under two aspects: an act of love for his followers, and victory because of Jesus' return to the Father. In verse 2, the author links the foot washing with Jesus' death by noting the betrayal of Jesus and, in verse 3, by emphasizing Jesus' return to God. In verses 4-5, the foot washing is an act of humility by Jesus, in that he plays the role of a servant, a role that symbolizes his humiliation in death. Verses 6-10a give the first interpretation of Jesus' action, i.e., the foot washing makes the disciple capable of sharing eternal life with Jesus. This is further developed in verses 9-10a, which speak of bathing, i.e., baptism.

Verses 12-15 give the second interpretation of Jesus' action. The foot washing demonstrates Jesus' service for others—something that the followers of Jesus must imitate. Hence the foot washing is a reality that must be reproduced in the lives of the community. The authentic follower of Jesus will not shun washing the feet of other community members. To claim Jesus as Lord and Master means to make oneself servant and slave of all. Self-service is no service.

Today's Good News

The Passover ceremony of Exodus, the upbraiding of Paul at Corinth, and the symbolic action of Jesus in the gospel story are powerful reminders on Holy Thursday that we must look beyond ourselves and discover the world of pain and frustration of our sisters and brothers. They urge us to liberate our ego by service on behalf of others.

Husbands and wives who consistently consider each other's needs show the Christian way. Family members who regularly seek to alleviate problems reveal Christian values. Leaders who habitually spend time and energy in promoting the good of their people demonstrate genuine Christianity. Such people set examples for us; examples which show that self-service is no service.

Eucharist reflects a Lord and Master who is servant and slave. Eucharist takes Jesus' death-style and offers it as the community's lifestyle. To eat and drink with Jesus is to arise and offer oneself as food and drink for others. Eucharist clearly states that self-service is no service.

Points for Reflection and Discussion

1. Whom do you believe was most humbled by Jesus' washing of Peter's feet: Jesus or Peter? Why?

_____

_____

_____

2. Do you believe it is possible to truly celebrate Eucharist apart from a community? Why or why not?

_____

_____

_____

Themes

Community
   L4, The Nicene Creed
   L8, Catechumenate Retreat Day
Eucharist
   L2, Saying Yes to Jesus
   L7, The Meaning of Holy Week
Service
   L3, Take a Look

Reading 1 (ABC), Isaiah 52:13—53:12

See, my servant shall prosper; he shall be exalted and lifted up, and shall be very high. Just as there were many who were astonished at him—so marred was his appearance, beyond human semblance, and his form beyond that of mortals—so he shall startle many nations; kings shall shut their mouths because of him; for that which had not been told them they shall see, and that which they had not heard they shall contemplate.

Who has believed what we have heard? And to whom has the arm of the Lord been revealed? For he grew up before him like a young plant, and like a root out of dry ground; he had no form or majesty that we should look at him, nothing in his appearance that we should desire him. He was despised and rejected by others; a man of suffering and acquainted with infirmity; and as one from whom others hide their faces he was despised, and we held him of no account. Surely he has borne our infirmities and carried our diseases; yet we accounted him stricken, struck down by God, and afflicted. But he was wounded for our transgressions, crushed for our iniquities; upon him was the punishment that made us whole, and by his bruises we are healed. All we like sheep have gone astray; we have all turned to our own way, and the Lord has laid on him the iniquity of us all. He was oppressed, and he was afflicted, yet he did not open his mouth; like a lamb that is led to the slaughter, and like a sheep that before its shearers is silent, so he did not open his mouth. By a perversion of justice he was taken away. Who could have imagined his future? For he was cut off from the land of the living, stricken for the transgression of my people. They made his grave with the wicked and his tomb with the rich, although he had done no violence, and there was no deceit in his mouth. Yet it was the will of the Lord to crush him with pain.

When you make his life an offering for sin, he shall see his offspring, and shall prolong his days; through him the will of the Lord shall prosper. Out of his anguish he shall see light; he shall find satisfaction through his knowledge. The righteous one, my servant, shall make many righteous, and he shall bear their iniquities. Therefore I will allot him a portion with the great, and he shall divide the spoil with the strong; because he poured out himself to death, and was numbered with the transgressors; yet he bore the sin of many, and made intercession for the transgressors.

Psalm 31:1,5,11-12,14-15,16,24 (R Lk 23:46)

Reading 2 (ABC), Hebrews 4:14-16;5:7-9

Since we have a great high priest who has passed through the heavens, Jesus, the Son of God, let us hold fast to our confession. For we do not have a high priest who is unable to sympathize with our weaknesses, but we have one who in every respect has been tested as we are, yet without sin. Let us therefore approach the throne of grace with boldness, so that we may receive mercy and find grace to help in time of need.

In the days of his flesh, Jesus offered up prayers and supplications, with loud cries and tears, to the one who was able to save him from death, and he was heard because of his reverent submission. Although he was a Son, he learned obedience through what he suffered; and having been made perfect, he became the source of eternal salvation for all who obey him.

Gospel (ABC), John 18:1—19:42

Jesus went out with his disciples across the Kidron valley to a place where there was a garden, which he and his disciples entered. Now Judas, who betrayed him, also knew the place, because Jesus often met there with his disciples. So Judas brought a detachment of soldiers together with police from the chief priests and the Pharisees, and they came there with lanterns and torches and weapons. Then Jesus, knowing all that was to happen to him, came forward and asked them, "Whom are you looking for?" They answered, "Jesus of Nazareth." Jesus replied, "I am he." Judas, who betrayed him, was standing with them. When Jesus said to them, "I am he," they stepped back and fell to the ground. Again he asked them, "Whom are you looking for?" And they said, "Jesus of Nazareth." Jesus answered, "I told you that I am he. So if you are looking for me, let these men go." This was to fulfill the word that he had spoken, "I did not lose a single one of those whom you gave me."

Then Simon Peter, who had a sword, drew it, struck the high priest's slave, and cut off his right ear. The slave's name was Malchus. Jesus said to Peter, "Put your sword back into its sheath. Am I not to drink the cup that the Father has given me?" So the soldiers, their officer, and the Jewish police arrested Jesus and bound him. First they took him to Annas, who was the father-in-law of Caiaphas, the high priest that year. Caiaphas was the one who had advised the Jews that it was better to have one person die for the people.

Simon Peter and another disciple followed Jesus. Since that disciple was known to the high priest, he went with Jesus into the courtyard of the high priest, but Peter was standing outside at the gate. So the other disciple, who was known to the high priest, went out, spoke to the woman who guarded the gate, and brought Peter in. The woman said to Peter, "You are not also one of this man's disciples, are you?" He said, "I am not." Now the slaves and the police had made a charcoal fire because it was cold, and they were standing around it and warming themselves. Peter also was standing with them and warming himself.

Then the high priest questioned Jesus about his disciples and about his teaching. Jesus answered, "I have spoken openly to the world; I have always taught in synagogues and in the temple, where all the Jews come together. I have said nothing in secret. Why do you ask me? Ask those who heard what I said to them; they know what I said." When he had said this, one of the police standing nearby struck Jesus on the face, saying, "Is that how you answer the high priest?" Jesus answered, "If I have spoken wrongly, testify to the wrong. But if have spoken rightly, why do you strike me?" Then Annas sent him bound to Caiaphas the high priest.

Now Simon Peter was standing and warming himself. They asked him, "You are not also one of his disciples, are you?" He denied it and said, "I am not." One of the slaves of the high priest, a relative of the man whose ear Peter had cut off, asked, "Did I not see you in the garden with him?" Again Peter denied it, and at that moment the cock crowed.

Then they took Jesus from Caiaphas to Pilate's headquarters. It was early in the morning. They themselves did not enter the headquarters, so as to avoid ritual defilement and to be able to eat the Passover. So Pilate went out to them and said, "What accusation do you bring against this man?" They answered, "If this man were not a criminal, we would not have handed him over to you." Pilate said to them, "Take him yourselves and judge him according to your law." The Jews replied, "We are not permitted to put anyone to death." (This was to fulfill what Jesus had said when he indicated the kind of death he was to die.) Then Pilate entered the headquarters again, summoned Jesus, and asked him, "Are you the King of the Jews?" Jesus answered, "Do you ask this on your own, or did others tell you about me?" Pilate replied, "I am not a Jew, am I? Your own nation and the chief priests have handed you over to me. What have you done?" Jesus answered, "My kingdom is not from this world. If my kingdom were from this world, my followers would be fighting to keep me from being handed over to the Jews. But as it is, my kingdom is not from here." Pilate asked him, "So you are a king?" Jesus answered, "You say that I am a king. For this I was born, and for this I came into the world, to testify to the truth. Everyone who belongs to the truth listens to my voice." Pilate asked him, "What is truth?"

After he had said this, he went out to the Jews again and told them, "I find no case against him. But you have a custom that I release someone for you at the Passover. Do you want me to release for you the King of the Jews?" They shouted in reply, "Not this man, but Barabbas!" Now Barabbas was a bandit. Then Pilate took Jesus and had him flogged. And the soldiers wove a crown of thorns and put it on his head, and they dressed him in a purple robe. They kept coming up to him, saying, "Hail, King of the Jews!" and striking him on the face. Pilate went out again and said to them, "Look, I am bringing him out to you to let you know that I find no case against him." So Jesus came out, wearing the crown of thorns and the purple robe. Pilate said to them, "Here is the man!" When the chief priests and the police saw him, they shouted, "Crucify him! Crucify him!" Pilate said to them, "Take him yourselves and crucify him; I find no case against him." The Jews answered him, "We have a law, and according to that law he ought to die because he has claimed to be the Son of God." Now when Pilate heard this, he was more afraid than ever. He entered his headquarters again and asked Jesus, "Where are you from?" But Jesus gave him no answer. Pilate therefore said to him, "Do you refuse to speak to me? Do you not know that I have power to release you, and power to crucify you?" Jesus answered him, "You would have no power over me unless it had been given you from above; therefore the one who handed me over to you is guilty of a greater sin." From then on Pilate tried to release him, but the Jews cried out, "If you release this man, you are no friend of the emperor. Everyone who claims to be a king sets himself against the emperor."

When Pilate heard these words, he brought Jesus outside and sat on the judge's bench at a place called The Stone Pavement, or in Hebrew Gabbatha. Now it was the day of Preparation for the Passover; and it was about noon. He said to the Jews, "Here is your King!" They cried out, "Away with him! Away with him! Crucify him!" Pilate asked them, "Shall I crucify your King?" The chief priests answered, "We have no king but the emperor." Then he handed him over to them to be crucified.

So they took Jesus; and carrying the cross by himself, he went out to what is called The Place of the Skull, which in Hebrew is called Golgotha. There they crucified him, and with him two others, one on either side, with Jesus between them. Pilate also had an inscription written and put on the cross. It read, "Jesus of Nazareth, the King of the Jews." Many of the Jews read this inscription, because the place where Jesus was crucified was near the city; and it was written in Hebrew, in Latin, and in Greek. Then the chief priests of the Jews said to Pilate, "Do not write, 'The King of the Jews,' but, 'This man said, I am King of the Jews.'" Pilate answered, "What I have written I have written."

When the soldiers had crucified Jesus, they took his clothes and divided them into four parts, one for each soldier. They also took his tunic; now the tunic was seamless, woven in one piece from the top. So they said to one another, "Let us not tear it, but cast lots for it to see who will get it." This was to fulfill what the scripture says, "They divided my clothes among themselves, and for my clothing they cast lots." And that is what the soldiers did.

Meanwhile, standing near the cross of Jesus were his mother, and his mother's sister, Mary the wife of Clopas, and Mary Magdalene. When Jesus saw his mother and the disciple whom he loved standing beside her, he said to his mother, "Woman, here is your son." Then he said to the disciple, "Here is your mother." And from that hour the disciple took her into his own home. After this, when Jesus knew that all was now finished, he said (in order to fulfill the scripture), "I am thirsty." A jar full of sour wine was standing there. So they put a sponge full of the wine on a branch of hyssop and held it to his mouth. When Jesus had received the wine, he said, "It is finished." Then he bowed his head and gave up his spirit.

Since it was the day of Preparation, the Jews did not want the bodies left on the cross during the sabbath, especially because that sabbath was a day of great solemnity. So they asked Pilate to have the legs of the crucified men broken and the bodies removed. Then the soldiers came and broke the legs of the first and of the other who had been crucified with him. But when they came to Jesus and saw that he was already dead, they did not break his legs. Instead, one of the soldiers pierced his side with a spear, and at once blood and water came out. (He who saw this has testified so that you also may believe. His testimony is true, and he knows that he tells the truth.) These things occurred so that the scripture might be fulfilled, "None of his bones shall be broken." And again another passage of scripture says, "They will look on the one whom they have pierced."

After these things, Joseph of Arimathea, who was a disciple of Jesus, though a secret one because of his fear of the Jews, asked Pilate to let him take away the body of Jesus. Pilate gave him permission; so he came and removed his body. Nicodemus, who had at first come to Jesus by night, also came, bringing a mixture of myrrh and aloes, weighing about a hundred pounds. They took the body of Jesus and wrapped it with the spices in linen cloths, according to the burial custom of the Jews. Now there was a garden in the place where he was crucified, and in the garden there was a new tomb in which no one had ever been laid. And so, because it was the Jewish day of Preparation, and the tomb was nearby, they laid Jesus there.

Death Unto Life

JOHN F. CRAGHAN

Death brings life to the community. All too often we subscribe to the view that we are born for ourselves and we die for ourselves. Perhaps we also accept a dog-eat-dog philosophy and may even endorse belief in the survival of the fittest. We may tend to be isolationists, even when we interact with others. We may find it impossible to accept the paradoxical doctrine that death brings life to the community.

Today's readings are the very opposite of the isolationist philosophy. They point us in the direction of two individuals whose death culminated in life. Their death, however, was not a purely personal achievement. Rather, it was one that brought life to their community.

The first reading is the fourth Servant Song from the work of the anonymous exilic author of the Second Isaiah (chapters 40—55). The Suffering Servant is quite likely the prophet himself and all those followers who heed God's word to leave exile in Babylon for a new life in Israel.

The song begins on a note of triumph, the exaltation of the Servant and the accomplishment of his mission. The song then describes the would-be triumph of the Servant's enemies, i.e., the disfigurement, death, and burial of the Servant as a criminal. Such a catastrophe obviously indicated the presence of sin. It was not the prophet's sin, however, but Israel's ("wounded for *our* transgressions, crushed for *our* iniquities"). The Servant, therefore, bore Israel's guilt and gave his life as a sin-offering (verse 10). The outcome of the Servant's action is redemption for Israel. In this passage death brings life to the community.

The second reading consists of two passages from Hebrews that emphasize Jesus' high-priestly office and its implications for believers. While the author acknowledges Jesus' special relationship with God, however, he also underlines the utter humanity of this high priest. Hence Jesus can fully understand the weakness of his people since he himself was often tempted.

In 5:7-9, while the author returns to the theme of Jesus' humanity ("loud cries and tears"), he also connects it with the theme of Jesus' exaltation. Jesus' obedience to the Father results in his priestly consecration. In turn, that consecration enables him to save those who obey him. Jesus' ultimate weakness, death on the cross, climaxes in his power as high priest whereby believers experience the source of salvation. Death brings life to the community.

A Lifegiving Passion

John's passion account has three main elements: Jesus' arrest and questioning (18:1-27), his trial before Pilate (18:28—19:16a), and his crucifixion (19:16b-42). Actually the word "passion" is something of a misnomer since Jesus' painful experience is only an aspect of his royal character. The reason for the crowning and mocking of Jesus, for example (19:2-3), is that Pilate has already proclaimed him a king (18:37). The cry, "Here is the man," is also part of the ritual of coronation—the people acknowledge Jesus as king. Finally, the crucifixion itself is Jesus' actual enthronement because the trilingual inscription (19:19-20) announces his kingship to the international community.

John presents an absolutely free and self-possessed Jesus who is the master of his own fate. Only in this gospel does Jesus respond to the indignities before the Jewish officials (18:21). In "lecturing" Pilate (19:9-11), Jesus implies that no one really takes his life away—rather, he lays it down freely. Unlike Matthew, Mark, and Luke, John has no Simon to help Jesus carry his cross. Jesus accepts his destiny alone in absolute freedom (19:17).

Among other special moments in this gospel is the flow of blood and water (19:34). The flow of water is linked to Jesus' own prophecy that from within him there would flow rivers of living water (7:37-38). John relates this to Jesus' giving up of his spirit (19:30). Jesus' death, therefore, is that moment of glorification when the Spirit is released upon the new community (7:39;20:22). Clearly, for the author of John, death brings life to the community.

Today's Good News

The Suffering Servant and the Jesus of both the Letter to the Hebrews and the Gospel of John must influence our way of thinking about life and death. These two realities are not isolated but intertwined. The experience of pain in self-giving must say something about genuine living.

There are the parents who provide for the total well-being of their families by daily sacrificing themselves. There are the politicians and other leaders who drain themselves for the people entrusted to their care. There are the friends of the sick, the lonely, the disabled; those who mend broken bones and broken hearts and broken spirits. These people, and all those like them, recognize that death truly does bring life to the community.

Points for Reflection and Discussion

1. Our Church does not celebrate the Liturgy of the Eucharist on Good Friday—the only day of the year that there is no eucharistic feast—because on this day we commemorate the death of the Lord Jesus. Allow his suffering and death to pierce your heart. Grieve for him—and for all God's people who suffer and die at the hands of ignorance and injustice.

_____

_____

_____

_____

2. Do you find the passion according to John to be more of a "celebration" than the passions according to Mark and Matthew and Luke? Is it possible to really "celebrate" Christ's passion? Why or why not?

_____

_____

_____

_____

Themes

Death
    L4, The Nicene Creed
    L7, The Meaning of Holy Week
Pain, Suffering
    L5, The Way of the Cross
Sin
    L1, What Is Lent?
    L3, Take a Look
    L8, Catechumenate Retreat Day

Reading 1 (ABC), Genesis 1:1—2:2

In the beginning when God created the heavens and the earth, the earth was a formless void and darkness covered the face of the deep, while a wind from God swept over the face of the waters. Then God said, "Let there be light"; and there was light. And God saw that the light was good; and God separated the light from the darkness. God called the light Day, and the darkness he called Night. And there was evening and there was morning, the first day.

And God said, "Let there be a dome in the midst of the waters, and let it separate the waters from the waters." So God made the dome and separated the waters that were under the dome from the waters that were above the dome. And it was so. God called the dome Sky. And there was evening and there was morning, the second day.

And God said, "Let the waters under the sky be gathered together into one place, and let the dry land appear." And it was so. God called the dry land Earth, and the waters that were gathered together he called Seas. And God saw that it was good. Then God said, "Let the earth put forth vegetation: plants yielding seed, and fruit trees of every kind on earth that bear fruit with the seed in it." And it was so. The earth brought forth vegetation: plants yielding seed of every kind, and trees of every kind bearing fruit with the seed in it. And God saw that it was good. And there was evening and there was morning, the third day.

And God said, "Let there be lights in the dome of the sky to separate the day from the night; and let them be for signs and for seasons and for days and years, and let them be lights in the dome of the sky to give light upon the earth." And it was so. God made the two great lights—the greater light to rule the day and the lesser light to rule the night—and the stars. God set them in the dome of the sky to give light upon the earth, to rule over the day and over the night, and to separate the light from the darkness. And God saw that it was good. And there was evening and there was morning, the fourth day.

And God said, "Let the waters bring forth swarms of living creatures, and let birds fly above the earth across the dome of the sky." So God created the great sea monsters and every living creature that moves, of every kind, with which the waters swarm, and every winged bird of every kind. And God saw that it was good. God blessed them, saying, "Be fruitful and multiply and fill the waters in the seas, and let birds multiply on the earth." And there was evening and there was morning, the fifth day.

And God said, "Let the earth bring forth living creatures of every kind: cattle and creeping things and wild animals of the earth of every kind." And it was so. God made the wild animals of the earth of every kind, and the cattle of every kind, and everything that creeps upon the ground of every kind. And God saw that it was good. Then God said,

"Let us make humankind in our image, according to our likeness; and let them have dominion over the fish of the sea, and over the birds of the air, and over the cattle, and over all the wild animals of the earth, and over every creeping thing that creeps upon the earth." So God created humankind in his image, in the image of God he created them; male and female he created them. God blessed them, and God said to them, "Be fruitful and multiply, and fill the earth and subdue it; and have dominion over the fish of the sea and over the birds of the air and over every living thing that moves upon the earth." God said, "See, I have given you every plant yielding seed that is upon the face of all the earth, and every tree with seed in its fruit; you shall have them for food. And to every beast of the earth, and to every bird of the air, and to everything that creeps on the earth, everything that has the breath of life, I have given every green plant for food." And it was so. God saw everything that he had made, and indeed, it was very good. And there was evening and there was morning, the sixth day.

Thus the heavens and the earth were finished, and all their multitude. And on the seventh day God finished the work that he had done, and he rested on the seventh day from all the work that he had done.

Psalm 104:1-2,5-6,10,12,13-14,24,35 (R verse 30)

(or) Psalm 33:4-5,6-7,12-13,20,22 (R verse 5)

Reading 3 (ABC), Exodus 14:15—15:1

The Lord said to Moses, "Why do you cry out to me? Tell the Israelites to go forward. But you lift up your staff, and stretch out your hand over the sea and divide it, that the Israelites may go into the sea on dry ground. Then I will harden the hearts of the Egyptians so that they will go in after them; and so I will gain glory for myself over Pharaoh and all his army, his chariots, and his chariot drivers. And the Egyptians shall know that I am the Lord, when I have gained glory for myself over Pharaoh, his chariots, and his chariot drivers."

The angel of God who was going before the Israelite army moved and went behind them; and the pillar of cloud moved from in front of them and took its place behind them. It came between the army of Egypt and the army of Israel. And so the cloud was there with the darkness, and it lit up the night; one did not come near the other all night. Then Moses stretched out his hand over the sea. The Lord drove the sea back by a strong east wind all night, and turned the sea into dry land; and the waters were divided. The Israelites went into the sea on dry ground, the waters forming a wall for them on their right and on their left. The Egyptians pursued, and went into the sea after them, all of Pharaoh's horses, chariots, and chariot drivers.

At the morning watch the Lord in the pillar of fire and cloud looked down upon the Egyptian army, and threw the Egyptian army into panic. He clogged their chariot wheels so that they turned with difficulty. The Egyptians said, "Let us flee from the Israelites, for the Lord is fighting for them against Egypt." Then the Lord said to Moses, "Stretch out your hand over the sea, so that the water may come back upon the Egyptians, upon their chariots and chariot drivers." So Moses stretched out his hand over the sea, and at dawn the sea returned to its normal depth. As the Egyptians fled before it, the Lord tossed the Egyptians into the sea. The waters returned and covered the chariots and the chariot drivers, the entire army of Pharaoh that had followed them into the sea; not one of them remained. But the Israelites walked on dry ground through the sea, the waters forming a wall for them on their right and on their left.

Thus the Lord saved Israel that day from the Egyptians; and Israel saw the Egyptians dead on the seashore. Israel saw the great work that the Lord did against the Egyptians. So the people feared the Lord and believed in the Lord and in his servant Moses.

Then Moses and the Israelites sang this song to the Lord: "I will sing to the Lord, for he has triumphed gloriously; horse and rider he has thrown into the sea."

Exodus 15:1-2,3-5,6-7,17-18 (R verse 1)

Epistle (ABC), Romans 6:3-11

Do you not know that all of us who have been baptized into Christ Jesus were baptized into his death? Therefore we have been buried with him by baptism into death, so that, just as Christ was raised from the dead by the glory of the Father, so we too might walk in newness of life. For if we have been united with him in a death like his, we will certainly be united with him in a resurrection like his. We know that our old self was crucified with him so that the body of sin might be destroyed, and we might no longer be enslaved to sin. For whoever has died is freed from sin. But if we have died with Christ, we believe that we will also live with him. We know that Christ, being raised from the dead, will never die again; death no longer has dominion over him. The death he died, he died to sin, once for all; but the life he lives, he lives to God. So you also must consider yourselves dead to sin and alive to God in Christ Jesus.

Psalm 118:1-2,16-17,22-23 (R Alleluia! Alleluia!)

Gospel (A), Matthew 28:1-10

After the sabbath, as the first day of the week was dawning, Mary Magdalene and the other Mary went to see the tomb. And suddenly there was a great earthquake; for an angel of the Lord, descending from heaven, came and rolled back the stone and sat on it. His appearance was like lightning, and his clothing white as snow. For fear of him the guards shook and became like dead men. But the angel said to the women, "Do not be afraid; I know that you are looking for Jesus who was crucified. He is not here; for he has been raised, as he said. Come, see the place where he lay. Then go quickly and tell his disciples, 'He has been raised from the dead, and indeed he is going ahead of you to Galilee; there you will see him.' This is my message for you." So they left the tomb quickly with fear and great joy, and ran to tell his disciples. Suddenly Jesus met them and said, "Greetings!" And they came to him, took hold of his feet, and worshiped him. Then Jesus said to them, "Do not be afraid; go and tell my brothers to go to Galilee; there they will see me."

Gospel (B), Mark 16:1-8

When the sabbath was over, Mary Magdalene, and Mary the mother of James, and Salome bought spices, so that they might go and anoint [Jesus]. And very early on the first day of the week, when the sun had risen, they went to the tomb. They had been saying to one another, "Who will roll away the stone for us from the entrance to the tomb?" When they looked up, they saw that the stone, which was very large, had already been rolled back. As they entered the tomb, they saw a young man, dressed in a white robe, sitting on the right side; and they were alarmed. But he said to them, "Do not be alarmed; you are looking for Jesus of Nazareth, who was crucified. He has been raised; he is not here. Look, there is the place they laid him. But go, tell his disciples and Peter that he is going ahead of you to Galilee; there you will see him, just as he told you."

So they went out and fled from the tomb, for terror and amazement had seized them; and they said nothing to anyone, for they were afraid.

Gospel (C), Luke 24:1-12

On the first day of the week, at early dawn, [the women] came to the tomb, taking the spices that they had prepared. They found the stone rolled away from the tomb, but when they went in, they did not find the body. While they were perplexed about this, suddenly two men in dazzling clothes stood beside them. The women were terrified and bowed their faces to the ground, but the men said to them, "Why do you look for the living among the dead? He is not here, but has risen. Remember how he told you, while he was still in Galilee, that the Son of Man must be handed over to sinners, and be crucified, and on the third day rise again." Then they remembered his words, and returning from the tomb, they told all this to the eleven and to all the rest. Now it was Mary Magdalene, Joanna, Mary the mother of James, and the other women with them who told this to the apostles. But these words seemed to them an idle tale, and they did not believe them. But Peter got up and ran to the tomb; stooping and looking in, he saw the linen cloths by themselves; then he went home, amazed at what had happened.

Victory

JOHN F. CRAGHAN

To celebrate Easter is to celebrate God's victory over death. Easter smacks of eggs, new clothes, and the promise of spring. In these examples the least common denominator is life of some type. From a biblical point of view, however, life and death take on special nuances. Thus life is the reality of community with God while death is the absence of community with God (see Ez 33:1-16). To celebrate Easter, therefore, is to celebrate the restoration of community with God through Jesus.

The Easter Vigil offers a wealth of biblical passages dealing with the theme of God's victory over death. Here we will limit our consideration to God's victory at the Red Sea (Ex 14:15—15:1), Paul's proclamation of victory over sin and death in baptism (Rom 6:3-11), and the discovery of the empty tomb (Mt 28:1-10; Mk 16:1-8; Lk 24:1-12).

The biblical traditions do not offer a blow-by-blow account of Israel's crossing of the Red Sea simply because the necessary sources are wanting. The Bible does provide a variety of traditions depicting the Lord as the Divine Warrior who uses military prowess to deliver his people. In this Easter Vigil passage there are three such traditions.

In the earliest account (15:1-18,21) the Lord defeats the Egyptians by creating a storm at sea that sinks their chariots and contributes to their death by drowning (15:8-10). While there is only an allusion to the safe passage of the Israelites, there is the clear statement of the utter destruction of the enemy.

In the second account (14:19-20,21b,24-25,27b,30-31) the Lord drives back the sea with a strong easterly wind and just before dawn startles the Egyptians with a glance that provokes military chaos. When the sea resumes its normal depth, the Lord throws the retreating Egyptians into its midst.

In the third account (14:21a,22-23,26-27a,28-29) dry land appears for the safe passage of the Israelites with the water forming something like walls to their right and left. The Egyptians pursue the Israelites on this dry land but the returning waters then engulf the entire Egyptian army.

In the celebration of the Easter Vigil this biblical text takes on special meaning. The waters of the Red Sea now refer to Jesus' experience of death and new life. God intervenes to turn the waters into a destructive force for the Egyptians. The Lord's victory over death is the Resurrection of Jesus. Hence to celebrate Easter is to celebrate this victory over death.

Past, Present, Future

In the passage from Romans, Paul deals with three time zones. The past is the time of baptism and hence immersion into Jesus' passion, death, and Resurrection. The future is the time of completion when the Second Coming of Jesus will occur. The present is the moment of ethical action. The Christian who has a past in Christ and so awaits the Second Coming must demonstrate life in Christ here and now.

Through baptism the Christian shares the transforming experiences of Jesus' death and Resurrection. Passing over our being raised together with Christ, Paul focuses on the implications of baptism. We thus begin a new mode of being that looks forward to the Second Coming. Though death has been vanquished, we can still sin. It is only an ongoing Christian life that demonstrates Jesus' death and Resurrection experience. Hence to celebrate Easter is to celebrate this victory over death.

The Empty Tomb

In Mark, the young man announces the Christian belief in the death and Resurrection of Jesus. While Jesus of Nazareth is the Crucified One, he is now the Raised One. In the Christian paradox death gives way to life. Omitting any post-resurrection appearances, Mark seems to suggest that the Resurrection is not the final moment—indeed life must go on. But it must be a life influenced by Jesus' triumph over death. To celebrate Easter is to celebrate this victory over death.

In Matthew, at the approach of the women there is an earthquake that calls to mind the earthquake at the time of Jesus' death (27:51-54). It announces the shaking of the world's foundations at Jesus' conquest of death. The posture of the angel, i.e., sitting on the stone, also underlines Jesus' victory. The message of the angel proclaims the startling reality in Mark that the Crucified One is now the Raised One. To celebrate Easter is to celebrate this victory over death.

In Luke, the story of the empty tomb is a study in contrasts. Although the women are authoritative witnesses, they do not arrive at faith. The two men scold the women for not understanding the message of Jesus that spoke of his Resurrection. The women then report their findings to the Eleven but encounter only ridicule. Finally *the* authority of the group, Peter, is overwhelmed by his own visit to the tomb but still cannot grasp the meaning of the event. It is only the presence of the Lord that will make Peter (24:34) and the others (24:13-32, 35-49) believers. Only then will the disciples be able to accept the truth that to celebrate Easter is to celebrate victory over death.

Today's Good News

This victory over death announced so powerfully in Romans and the gospels and reinterpreted in the crossing of the Red Sea must have profound repercussions on us. We are bidden to break out into *Alleluias* of Easter joy. However, the *Alleluias* must be more than the expression of happiness at the Easter Vigil. They must pervade our entire lives.

Perhaps we need to reflect on this question: Where is death (i.e., the absence of community with God) present in our daily lives? This may force us to examine our relationships. We may be led to examine our marriages, our ways of dealing with family members, our interaction with others at work, or any number of other relationships. If we seriously hamper community with our sisters and brothers, we seriously hurt our community with God. Against the background of *Alleluias*, we must bring about genuine life in these and other situations. Only then will we be able to state that to celebrate Easter is to celebrate this victory over death.

Points for Reflection and Discussion

1. Reflect on the question posed above: Where is death (i.e., absence of community with God) present in your daily life? What will you do to change death into life?

_____

_____

_____

_____

2. Take some time to read and reflect on all the readings that can be used in the Easter Vigil celebration: #2, Gn 22:1-18: #4, Is 54:5-14; #5, Is 55:1-11; #6, Bar 3:9-15,32–4:4; #7 Ez 36:16-28.

_____

_____

_____

_____

Themes

Life, Resurrection
   M1, Conversion: A Lifelong Process
   M3, Your Special Gifts
   M6, Discernment
   M7, Holiness
Relationships
   M2, The Laity: Called to Build God's Kingdom
   M4, Family Life
   M5, Your Prayer Life
   M8, Evangelization

Reading 1 (ABC), Acts 1:1-11

In the first book, Theophilus, I wrote about all that Jesus did and taught from the beginning until the day when he was taken up to heaven, after giving instructions through the Holy Spirit to the apostles whom he had chosen. After his suffering he presented himself alive to them by many convincing proofs, appearing to them during forty days and speaking about the kingdom of God. While staying with them, he ordered them not to leave Jerusalem, but to wait there for the promise of the Father. "This," he said, "is what you have heard from me; for John baptized with water, but you will be baptized with the Holy Spirit not many days from now." So when they had come together, they asked him, "Lord, is this the time when you will restore the kingdom to Israel?" He replied, "It is not for you to know the times or periods that the Father has set by his own authority. But you will receive power when the Holy Spirit has come upon you; and you will be my witnesses in Jerusalem, in all Judea and Samaria, and to the ends of the earth."

When he had said this, as they were watching, he was lifted up, and a cloud took him out of their sight. While he was going and they were gazing up toward heaven, suddenly two men in white robes stood by them. They said, "Men of Galilee, why do you stand looking up toward heaven? This Jesus, who has been taken up from you into heaven, will come in the same way as you saw him go into heaven."

Psalm 47:1-2,5-6,7-8 (R verse 5)

Reading 2 (ABC), Ephesians 1:17-23*

I pray that the God of our Lord Jesus Christ, the Father of glory, may give you a spirit of wisdom and revelation as you come to know him, so that, with the eyes of your heart enlightened, you may know what is the hope to which he has called you, what are the riches of his glorious inheritance among the saints, and what is the immeasurable greatness of his power for us who believe, according to the working of his great power. God put this power to work in Christ when he raised him from the dead and seated him at his right hand in the heavenly places, far above all rule and authority and power and dominion, and above every name that is named, not only in this age but also in the age to come. And he has put all things under his feet and has made him the head over all things for the church, which is his body, the fullness of him who fills all in all.

*In Canada the Second Reading for *Cycle B* is Ephesians 4:1-13; the Second Reading for *Cycle C* is Hebrews 9:24-28;10:19-23

Gospel (A), Matthew 28:16-20

The eleven disciples went to Galilee, to the mountain to which Jesus had directed them. When they saw him, they worshiped him; but some doubted. And Jesus came and said to them, "All authority in heaven and on earth has been given to me. Go therefore and make disciples of all nations, baptizing them in the name of the Father and of the Son and of the Holy Spirit, and teaching them to obey everything that I have commanded you. And remember, I am with you always, to the end of the age."

Gospel (B), Mark 16:15-20

[Jesus] said to [the apostles], "Go into all the world and proclaim the good news to the whole creation. The one who believes and is baptized will be saved; but the one who does not believe will be condemned. And these signs will accompany those who believe: by using my name they will cast out demons; they will speak in new tongues; they will pick up snakes in their hands, and if they drink any deadly thing, it will not hurt them; they will lay their hands on the sick, and they will recover." So then the Lord Jesus, after he had spoken to them, was taken up into heaven and sat down at the right hand of God. And they went out and proclaimed the good news everywhere, while the Lord worked with them and confirmed the message by the signs that accompanied it.

Gospel (C), Luke 24:46-53

[Jesus] said to [the apostles], "Thus it is written, that the Messiah is to suffer and to rise from the dead on the third day, and that repentance and forgiveness of sins is to be proclaimed in his name to all nations, beginning from Jerusalem. You are witnesses of these things. And see, I am sending upon you what my Father promised; so stay here in the city until you have been clothed with power from on high." Then he led them out as far as Bethany, and, lifting up his hands, he blessed them. While he was blessing them, he withdrew from them and was carried up into heaven. And they worshiped him, and returned to Jerusalem with great joy; and they were continually in the temple blessing God.

The Promise

ELSIE HAINZ MCGRATH

It was necessary that the risen Jesus spend some time with his friends. They needed the reassurance that seeing and touching gives to people—the proof that he truly had been raised to new, transfigured life-after-death. Thomas was not the only one who had to see in order to believe!

But if Jesus had just hung around earth for the rest of his risen life, what would we—who hadn't seen him die to begin with—accept as proof of new, transfigured life-after-death? What would we have learned about our own lives? And what would Jesus have done with his promise?

The Power

The disciples were anxious for answers. They asked, "Lord, is this the time when you will restore the kingdom to Israel?" They thought "the promise of the Father" would bring about an age of political sovereignty such as the nation had enjoyed under the reign of King David. Jesus' answer made clear that this was not what the promise was all about. Neither would the promise give them a glimpse of the *eschaton*, for "it is not for you to know the times or periods that the Father has set" for the end of time. The promise was not going to make their lives easier by restoring national dominance or by granting divine insight; it was, in fact, destined to "muddy the waters" of their baptisms. When they received the Spirit they too, would be baptized in fire. They would be empowered to take on the role of Christ: to teach and to nourish and to serve; to be ignored and to hunger and to die.

The larger purpose of Jesus' Resurrection is revealed to us in the story of his Ascension: the Church and its mission. That mission is the *kerygma*, the proclamation of the Good News throughout the entire world, and it is to be done by people who are afraid and filled with doubts. Only Jesus' passion and death, Resurrection and Ascension can overcome the skepticism and unbelief of his most ardent followers.

Today's Good News

The promise of the Spirit was a promise that was to be fulfilled on Pentecost, but which continues to be fulfilled *every* day in *every* lifetime. The Holy Spirit gives us the very mind and heart and power of our Lord, enabling us to carry on his work of redemption in our sinful world. That mission is the most striking manifestation of the triumphant power of God.

Ascension brings our Lord closer to us than he was to the apostles in his risen body. Ascension is less about what God has done for the Son than it is about what God has done—and continues to do—for us through the Son. As the Letter to the Ephesians tells us: "[the Father] has put all things under [Jesus'] feet and has made him the head over all things for the church, which is his body, the fullness of him who fills all in all."

Points for Reflection and Discussion

1. Have you ever thought that the apostles were "lucky" to have known Jesus?; that belief would be easier "if only" you could see him face-to-face? Have you ever wondered why it took them so long to "get it"?

_____

_____

_____

_____

2. Think about the awesomeness of God being "just one of the guys." Imagine that your best friend is God Incarnate. What would you do differently if you knew he or she was God? Would belief be easier?

_____

_____

_____

_____

Themes

Ascension, Christ, Holy Spirit
    M3, Your Special Gifts
    M6, Discernment
Church
    M2, The Laity: Called to Build God's Kingdom
    M4, Family Life
    M7, Holiness
    M8, Evangelization

Reading 1 (ABC), Isaiah 49:1-6

Listen to me, O coastlands, pay attention, you peoples from far away! The Lord called me before I was born, while I was in my mother's womb he named me. He made my mouth like a sharp sword, in the shadow of his hand he hid me; he made me a polished arrow, in his quiver he hid me away. And he said to me, "You are my servant, Israel, in whom I will be glorified." But I said, "I have labored in vain, I have spent my strength for nothing and vanity; yet surely my cause is with the Lord, and my reward with my God."

And now the Lord says, who formed me in the womb to be his servant, to bring Jacob back to him, and that Israel might be gathered to him, for I am honored in the sight of the Lord, and my God has become my strength—he says, "It is too light a thing that you should be my servant to raise up the tribes of Jacob and to restore the survivors of Israel; I will give you as a light to the nations, that my salvation may reach to the end of the earth."

Psalm 139:1-3,13-14,14-15 (*R verse 14*)

Reading 2 (ABC), Acts 13:22-26

Paul spoke in the synagogue: "[God] made David…king [of our ancestors]. In his testimony about him [God] said, 'I have found David, son of Jesse, to be a man after my heart, who will carry out all my wishes.' Of this man's posterity God has brought to Israel a Savior, Jesus, as he promised; before his coming John had already proclaimed a baptism of repentance to all the people of Israel. And as John was finishing his work, he said, 'What do you suppose that I am? I am not he. No, but one is coming after me; I am not worthy to untie the thong of the sandals on his feet.'

"You descendants of Abraham's family, and others who fear God, to us the message of this salvation has been sent."

Gospel (ABC), Luke 1:57-66,80

The time came for Elizabeth to give birth, and she bore a son. Her neighbors and relatives heard that the Lord had shown his great mercy to her, and they rejoiced with her. On the eighth day they came to circumcise the child, and they were going to name him Zechariah after his father. But his mother said, "No; he is to be called John." They said to her, "None of your relatives has this name."

Then they began motioning to his father to find out what name he wanted to give him. He asked for a writing tablet and wrote, "His name is John." And all of them were amazed. Immediately his mouth was opened and his tongue freed, and he began to speak, praising God.

Fear came over all their neighbors, and all these things were talked about throughout the entire hill country of Judea. All who heard them pondered them and said, "What then will this child become?" For, indeed, the hand of the Lord was with him.

The child grew and became strong in spirit, and he was in the wilderness until the day he appeared publicly to Israel.

Being a Prophet

JOHN F. CRAGHAN

Prophetic title means prophetic service. Prophet is both the title and the challenge that we receive at baptism. We are pleased with the title but often displeased with the service involved. We are elated to be known as God's spokespersons but less elated to act as spokespersons, i.e., by reaching out to others. We are gratified to be called God's criticizers (we tell it the way it really is) and God's energizers (we tell it the way it can be). But we are less gratified when we must actually involve ourselves in the plight of others. We bask in the beauty of the name "prophet" but we cower in the reality of that title.

Today's readings deal with the reality of being prophets. They situate the prophetic role within the context of the community. The one who is called by God is called to serve the community. Hence the movement is ever outward—from the prophet to the people. Prophetic title means prophetic service.

A Light to the Nations

The first reading is the second Servant Song from the work of the anonymous exilic author of the Second Isaiah (chapters 40—55). The Suffering Servant is quite likely the prophet himself and all those followers who heed God's word to leave exile in Babylon for a new life in Israel. As the passage points out, however, the prophetic vocation of the Servant necessarily involves service.

In Second Isaiah both name and reality of prophet come together in terms of service. After the prophet mentions his prophetic calling from his mother's womb (see Jer 1:5), he describes the implications of that calling. He is the one through whom the Lord will show his glory (verse 3), through whom Jacob will be brought back (verse 5), through whom the survivors of Israel will be restored (verse 6). His vocation also includes the Gentiles, however—he will serve as their light (verse 6). Despite God's protection and care ("sharp sword" and "polished arrow"), he is afflicted and discouraged. He feels as though he has labored and spent himself in vain.

But he is confident that the Lord will sustain him in his trial with his enemy. Here prophetic title means prophetic service.

In Acts, Paul's sermon in the synagogue at Pisidian Antioch is Luke's model sermon for the proclamation of the Good News to Israel. Here Paul addresses Jews living outside the Holy Land and pagans who accepted Israel's ethical monotheism but did not keep the entire Mosaic law ("others who fear God"). In verses 16-25, Luke develops God's plan as it leads from Israel to the Christian Church.

A Voice in the Wilderness

In verses 22-23, Luke moves quickly from David to Jesus by way of John the Baptist. John's prophetic career is one of service, i.e., he is to prepare God's people by preaching a baptism of repentance (see Lk 1:76-77). He is a herald who announces the coming of "one who is more powerful" (Lk 3:16). John acknowledges that his whole career is in view of the one the thong of whose sandals he is not worthy to untie (verse 25). Prophetic title means prophetic service.

The gospel is the account of the birth and naming of the Baptist. Elizabeth's delivery is reminiscent of the Hebrew Scriptures where the barren wives of the patriarchs bear a child (or children) and thus provoke an atmosphere of great joy. On the occasion of John's circumcision and name-giving the neighbors learn of the divinely-arranged conception/birth. These neighbors also begin to grasp the future greatness of this child when Elizabeth and Zechariah agree on his unexpected name of John. Zechariah's regained speech increases the neighbors' amazement. This is also Luke's device for anticipating John's greatness.

In verse 80, Luke adopts another motif from the Hebrew Scriptures, i.e., the growth and maturity of the child (see Gn 21:8; Jgs 13:24-25; 1 Sm 2:21). The phrase "in spirit" suggests John's spirit-influenced prophetic mission. It may also, however, imply the Holy Spirit (see Lk 1:15,41,67). What is certainly clear is John's sojourn in the desert, the place of revelation. As a prophet, he will remain there until his heraldic proclamation of "the one who is coming" (see Lk 3:15-17).

Today's Good News

These readings draw us away from an ego-centered notion of prophetic ministry to one of communal service. The figures of the Suffering Servant and John the Baptist evoke the image of one called by God to attend to the needs and concerns of the community.

Family members who devote their time and energy to minister to each other vindicate their prophetic title, for example, as do workers who see their jobs as the opportunity to contribute to the common good. All those in leadership positions who employ their influence and power to promote justice for all justify their prophetic title, as do peacemakers who use their talents to overcome hate and foster reconciliation between families and friends. All such people insist on the proper and sacramental marriage of prophecy and service. For them prophetic title means prophetic service.

Points for Reflection and Discussion

1. Have you ever thought of yourself as "prophet"? As "servant"?

_____

_____

_____

_____

2. Prophets point the way to persons greater than themselves. Talk about some modern-day prophets and the world's general response to them.

_____

_____

_____

_____

Themes
Baptism
    Q2, What Do Catholics Believe?
    M1, Conversion: A Lifelong Process
Prophet
    Q12, Catholics and Church
    M3, Your Special Gifts
    M6, Discernment
Service
    Q6, The Saints
    Q7, Mary
    Q9, Who's Who in the Church
    M2, The Laity: Called to Build God's Kingdom
    M8, Evangelization

Reading 1 (ABC), Acts 12:1-11

King Herod laid violent hands upon some who belonged to the church. He had James, the brother of John, killed with the sword. After he saw that it pleased the Jews, he proceeded to arrest Peter also. (This was during the festival of Unleavened Bread.) When he had seized him, he put him in prison and handed him over to four squads of soldiers to guard him, intending to bring him out to the people after the Passover. While Peter was kept in prison, the church prayed fervently to God for him. The very night before Herod was going to bring him out, Peter, bound with two chains, was sleeping between two soldiers, while guards in front of the door were keeping watch over the prison. Suddenly an angel of the Lord appeared and a light shone in the cell. He tapped Peter on the side and woke him, saying, "Get up quickly." And the chains fell off his wrists. The angel said to him, "Fasten your belt and put on your sandals." He did so. Then he said to him, "Wrap your cloak around you and follow me."

Peter went out and followed him; he did not realize that what was happening with the angel's help was real; he thought he was seeing a vision. After they had passed the first and the second guard, they came before the iron gate leading into the city. It opened for them of its own accord, and they went outside and walked along a lane, when suddenly the angel left him.

Then Peter came to himself and said, "Now I am sure that the Lord has sent his angel and rescued me from the hands of Herod and from all that the Jewish people were expecting."

Psalm 34:1-2,3-4,5-6,7-8 (R verse 4)

Reading 2 (ABC), 2 Timothy 4:6-8,17-18

Paul wrote: As for me, I am already being poured out as a libation, and the time of my departure has come. I have fought the good fight, I have finished the race, I have kept the faith. From now on there is reserved for me the crown of righteousness, which the Lord, the righteous judge, will give me on that day, and not only to me but also to all who have longed for his appearing.

The Lord stood by me and gave me strength, so that through me the message might be fully proclaimed and all the Gentiles might hear it. So I was rescued from the lion's mouth. The Lord will rescue me from every evil attack and save me for his heavenly kingdom. To him be the glory forever and ever. Amen.

Gospel (ABC), Matthew 16:13-19

When Jesus came into the district of Caesarea Philippi, he asked his disciples, "Who do people say that the Son of Man is?" And they said, "Some say John the Baptist, but others Elijah, and still others Jeremiah or one of the prophets." He said to them, "But who do you say that I am?" Simon Peter answered, "You are the Messiah, the Son of the living God."

And Jesus answered him, "Blessed are you, Simon son of Jonah! For flesh and blood has not revealed this to you, but my Father in heaven. And I tell you, you are Peter, and on this rock I will build my church, and the gates of Hades will not prevail against it. I will give you the keys of the kingdom of heaven, and whatever you bind on earth will be bound in heaven, and whatever you loose on earth will be loosed in heaven."

Giving Gifts

JOHN F. CRAGHAN

If we are not careful, we can hoard our talents, our gifts, our possessions and property. We somehow think that our efforts to acquire them preclude sharing them with others. Today's readings demand that we reassess our attitudes towards gifts, talents, and personal possessions. The example of Peter and Paul drives us from the limited domain of private possessions into the greater area of communal concern. These examples state unequivocally that private gifts and talents are really public property.

In the Acts of the Apostles, Luke selects Peter as his first hero (to be followed by Paul in chapters 16—21). Peter shares the gift of the Good News he received from Jesus with the Gentiles (chapters 10—11). Peter's personal experience of the Christian message becomes his gift to Jews and Gentiles alike.

Since persecution is often the catalyst for growth (Acts 12:24), Luke tells the story of Peter's imprisonment and miraculous escape. Despite the tight security, God masterminds the escape, while Peter remains completely passive.

Luke asserts that God will provide for the people in times of persecution. He also implies that the escape is calculated to allow Peter to continue his mission. Luke observes that after explaining his miraculous deliverance to the local Christian community, Peter left them to go off to another place. The deliverance, a genuine gift from God, becomes part of Peter's message to be shared with others.

The Legacy of Leadership

In exhorting his audience to preach solid doctrine, to accept suffering, and to continue their ministry faithfully, the author of Second Timothy offers the example of the apostle Paul. He presents this plea as if it were Paul's last will and testament. Noting Paul's sacrificial death ("libation"), he encourages the readers to use their gifts and talents for others as Paul did.

The author recounts the apostle's deliverance, noting that the rescue from the lion's jaws was not merely a personal favor. Paul's talents and gifts benefited the common good, "so that through me the preaching task might be completed and all the nations might hear the gospel" (4:17). Paul's example of self-giving is to become the contagious legacy of the community. We are not to retain the Lord's gifts for ourselves but to share them with others.

The gospel passage is recorded by all three synoptic authors (Mark, Matthew, Luke). In Mark, Peter identified Jesus as the Messiah (8:29). In Luke, Peter calls Jesus the Messiah of God (9:20). In Matthew, Peter adds, "[you are] the Son of the living God!" (16:16). Peter's perception of Jesus as the transcendent Son of God is due, not to mere human nature (literally "flesh and blood") but to a revelation from the Father (16:17; see Gal 1:15-16). This realization of Peter's giftedness prompts Matthew to have Jesus confer a leadership role on Peter. "Rock" suggests the unshakableness he will provide for Jesus' community (Mt 7:24-27). Not even the insatiable appetite of the nether world ("the jaws of death," Song 8:6) will prevail against it.

The reference to the keys of the kingdom recalls the authority of a prime minister (Is 22:22) and indicates that Peter has the power to teach people the way to reach the kingdom (Mt 23:13).

For Matthew, Peter does not stand in splendid isolation from the rest of the community. His position as rock and his power of binding and loosing are not purely personal privileges. They presume the welfare of the entire community. In the Gospel of Matthew, therefore, Peter gives an example of how personal gifts are to be shared with the entire Christian community.

Today's Good News

Our personal gifts are manifold. We may find that we have talents for consoling, healing, teaching, leading, and so forth. These may be talents that have been acquired only at great price and after much sacrifice. While we tend to clutch them as a miser's booty, Peter and Paul suggest that these talents are not ours alone. Since we are all members of the community, the talents and gifts that we possess become the common possession of the entire Christian community.

When talents are hoarded for personal use, they atrophy. Sharing one's talents, gifts, and possessions enriches them. Such an awareness calls for a new set of priorities. The question must now be, how can I share my gift with you?; not, how can I use my gift for personal gain? The gift is perfected in the act of giving, not in the act of hoarding. Ultimately, to receive a gift from God is to receive a call to give that gift to the human community. Personal gifts, by Christian definition, are to be shared with others.

Points for Reflection and Discussion

1. What special gifts and talents have you been given by God? How do you best share them with others?

_____

_____

_____

_____

2. Today's readings remind us that authority and power ("crown of righteous"; "rock") can only work if used in service to others ("bound in chains"; "poured out like a libation"). What authority and power do you have? How do you exercise it?

_____

_____

_____

_____

_____

Themes

Authority
    Q9, Who's Who in the Church
Gifts
    M3, Your Special Gifts
Ministry
    Q12, Catholics and Church
    M2, The Laity: Called to Build God's Kingdom
    M8, Evangelization

Reading 1 (ABC), Daniel 7:9-10,13-14

As I watched, thrones were set in place, and an Ancient One took his throne, his clothing was white as snow, and the hair of his head like pure wool; his throne was fiery flames, and its wheels were burning fire. A stream of fire issued and flowed out from his presence. A thousand thousands served him, and ten thousand times ten thousand stood attending him. The court sat in judgment, and the books were opened.

As I watched in the night visions, I saw one like a human being coming with the clouds of heaven. And he came to the Ancient One and was presented before him. To him was given dominion and glory and kingship, that all peoples, nations, and languages should serve him. His dominion is an everlasting dominion that shall not pass away, and his kingship is one that shall never be destroyed.

Psalm 97:1-2,5-6,9,12 (*R verses 1 and 9*)

Reading 2 (ABC), 2 Peter 1:16-19

We did not follow cleverly devised myths when we made known to you the power and coming of our Lord Jesus Christ, but we had been eyewitnesses of his majesty. For he received honor and glory from God the Father when that voice was conveyed to him by the Majestic Glory, saying, "This is my Son, my Beloved, with whom I am well pleased." We ourselves heard this voice come from heaven, while we were with him on the holy mountain. So we have the prophetic message more fully confirmed. You will do well to be attentive to this as to a lamp shining in a dark place, until the day dawns and the morning star rises in your hearts.

Gospel (A), Matthew 17:1-9

Jesus took with him Peter and James and his brother John and led them up a high mountain, by themselves. And he was transfigured before them, and his face shone like the sun, and his clothes became dazzling white. Suddenly there appeared to them Moses and Elijah, talking with him. Then Peter said to Jesus, "Lord, it is good for us to be here; if you wish, I will make three dwellings here, one for you, one for Moses, and one for Elijah."

While he was still speaking, suddenly a bright cloud overshadowed them, and from the cloud a voice said, "This is my Son, the Beloved; with him I am well pleased; listen to him!" When the disciples heard this, they fell to the ground and were overcome by fear. But Jesus came and touched them, saying, "Get up and do not be afraid." And when they looked up, they saw no one except Jesus himself alone.

As they were coming down the mountain, Jesus ordered them, "Tell no one about the vision until after the Son of Man has been raised from the dead."

Gospel (B), Mark 9:2-10

Jesus took with him Peter and James and John, and led them up a high mountain apart, by themselves. And he was transfigured before them, and his clothes became dazzling white, such as no one on earth could bleach them. And there appeared to them Elijah with Moses, who were talking with Jesus. Then Peter said to Jesus, "Rabbi, it is good for us to be here; let us make three dwellings, one for you, one for Moses, and one for Elijah." He did not know what to say, for they were terrified.

Then a cloud overshadowed them, and from the cloud there came a voice, "This is my Son, the Beloved; listen to him!" Suddenly when they looked around, they saw no one with them any more, but only Jesus.

As they were coming down the mountain, he ordered them to tell no one about what they had seen, until after the Son of Man had risen from the dead. So they kept the matter to themselves, questioning what this rising from the dead could mean.

Gospel (C), Luke 9:28-36

Jesus took with him Peter and John and James, and went up on the mountain to pray. And while he was praying, the appearance of his face changed, and his clothes became dazzling white. Suddenly they saw two men, Moses and Elijah, talking to him. They appeared in glory and were speaking of his departure, which he was about to accomplish at Jerusalem.

Now Peter and his companions were weighed down with sleep; but since they had stayed awake, they saw his glory and the two men who stood with him. Just as they were leaving him, Peter said to Jesus, "Master, it is good for us to be here; let us make three dwellings, one for you, one for Moses, and one for Elijah"—not knowing what he said. While he was saying this, a cloud came and overshadowed them; and they were terrified as they entered the cloud.

Then from the cloud came a voice that said, "This is my Son, my Chosen; listen to him!" When the voice had spoken, Jesus was found alone. And they kept silent and in those days told no one any of the things they had seen.

To Be Transfigured

ELSIE HAINZ McGRATH

What did the transfiguration mean for Peter and James and John? What does it mean for us? We catch a clue in today's second reading. The Letter of Peter was clearly written in hindsight—after the Resurrection. It reiterates the events of the mountaintop as fact—an eye-witness account being put forward as proof of the *Parousia,* the Second Coming of Christ. Peter and James and John, in looking back on the events of that glorious day, interpret the transfiguration in light of the Resurrection. They were given a glimpse of the King of Glory while he was still among them as a mere man. Clearly, Jesus reigns in transfigured splendor with his *Abba* Father. God attested to this when stating that Jesus was "my Son." Clearly, Jesus will make a second transfigured appearance.

An Everlasting Dominion

The first reading today gives us a sample of *apocalyptic,* that style of writing which was to exert tremendous influence during the next few centuries in the Church. Its means is to use events from past and present history in such a way that they are perceived as future prophecies; its purpose is to provide hope to people who are facing seemingly insurmountable crises.

As the story establishes before today's reading picks it up, four beasts have to be destroyed before "one like a human being" is given everlasting dominion by the "Ancient One." These four beasts have been identified by scholars as the four successive pagan empires of the Babylonians, the Medes, the Persians, and the Greeks. The readers knew that *only* the Greek empire, under the obsessively cruel rule of Antiochus IV Epiphanes, still oppressed them. The message of hope was clear to them, therefore: the others eventually fell, so will this one.

The Christian interpretation of today's reading has remained unchanged throughout the centuries: *all* injustice will eventually cease, *all* evil rulers will eventually fall, and Christ will come again to reign in glory forever.

Today's Good News

Peter wanted to stay on the mountaintop, to pitch tents and maybe start a campfire. And why not? The apostles heard the voice of God, and they believed, and they obeyed—but they didn't understand. (Such a thing could not have been understood on the other side of the Resurrection.) Still they went back down the mountain, back to the "real" world of work and worry, of temptation and rejection. But they had only to close their eyes and bring back the vision of the mountaintop to feel the closeness they had shared.

And so do we. The message of the transfiguration story—for us today and for Peter and James and John two thousand years ago—is that the Son of God brings change and turns death into life. And sometimes we are graced with glimpses of the reign of God. They get us through the hard times down in the valleys; they take us to the heady and transfiguring peaks of the mountaintops.

Points for Reflection and Discussion

1. Talk about a transfiguring experience in your life. Did you want to leave the experience? Did leaving it bring new and unexpected spiritual growth?

——————————————————

——————————————————

——————————————————

——————————————————

2. Some Scripture scholars think the transfiguration story is actually a post-resurrection story; that it didn't happen before Easter. What do you think? Why?

——————————————————

——————————————————

——————————————————

——————————————————

Themes

Revelation
    Q12, Catholics and Church
    M1, Conversion: A Lifelong Process
Second Coming
    Q2, What Do Catholics Believe?
    M8, Evangelization
Transfiguration
    Q5, How Do Catholics Interpret the Bible?
    M7, Holiness

Reading 1 (ABC), Revelation 11:19;12:1-6,10

God's temple in heaven was opened, and the ark of his covenant was seen within his temple. A great portent appeared in heaven: a woman clothed with the sun, with the moon under her feet, and on her head a crown of twelve stars. She was pregnant and was crying out in birthpangs, in the agony of giving birth.

Then another portent appeared in heaven: a great red dragon, with seven heads and ten horns, and seven diadems on his heads. His tail swept down a third of the stars of heaven and threw them to the earth. Then the dragon stood before the woman who was about to bear a child, so that he might devour her child as soon as it was born.

And she gave birth to a son, a male child, who is to rule all the nations with a rod of iron. But her child was snatched away and taken to God and to his throne; and the woman fled into the wilderness, where she has a place prepared by God, so that there she can be nourished for one thousand two hundred sixty days.

Then I heard a loud voice in heaven, proclaiming, "Now have come the salvation and the power and the kingdom of our God and the authority of his Messiah."

Psalm 45:9-10,11,12,14,15,17 (*R* verse 9)

Reading 2 (ABC), 1 Corinthians 15:20-26

Christ has been raised from the dead, the first fruits of those who have died. For since death came through a human being, the resurrection of the dead has also come through a human being; for as all die in Adam, so all will be made alive in Christ. But each in his own order: Christ the first fruits, then at his coming those who belong to Christ. Then comes the end, when he hands over the kingdom to God the Father, after he has destroyed every ruler and every authority and power. For he must reign until he has put all his enemies under his feet. The last enemy to be destroyed is death.

Gospel (ABC), Luke 1:39-56

Mary set out and went with haste to a Judean town in the hill country, where she entered the house of Zechariah and greeted Elizabeth. When Elizabeth heard Mary's greeting, the child leaped in her womb. And Elizabeth was filled with the Holy Spirit and exclaimed with a loud cry, "Blessed are you among women, and blessed is the fruit of your womb. And why has this happened to me, that the mother of my Lord comes to me? For as soon as I heard the sound of your greeting, the child in my womb leaped for joy. And blessed is she who believed that there would be a fulfillment of what was spoken to her by the Lord."

And Mary said, "My soul magnifies the Lord, and my spirit rejoices in God my Savior, for he has looked with favor on the lowliness of his servant. Surely, from now on all generations will call me blessed; for the Mighty One has done great things for me, and holy is his name. His mercy is for those who fear him from generation to generation. He has shown strength with his arm; he has scattered the proud in the thoughts of their hearts. He has brought down the powerful from their thrones, and lifted up the lowly; he has filled the hungry with good things, and sent the rich away empty. He has helped his servant Israel, in remembrance of his mercy, according to the promise he made to our ancestors, to Abraham and to his descendants forever." And Mary remained with her about three months and then returned to her home.

The Assumption

ELSIE HAINZ MCGRATH

As early as the fifth century, Christians celebrated a "Memorial of Mary" on the fifteenth of August. This evolved into what was called the feast of the Dormition (or "falling asleep") of the Virgin. In other words, Mary died but her body did not corrupt; rather, it was assumed into heaven. The Assumption, then, is a truth that emerged from the faith of the people because Christians simply could not imagine that Mary's body was separated from her soul and suffered decay when she died. It has been a part of the Church's lived Tradition and, as such, was proclaimed dogma in 1950. The Church believes that "Mary is one with the risen Christ in the fullness of her personality" (*Behold Your Mother* [1973], National Council of Catholic Bishops).

Queen of Heaven

The Book of Revelation dates back to the Church's beginnings. It is believed to have been written during the Roman reign of Domitian (A.D. 81-96), a particularly violent persecutor of Christians. The literary genre of *apocalyptic* was well-known in times of crises; it gave the people cause for hope in the midst of despair. With symbolic numbers and colors, clothing and metals, writers conveyed the promise that God would be the ultimate victor in whatever war was being waged against them.

As today's reading indicates, Revelation, which is the only wholly apocalyptic writing in the New Testament, is also filled with images of a woman who is the queen of heaven. The characteristic sun, moon, and stars are typical of high goddesses in the ancient world. While the woman's identity is not fully revealed, Church Tradition has universally held her to be Mary.

Today's reading has the queen of heaven (thus the spouse of the king—God) suffering the pains of childbirth for the sake of delivering the Messiah—the Savior of the world. She faces the mythological dragon, used in ancient literature to represent the oppressor, whether Nero or Satan, and when the baby is born he is immediately rescued from the grips of the oppressor by God. This is a sign that the child will truly usher in world peace and justice, a sign here reinforced by the heavenly proclamation. The woman, having successfully birthed her godly son, is transported to the desert where she may in safety and privileged privacy complete her time of ritual purification.

The Canticle of Mary

Luke's Gospel tells the story of Mary's visitation. She enters the home of Elizabeth and Zechariah, and the babe in Elizabeth's womb immediately recognizes the babe in Mary's womb. If that isn't amazing enough, Elizabeth herself recognizes the babe in Mary's womb—and no one even knew she was pregnant yet! But the focus is not on the special children—neither Jesus the Christ nor John the Baptizer. The focus is on *Mary*—the *mother* of the Lord. Mary herself recognizes this, and sings a canticle of praise. "Surely, from now on all generations will call *me* blessed; for the Mighty One has done great things *for me.*"

This canticle has been the Church's prayer, in the Liturgy of the Hours, for "all generations." Recited daily, it stands as a reminder of perfect faithfulness to those who would be faithful—Mary's own humble testimony to the greatness of God and the wonderful things God will wrought in the lives of those who trust.

Today's Good News

Saint Paul tells us that "Christ has been raised from the dead, the first fruits of those who have died." In other words, what was done for Christ will be done for all of us. When he comes again we will be raised to heaven with him, body and soul, but this cannot happen until all the forces that stint our full humanity ("rule, authority, and power") are destroyed. In other words, we must become perfect, as our Lord is perfect, in order to attain our heavenly home.

Mary's assumption into heaven, then, theologically points to what we believe God will do for us. She was "the handmaid of the Lord" who agreed that "it be done to me according to your will." Perfect humanity mirrors divinity, and so she has taken her rightful place beside God—as Mother of the Redeemer, as spouse of the Creator, as representative of the Church—as Queen of Heaven. Body and soul, we too will someday be raised to new life in the kingdom of God.

Points for Reflection and Discussion

1. How is Mary most relatable for you (as mother or sister...as human or super-human...as accessible or unreachable...)?

_____

_____

_____

_____

2. Pray the canticle of Mary slowly and reverently. Try to imagine that you are Mary as you say the words. How do you feel?

_____

_____

_____

_____

Themes
Assumption, Mary
    Q7, Mary
    M7, Holiness
Redemption
    Q2, What Do Catholics Believe?
    M1, Conversion: A Lifelong Process

Reading 1 (ABC), Numbers 21:4-9

From Mount Hor they set out by the way to the Red Sea, to go around the land of Edom; but the people became impatient on the way. The people spoke against God and against Moses, "Why have you brought us up out of Egypt to die in the wilderness? For there is no food and no water, and we detest this miserable food." Then the Lord sent poisonous serpents among the people, and they bit the people, so that many Israelites died. The people came to Moses and said, "We have sinned by speaking against the Lord and against you; pray to the Lord to take away the serpents from us." So Moses prayed for the people.

And the Lord said to Moses, "Make a poisonous serpent, and set it on a pole; and everyone who is bitten shall look at it and live." So Moses made a serpent of bronze, and put it upon a pole; and whenever a serpent bit someone, that person would look at the serpent of bronze and live.

Psalm 78:1-2,34-35,36-37,38 (R verse 7)

Reading 2 (ABC), Philippians 2:6-11

Though he was in the form of God, [Jesus] did not regard equality with God as something to be exploited, but emptied himself, taking the form of a slave, being born in human likeness. And being found in human form, he humbled himself and became obedient to the point of death—even death on a cross. Therefore God also highly exalted him and gave him the name that is above every name, so that at the name of Jesus every knee should bend, in heaven and on earth and under the earth, and every tongue should confess that Jesus Christ is Lord, to the glory of God the Father.

Gospel (ABC), John 3:13-17

Jesus said to Nicodemus: "No one has ascended into heaven except the one who descended from heaven, the Son of Man. And just as Moses lifted up the serpent in the wilderness, so must the Son of Man be lifted up, that whoever believes in him may have eternal life.

"For God so loved the world that he gave his only Son, so that everyone who believes in him may not perish but may have eternal life. Indeed, God did not send the Son into the world to condemn the world, but in order that the world might be saved through him."

Reaching the Top

JOHN F. CRAGHAN

In our conversations and perhaps even in our prayers we dream about making it big and getting to the top. We rehearse the steps necessary for our climb upward. If other people become obstacles in our path, we quietly yet effectively set them aside. We give gifts only to the extent that they will enhance our prestige. We have failed to learn that giving oneself is the way to reach the top.

Today's readings focus on the challenge of giving oneself for the sake of others. They offer us a different formula for success and prosperity. Only those who give themselves in service for others really win esteem. Paradoxically, it is the symbol of the cross that casts its shadow across our gift-giving and provides a model of action for reaching the top. It implies that self-giving can be truly self-fulfilling.

Psalm 78 is a historical epic that provides a lesson for modern living. The psalmist invites the audience to reflect on Israel's history and learn from it. In verses 12-32, the psalmist recites Israel's wilderness experience. Though God was exceedingly gracious during the years the people lived in the desert, Israel responded through rebellion, which in turn provoked God's anger. Anger, however, was not present in God's final reply. Despite Israel's rejection, Israel's God will not be outdone. In verses 33-39, the psalmist appeals to the audience to see God's marvelous plan at work. In this scenario, sin brings punishment, which then becomes the occasion for the people's repentance. In the end, the people's repentance moves God to grant forgiveness.

In this reflection, Israel's God grows in strength by understanding the weakness of Israel. Without condoning sin, the psalmist paints a picture of a God who achieves greatness by bending low to assist the weak people. God's concern for the people is rewarded by their reverence and esteem.

The Name Above All Names

In his letter, Paul seeks to motivate the charity of the Philippians by incorporating (with some additions) a Jewish-Christian hymn into his text. It stands to reason that since Jesus was totally sinless, he should not have been subject to death and corruption (see Wis 2:23). Nevertheless, he put aside his prerogatives and took on a life of suffering and frustration.

Rejecting his privileged status, Jesus went even further. He descended to the very depths of death through his death on the cross. But Jesus' death would not be God's last word. God accepted the self-giving of the Son and exalted him, conferring on him the title and authority previously reserved to God, namely, "Lord." Consequently, everyone that is in the heavens, on the earth, and under the earth (see Is 45:2) must "confess that JESUS CHRIST IS LORD to the glory of God the Father." Jesus demonstrates that by giving oneself for the good of others, one can truly make it to the top.

To Be Lifted Up

In his conversation with Nicodemus, Jesus affirms that he alone has direct vision of God (Jn 3:13; see Prv 30:3-4). Next, Jesus addresses Nicodemus' question about being born again (see Jn 3:4). He explains how this new sense of being born flows from the mystery of the crucifixion/resurrection/ascension. Referring to Israel's experience in the desert mentioned in today's first reading, Jesus appeals to the crucifixion. Ironically, "being lifted up" on the cross is only the start of the process that will culminate in "being lifted up" in glory (see Jn 8:28;12:32). Ultimately all believers will experience this new life as a result of this total process of being uplifted (see Jn 7:37-39).

John next joins Jesus' exaltation with the notion of gift-giving. Like Abraham sacrificing Isaac, God the Father loves the world so much that he is willing to give his only Son so that all may benefit (see Gn 22:2,12,18). By giving his Son, the Father ultimately gives himself, that is, he sends his Son "that the world might be saved through him" (Jn 3:17). By linking the sending of the beloved Son ever so intimately with the self-giving on Calvary, John affirms that giving oneself in service is truly making it to the top.

Today's Good News

We naturally seek "to be lifted up." We want to be recognized as truly successful people. On a worldly level, this may lead us to disregard our responsibilities toward others and see them as mere stepping-stones in our upward climb. In such a pursuit, we have opted for only one interpretation of "being lifted up," namely, that of exaltation at the expense of others.

Today's feast challenges us by presenting an entirely different approach. The triumph of the cross affirms that only those who give themselves in the service of others ultimately make it to the top. In the language of Paul, it is only self-emptying that is self-fulfilling. The symbol of the cross shows that there is strength in weakness. Jesus demonstrates that it is in the giving of self that one really gains prominence. The Lord of glory is first the Jesus of pain. The cross is Christianity's most powerful symbol that giving oneself in service to others is truly the way to make it to the top.

Points for Reflection and Discussion

1. Seriously reflect on the fact that the humility of the cross is the triumph of the Church. Do you bear your cross humbly or triumphantly?

_____

_____

_____

_____

2. Do you find it hard to let go of your crosses? Why or why not? Does turning them over to Jesus lighten your load? If so, how?

_____

_____

_____

_____

_____

Themes
Cross, Lord, Salvation
Q2, What Do Catholics Believe?

Reading 1 (ABC), Revelation 7:2-4,9-14

I, [John], saw an angel ascending from the rising of the sun, having the seal of the living God, and he called with a loud voice to the four angels who had been given power to damage earth and sea, saying, "Do not damage the earth or the sea or the trees, until we have marked the servants of our God with a seal on their foreheads." And I heard the number of those who were sealed, one hundred forty-four thousand, sealed out of every tribe of the people of Israel.

After this I looked, and there was a great multitude that no one could count, from every nation, from all tribes and peoples and languages, standing before the throne and before the Lamb, robed in white, with palm branches in their hands. They cried out in a loud voice, saying, "Salvation belongs to our God who is seated on the throne, and to the Lamb!" And all the angels stood around the throne and around the elders and the four living creatures, and they fell on their faces before the throne and worshiped God, singing, "Amen! Blessing and glory and wisdom and thanksgiving and honor and power and might be to our God forever and ever! Amen."

Then one of the elders addressed me, saying, "Who are these, robed in white, and where have they come from?" I said to him, "Sir, you are the one that knows." Then he said to me, "These are they who have come out of the great ordeal; they have washed their robes and made them white in the blood of the Lamb."

Psalm 24:1-2,3-4,5-6 (R verses 7 and 10)

Reading 2 (ABC), 1 John 3:1-3

See what love the Father has given us, that we should be called children of God; and that is what we are. The reason the world does not know us is that it did not know him. Beloved, we are God's children now; what we will be has not yet been revealed. What we do know is this: when he is revealed, we will be like him, for we will see him as he is. And all who have this hope in him purify themselves, just as he is pure.

Gospel (ABC), Matthew 5:1-12

When Jesus saw the crowds, he went up the mountain; and after he sat down, his disciples came to him. Then he began to speak, and taught them, saying:

"Blessed are the poor in spirit, for theirs is the kingdom of heaven.

"Blessed are those who mourn, for they will be comforted.

"Blessed are the meek, for they will inherit the earth.

"Blessed are those who hunger and thirst for righteousness, for they will be filled.

"Blessed are the merciful, for they will receive mercy.

"Blessed are the pure in heart, for they will see God.

"Blessed are the peacemakers, for they will be called children of God.

"Blessed are those who are persecuted for righteousness' sake, for theirs is the kingdom of heaven.

"Blessed are you when people revile you and persecute you and utter all kinds of evil against you falsely on my account. Rejoice and be glad, for your reward is great in heaven."

Freedom Fighters

JOHN F. CRAGHAN

We sometimes imagine the saints to be rather esoteric types. We see them as the recipients of special revelations and the devotees of mystical experiences. We imagine them to be divorced from our "real" world. We cannot conceive of them as people with a crusade or a cause. Since saints populate never-never land, we automatically exclude the possibility that they are freedom fighters.

Today's readings see the saints in the context of freedom. They are the people who decide upon a course of action and pursue it relentlessly. Since they opt for God's vision, they refuse to be tied down by any force or power opposed to that vision. Each day they reject whatever detracts from the love of God and of others. In this setting saints are clearly freedom fighters.

Robes of White

The Book of Revelation responds to a persecution of Christians in Asia Minor toward the end of the first century A.D. The refusal to worship the Roman emperor could have dire consequences, including death. Writing from Patmos, some fifty miles southwest of Ephesus, the author provides an interlude between the breaking of the sixth (6:12-17) and the seventh (8:1) seals. In 7:1-8, he speaks of God's care for the Church on earth and, in 7:9-17, of God's reception of glory from the Church in heaven. The seal shows that the elect are divine property. The number 144,000 attempts to capture—with no attempt at mathematical precision—the multitude of the true Israel.

In verses 9-12, the jubilant Christians appear in full glory. Their palm branches bespeak their victory. Verse 14 identifies them further. They have survived the great period of trial, namely, the persecution. While the martyrs are certainly included, this verse also envisions all Christians who choose to be faithful during crises. By sharing in Christ's death, they have kept themselves pure ("white robes"). Saints are freedom fighters.

The author of First John, writing around A.D. 100, sometime after the composition of the fourth gospel, addresses the question of secession within his community. Some groups have left the community and established independent associations to preach and teach a doctrine different from the author's. Such groups have rejected basic beliefs about Jesus (see 4:1-3). Moreover, there are fundamental differences between the author's community and these dissident groups over matters of sin and judgment.

In the midst of troubles, the community is urged to reflect on their relationship with the Father through the Son and to act upon it. In effect, the invitation is a call to exercise freedom by mirroring the perfection ("pure") of God.

Inheriting the Kingdom

In this keynote address, namely, the Sermon on the Mount, Matthew presents Jesus' vision of the kingdom. He brings together those qualities that pronounce a person truly fortunate or blessed. The first four beatitudes (5:3-6) emphasize a passive attitude (the mournful, the meek...) while the fifth, sixth, and seventh (verses 7-10) stress an active involvement (merciful, peacemakers...). The final beatitude (verses 11-12) focuses on persecution.

The eighth beatitude probably refers to the situation of Matthew's Jewish-Christian community. They still bear scars connected to their separation from Judaism. Developing this theme, Matthew has Jesus address the disciples directly, warning them about the harassment (persecution) they will endure in living the Christian life. He also underlines the personal relationship between Jesus and the disciples ("on my account").

Today's Good News

Today's feast is a marvelous opportunity to recall the "saints" in our own lives. We naturally think of parents, relatives, and friends who daily undertook the task of living the Christian life. They were freedom fighters insofar as they rejected other interests and pursuits to devote their time and energy to good. In their dedication, they experienced pain and frustration because freedom is not exempt from these. In recalling them on this feast, we truly honor them by applying their pursuit of freedom to our lives. In this way the chain of service is continued. We, the saints of the present world, are called to be freedom fighters.

Points for Reflection and Discussion

1. Who are the "saints" in your everyday life? Why?

_____

_____

_____

_____

2. How would you define "freedom" in light of sainthood?

_____

_____

_____

_____

Themes

Freedom
   M3, Your Special Gifts
   M7, Holiness

Revelation
   Q5, How Do Catholics Interpret the Bible?
   Q12, Catholics and Church
   M5, Your Prayer Life
   M6, Discernment

Saints
   Q6, The Saints
   M2, The Laity: Called to Build God's Kingdom

Reading 1 (ABC), Daniel 12:1-3

At that time Michael, the great prince, the protector of your people, shall arise. There shall be a time of anguish, such as has never occurred since nations first came into existence. But at that time your people shall be delivered, everyone who is found written in the book. Many of those who sleep in the dust of the earth shall awake, some to everlasting life, and some to shame and everlasting contempt. Those who are wise shall shine like the brightness of the sky, and those who lead many to righteousness, like the stars forever and ever.

Psalm 23:1-3,3-4,5,6 (*R verse 1*)

Reading 2 (ABC), Rom 8:31-35,37-39

If God is for us, who is against us? He who did not withhold his own Son, but gave him up for all of us, will he not with him also give us everything else? Who will bring any charge against God's elect? It is God who justifies. Who is to condemn? It is Christ Jesus, who died, yes, who was raised, who is at the right hand of God, who indeed intercedes for us. Who will separate us from the love of Christ? Will hardship, or distress, or persecution, or famine, or nakedness, or peril, or sword? In all these things we are more than conquerors through him who loved us. For I am convinced that neither death, nor life, nor angels, nor rulers, nor things present, nor things to come, nor powers, nor height, nor depth, nor anything else in all creation, will be able to separate us from the love of God in Christ Jesus our Lord.

Gospel (ABC), John 17:24-26

Jesus prayed and said: "Father, I desire that those also, whom you have given me, may be with me where I am, to see my glory, which you have given me because you loved me before the foundation of the world.

"Righteous Father, the world does not know you, but I know you; and these know that you have sent me. I made your name known to them, and I will make it known, so that the love with which you have loved me may be in them, and I in them."

*These are only suggested readings for All Souls Day. Any readings from the liturgical Masses for the Dead may be used today.

Life Everlasting

JOHN F. CRAGHAN

We have a penchant for forgetting. We easily succumb to the debilitating disease of "out of sight, out of mind." Though loved ones have graced our lives with support and dedication, we tend to forget them once they are dead. Somehow it is so difficult to bridge the chasm between the great deeds of our beloved dead and the faulty performance of our memories.

Today's readings are designed to jar our sense of recollection. They all converge on a God who does not forget the people and their accomplishments. They emphasize that God cannot overlook the goodness of others. We might say God has instant recall. The feats of the faithful departed are very much alive. By definition, in fact, God proclaims, "I will never forget my people."

A Glimmer of Hope

Around 165 B.C., the author of Daniel sought to offer encouragement to the Jews during the persecution of the Seleucid king, Antiochus IV Epiphanes (see 1 Mc 1—6; 2 Mc 4—9). Today's first reading is the conclusion of his most elaborate *apocalypse*. An angel explains the vision to Daniel, who in turn communicates the message of hope to his beleaguered community. The triumph of Michael is symbolic of the triumph of the faithful people of God.

This is the first biblical passage that clearly speaks about the resurrection of the dead. The author does not envision a universal resurrection: only those who merit eternal reward or punishment will rise. In this passage, the author singles out Israel's wise teachers among those who will rise in glory. He praises the example of the Maccabean martyrs who have offered their lives for their religious convictions (see Is 53:12).

Significantly, the author speaks about those whose names are written in the book. In both Israel (see Ex 32:32-33; Ps 69:29) and the ancient Near East such a book recorded the names of those who belonged to the community. In this instance those listed in the book are specifically those Jews who have persevered and who will, therefore, be delivered. The book and its record of loyal followers proclaims, "I will never forget my faithful people."

Nothing Can Separate Us From the Love of God

Today's passage from the second reading is Paul's triumphant conclusion to chapters 5—8. This section implicitly raises the questions: Will God continue to remember us?; will God continue to provide for us? At the great judgment scene the Judge will decide in favor of the faithful. Christ who died for all people will continue, in his risen life, to support them and serve as the advocate at their trial.

In this heavenly scene there is no obstacle that can separate loyal Christians from God's abiding love. No matter what the force, God's overwhelming love, manifest in the person of Christ Jesus, will continue to protect the faithful. This love clearly proclaims, "I will never forget my creatures."

Today's gospel is the end of Jesus' high-priestly prayer (Jn 17:1-26). As Moses blessed the Israelites before he died (see Dt 33), Jesus blesses his community for the final time. He expresses the wish that believers should be with him in heaven to share a final revelation of his own glory. Since these believers have been his intimates on earth, it is only right that they should enjoy lasting union with Jesus in eternity. The dynamic love between Father and Son is the basis of Christian unity. Such unity perpetuates that love and is the assurance that God is incapable of ever forgetting "my own."

Today's Good News

There are, of course, many ways in which we can remember our dead. We can page through family photo albums and review our home movies. We can recall both the humorous and the tragic events in their lives. We can reflect on their wise sayings and timely advice. The danger remains, however, that the past is condemned to be simply the past.

Let the past be the catalyst for the present and the future. Let the love and devotion of parents be the inspiration in our family circle. Let the patience and understanding of relatives and friends be the springboard for our gentleness and tolerance at our jobs. Let the generosity and self-giving of our forbearers in community have an impact on our social life. Ultimately, to remember is to let the past influence the present and the future. In such a way we are loyal to the author of Daniel, to Paul, and to John, all of whom clearly proclaim, "God never forgets the people and their goodness." We must likewise recall and benefit from the good deeds of our ancestors.

Points for Reflection and Discussion

1. After you get over missing them, do you often think about those who have died? Do you ever wonder where they are or what they are doing?

_____

_____

_____

_____

2. Stories keep memories alive—even for those who may never have known the stories' characters. Do you tell stories about long-ago relatives and friends—maybe even some you never knew but remember from the stories that were told to you?

_____

_____

_____

_____

Themes

Death
    Q2, What Do Catholics Believe?
Life
    Q6, The Saints
    M1, Conversion: A Lifelong Process
Remembrance
    Q3, What is the Meaning of the Mass?
    Q11, Catholic Practices

Reading 1 (ABC), 2 Chronicles 5:6-10,13—6:2

King Solomon and all the congregation of Israel, who had assembled before him, were before the ark, sacrificing so many sheep and oxen that they could not be numbered or counted. Then the priests brought the ark of the covenant of the Lord to its place, in the inner sanctuary of the house, in the most holy place, underneath the wings of the cherubim. For the cherubim spread out their wings over the place of the ark, so that the cherubim made a covering above the ark and its poles. The poles were so long that the ends of the poles were seen from the holy place in front of the inner sanctuary; but they could not be seen from outside; they are there to this day. There was nothing in the ark except the two tablets that Moses put there at Horeb, where the Lord made a covenant with the people of Israel after they came out of Egypt.

It was the duty of the trumpeters and singers to make themselves heard in unison in praise and thanksgiving to the Lord, and when the song was raised, with trumpets and cymbals and other musical instruments, in praise to the Lord, "For he is good, for his steadfast love endures forever," the house, the house of the Lord, was filled with a cloud, so that the priests could not stand to minister because of the cloud; for the glory of the Lord filled the house of God.

Then Solomon said, "The Lord has said that he would reside in thick darkness. I have built you an exalted house, a place for you to reside in forever."

Psalm 122:1-2,3-4,4-5,8-9 (R verse 1)

Reading 2 (ABC), 1 Corinthians 3:9-13,16-17

You are God's building. According to the grace of God given to me, like a skilled master builder I laid a foundation, and someone else is building on it. Each builder must choose with care how to build on it. For no one can lay any foundation other than the one that has been laid; that foundation is Jesus Christ. Now if anyone builds on the foundation with gold, silver, precious stones, wood, hay, straw—the work of each builder will become visible, for the Day will disclose it, because it will be revealed with fire, and the fire will test what sort of work each has done.

Do you not know that you are God's temple and that God's Spirit dwells in you? If anyone destroys God's temple, God will destroy that person. For God's temple is holy, and you are that temple.

Gospel (ABC), Luke 19:1-10

[Jesus] entered Jericho and was passing through it. A man was there named Zacchaeus; he was a chief tax collector and was rich. He was trying to see who Jesus was, but on account of the crowd he could not, because he was short in stature. So he ran ahead and climbed a sycamore tree to see him, because he was going to pass that way. When Jesus came to the place, he looked up and said to him, "Zacchaeus, hurry and come down; for I must stay at your house today."

So he hurried down and was happy to welcome him. All who saw it began to grumble and said, "He has gone to be the guest of one who is a sinner." Zacchaeus stood there and said to the Lord, "Look, half of my possessions, Lord, I will give to the poor; and if I have defrauded anyone of anything, I will pay back four times as much." Then Jesus said to him, "Today salvation has come to this house, because he too is a son of Abraham. For the Son of Man came to seek out and to save the lost."

* These readings have been selected from among the many Scripture readings designated as suitable for today from the Masses for the Dedication of a Church.

Building Churches

JOHN F. CRAGHAN

We seem to easily isolate ourselves from the woes of others, to deem aloofness a blessing. We preserve our personal relationship with our God but elect to bypass the community. Today's readings focus on the presence of God among the community of believers. They demonstrate a presence that goes beyond church walls to the heart of each believer. This presence is not a static presence, but one that provokes action. God's presence in and through believers is a contagious experience. It has the capacity to penetrate the world of others and offer new dimensions of hope. God's presence, therefore, means that we must reach out and touch someone.

Writing around 520 B.C., the author of today's passage from Second Chronicles attempts to involve God's community in the rebuilding of the Temple. (The neo-Babylonians had destroyed it in 586 B.C.) He paints a grandiose picture of the dedication of Solomon's temple. The priests place the Ark (the container for the two tablets and the footstool of Israel's invisible God) in the Holy of Holies, the innermost sanctuary. At this point the musicians celebrate the awesome spectacle by singing the refrain of Psalm 136. In turn, the Lord signals acceptance of this house by filling it with a cloud. The cloud manifests God's power and might. It shows God's "glory" (Ex 16:7; Nm 14:22). For the author, God's people enjoy this divine presence because they have busied themselves with the process of reconstruction. In so doing they have reached out and touched the presence of God.

The Holy Temple of God

For Paul, the Christian community is an organic unity (see 1 Cor 12:12-31). Everyone in this community both gives and receives. In today's passage Paul emphasizes the quality of the Corinthians' contributions. In addition to building on the right foundation, they are to employ adequate building materials. The materials necessary for building the community and making Christ present are love, joy, patience, peace, and the like (see Col 3:12-17).

The Second Coming of Christ ("the Day") will assess the quality of the workmanship. Worse than the use of substandard materials, however, is the attempt to destroy the Christian community. All such attempts are basically egocentric. They focus on self and not the community (see 1 Cor 8:11-12). Believers are to reveal God's presence within them by good works. This is the holiness that results from love in action (see Phil 2:14-16). For Paul too, the presence of Christ is recognized as Christians reach out and touch others in a spirit of love.

Salvation

In the gospel episode, Luke insists that the mission of Jesus of Nazareth is to search out and save the lost (see Ez 34:16). Jesus singles out a wealthy tax collector—an occupation that made Zacchaeus especially odious to fellow Jews. The Jews label Zacchaeus a sinner and conclude that it is improper for Jesus to lodge with him. At this point Zacchaeus bristles. He announces that henceforth he will give half of his wealth to the poor. He also states that in the event of extortion he offers four times the amount in question. In Luke's view, Zacchaeus has as great a claim on Jesus as any other descendant of Abraham.

By using the adverb "today" twice in the story, Luke insists on the presence of salvation in the person of Jesus (see also Lk 2:11;23:43). Jesus' coming to Zacchaeus' house is actually part of the Father's plan. "I must stay" implies necessity. It behooves Jesus to stay with Zacchaeus. Here the presence of Christ connotes mercy and forgiveness.

In this story there is a twofold reaching out. Despite the objections of the crowd, Jesus reaches out to Zacchaeus. Because of Jesus' generosity, Zacchaeus reaches out to the poor. The presence of Jesus in Zacchaeus' house is only fitting. For Luke too, the message is clearly stated: Reach out and touch someone.

Today's Good News

Our God is a God of disguises. God chooses individual believers as appropriate dwelling places. This is a God who transcends the sacred space of churches to reside in the body (temple) of individual Christians. God is not just present in churches and chapels. God is present in the kindly deeds of all Christian people. By their loving actions, Christians become living churches, dwelling places for God in today's world. Christians must reach out and touch all people who seek to enjoy the presence of the all-holy One of Israel. They must bring Christ's love to those who yearn to come in contact with the mercy and concern of this God.

Points for Reflection and Discussion

1. Think about being a holy temple of God. Imagine those who would come to you, as temple. What is your response to them?

_____

2. How would the world be different if everyone built churches of flesh—communities of people—instead of churches of stone?

_____

Themes
Church
Q8, Places in the Catholic Church
Q12, Catholics and Church
M2, The Laity: Called to Build God's Kingdom
Holiness
Q6, The Saints
M3, Your Special Gifts
M7, Holiness
Salvation
Q1, Journey of Faith
M1, Conversion: A Lifelong Process

Gathering Prayers During Inquiry

Prayer

Loving and merciful God, we gather today because we have faith in you. We want our faith to grow, as our knowledge of you and of one another grows. We ask your blessings on us and our efforts as we begin this new journey of faith in our lives. We pray in the name of Jesus.
Amen

Prayer

Gracious God, we gather once again as your people embarked on a journey of faith. We pray for the courage to voice those things we find troubling or confusing about the Catholic Church, so that our understanding may increase and our quest for knowledge may bring us ever closer to you who are All Knowing.
Amen

Prayer

God of all, we thank you for being with us on our journey of faith. We marvel at the friendships that are being formed as we share our stories—the fascinating ways in which they are different and yet the same. We are no longer alone in our desire for knowledge and understanding—for you are with us, and we are with one another.
Amen

Prayer

How marvelous are your ways, O Lord, our God! Again we ask your blessings upon us as our journey continues. Soon we will be making a turn in the road, pledging our faith-lives to the Catholic Church in fidelity and prayer and continued study. Our hearts are filled with gratitude and awe. How marvelous are your ways, O Lord, our God!
Amen

Gathering Prayers During Catechumenate

Prayer

Dear God, we gather together today and reflect upon your Word. It is another beginning for us, as each new day is another beginning. Please hear our prayer and help us to see that you are present and active in our lives today just as you were present and active in the lives of our ancestors—those whose stories we hear each week in the Liturgy of the Word.
Amen

Prayer

Creator God, we bow before you and ask your blessing upon our hearts and upon our minds, so that we may be drawn ever closer to your infinite love in our sharing of your scriptural presence. Our hearts are restless until they rest in you, O God, for you are our heart's one true desire. Speak your Words to us, O God; write them on our hearts.
Amen

Prayer

Eternal Lord, our appetites will not be sated, for you have put a hunger within us that can only be filled by your Word of everlasting life. You, who are all things to all people, speak to us out of our need. Give us the ears to hear so that our words can speak to our sisters and brothers in their need.
Amen

Prayer

Yahweh God, we have journeyed so far together with you! We have been challenged, and we have been consoled. We have been hurt, and we have been healed. We asked to know your ways, O Lord, and fleetingly we have. We approach another turn in the road. Abba, instill in us the steadfast faith that will allow us to stay the course.
Amen

Gathering Prayers During Lent

Prayer

Father-Mother God, help us to accept the suffering in our lives as faithfully as your Son did, as we begin our journey down his Lenten path. Sustain us in our own desert experience, so that our hunger for your life-giving sustenance may never be compromised by grasping at worldly riches and power. We pray these things of you in the blessed Name of Jesus.
Amen

Prayer

We pray, dear God, that you do not leave us orphaned on our journey. Hear us, O God, as we profess our faith in you, Father, Son, and Spirit; and in your living Church of yesterday, today, and tomorrow; and in the everlasting life of all your saints. Illumine our hearts and our minds with your love.
Amen

Prayer

Jesus, our friend and brother, we feel your agony and your anguish. We offer love, and the work of our hands, to sustain you on your Way—the way that we all must follow as we aspire to our own glorious resurrection. We are your body, the Church, and we place our hope in you.
Amen

Prayer

Sing Hosanna to our Lord! Gentle Jesus, we waffle between praises and curses, first celebrating with you and then hiding from you—while you steadfastly love us and serve us. We eventually bow down, paying homage to your bruised and lifeless body, for it is in you that we have our being. And, behold, you make all things new! Hosanna in the highest!
Amen

Gathering Prayers During Mystagogy

Prayer

Lord of life, what a glorious God you are! We now are truly a new creation, and still you have not finished with us! We begin to fathom the mysteries of our heart. We recognize you, eternal Lord, in the faces of one another, in the service of strangers, ...in the breaking of bread.
We say Alleluia! Amen!

Prayer

Giver of all good things, as we move along your Way we sense the path leads to everywhere and nowhere. We pray for the stillness that will allow our hearts to hear you in the midst of our noisiness. We pray for the grace to touch other's hearts with your tender mercy and steadfast love. We pray, Abba, and we do not know the words. Lord, hear our prayer.
Amen

Prayer

Prayer is a hunger that grows within us, Lord. We are trying to be your hands...your ears...your mouth—but sometimes it is so hard, Lord. We want nothing more than to be with you, but you demand more in order for that to happen. You demand that we BE you! Keep telling us we really can do it, Lord. Thy will be done!
Amen

Prayer

Eternal and loving God of all, though our journey is common its paths are divergent. You have given us means of sustaining one another along your Way, and what has been given us must now be distributed to those poor who have need of it. You promise the Spirit will guide us. We do believe, Lord; help our unbelief.
Amen

PRAYERS

Dismissal Prayers During Inquiry	*Dismissal Prayers During Catechumenate*
Prayer Loving and merciful God, as we come to the end of our time together today we give you thanks for sparks of insight. We believe you have blessed us with faith, and that you bless our efforts to come to know you better. We thank you in the name of Jesus. Amen	*Prayer* Dear God, as we have reflected on your Word today we have gained a new awareness of how the stories of our lives intertwine. In sharing your stories of yesterday, we experience your dynamic presence in our own stories of today. May we never tire of sharing your stories—and ours. Amen
Prayer Gracious God, we marvel at our increasing courage to speak and to question, and at the increase of peace that comes with our increase of understanding and knowledge about the Catholic Church. All-Knowing God, keep our appetites for knowledge and understanding whetted. Amen	*Prayer* Creator God, it seems your words are truly written upon our hearts. It is only our minds that impede their journey and keep us from the holy wholeness for which you have formed us. We are grateful for the opening of our minds that allows our restless hearts to beat more nearly with your own Sacred Heart. Amen
Prayer God of all, our stories of faith bind us ever more closely into a Christian community. As we invest in one another's lives we seem to be bolstered by a sense of unity even though we are surely a diverse group! We feel your presence among us, Lord; we give you thanks. Amen	*Prayer* Eternal God of all, hunger for your words of life grows with our sharing of those words. We thank you for all that we have heard today, and we ask that we continue to hear your words every day of our lives. We ask not only for ourselves, God, but for all those to whom we can speak in your holy Name. Amen
Prayer How marvelous are your ways, O Lord, our God! We ask your blessings, and we receive them. We are confident, as we face this turn in our journey-of-faith road, that you walk beside us, and so our journey becomes easier even as it becomes more difficult! How marvelous are your ways, O Lord, our God! Amen	*Prayer* Yahweh God, as the road makes another major turn in our journey of faith we breath deeply and say AMEN: Amen for all that has been, and Amen for all that will yet be. We approach a stretch of desert with anxious hearts. Amen, Abba!